# PERSPECTIVES ON ATHLETE-CENTRED COACHING

Underpinned by a philosophy of empowerment, athlete-centred approaches to coaching are defined by a style that promotes learning through ownership, responsibility, initiative and awareness. *Perspectives on Athlete-Centred Coaching* offers an in-depth theoretical examination of player-focused coaching models, and provides professional guidance for practising coaches.

Written by a cast of world-leading scholars and practitioners, and offering a breadth of approaches to, and critiques of, the application of athlete-centred coaching, the book covers topics including:

- athlete-centred coaching and holistic development
- coaching tactical creativity
- athlete-centred coaching in disability sport
- team culture and athlete-centred coaching
- developing thinking players through Game Sense coaching
- supporting athlete wellbeing
- athlete-centred coaching and Teaching Games for Understanding
- athlete-centred coaching in masters sport.

Based on the latest research and offering the most comprehensive enquiry into this central area of coaching theory, *Perspectives on Athlete-Centred Coaching* is important reading for any students and lecturers of sports coaching or physical education, and practising coaches across any sport.

**Shane Pill** is Associate Professor in Physical Education and Sport at Flinders University, Australia. He received a 2016 Australian Government Award for Outstanding Contributions to Student Learning and is author of the popular Play with Purpose resources for teachers and coaches.

# PERSPECTIVES ON ATHLETE-CENTRED COACHING

*Edited by Shane Pill*

Routledge
Taylor & Francis Group

LONDON AND NEW YORK

First published 2018
by Routledge
2 Park Square, Milton Park, Abingdon, Oxon OX14 4RN

and by Routledge
711 Third Avenue, New York, NY 10017

*Routledge is an imprint of the Taylor & Francis Group, an Informa business*

*British Library Cataloguing-in-Publication Data*
A catalogue record for this book is available from the British Library

*Library of Congress Cataloging-in-Publication Data*
A catalog record for this book has been requested

ISBN: 978-1-138-10389-4 (hbk)
ISBN: 978-1-138-10390-0 (pbk)
ISBN: 978-1-315-10245-0 (ebk)

Typeset in Bembo
by Apex CoVantage, LLC

# CONTENTS

# CONTRIBUTORS

**Deborah Agnew** is a senior lecturer in the School of Education at Flinders University. She teaches sport, coaching science and strength and conditioning in the Bachelor of Sport, Health and Physical Activity. Her primary research interest is athlete welfare and retirement from elite sport. Other research interests include Australian football, masculinity and men's health.

**John P. Alder** is a senior performance pathway scientist at the English Institute of Sport. He works with coaches, leaders and practitioners across the Olympic and Paralympic sports to support the development of people, pathways and systems that enhance the transition of athletes from talented juniors to world class international performers. His PhD research explored culture, leadership and change in the high performance unit of a National Sporting Organisation.

**Joy I. Butler** is Professor of Curriculum and Pedagogy at the University of British Columbia, Canada. She is Chair of Health, Outdoor and Physical Experiential Education program. She founded and was Chair of the TGfU Task Force in 2002 and developed its evolution as AIESEP's TGfU SIG in 2006. Joy has edited or co-edited eight TGfU books. She authored *Playing Fair: Using Student-Invented Games to Prevent Bullying, Teach Democracy, and Promote Social Justice* in 2016.

**Humberto Moreira Carvalho** teaches and researches at the Federal University of Sta. Catarina, Brazil. Humberto is an expert in advanced statistics and is interested in the path to expertise in youth sport.

**Luís Catarino** is working on his PhD project, studying the links between biological variables and decision-making in team sports.

**Ed Cope** is the Learning Design and Development Manager at the English Football Association. Previous to this he worked as lecturer in sports coaching and performance at the University of Hull. Ed's work is focussed on the development and application of effective pedagogy. Ed has written about this topic in relation to sports coaches' use of coaching behaviours, and how coaches' practices are received by children and players.

**Christopher Cushion** is a professor of coaching and pedagogy at Loughborough University. His research interests focus on understanding coach learning, coaching practice and coach behaviour, within a framework of developing a sociology of coaching. He has worked on projects with a number of governing body organisations and professional clubs, as well as developing coaching and coach education in non-sporting contexts, such as the police and the military.

**Ken Edwards** is an associate professor in health and physical education at the University of Southern Queensland (USQ), Australia. Ken is also a program coordinator in sport and education within the School of Health and Wellbeing. He currently teaches in the sport and exercise programs at USQ and researches in physical education and sport teaching styles, and indigenous Australian sport and games. He has written books and articles and developed the *Yulunga: Traditional Indigenous Games* program for the Australian Sports Commission.

**Greg Forrest** is a senior lecturer in physical education and sport at the University of Wollongong, Australia. He teaches and researches in physical education and sport coaching, and is currently working with a range of sports associations to enhance coaching practices in community sport. He is a previous recipient of the Australian College of Educator's Outstanding Achievement in Tertiary Education Award.

**Carlos Gonçalves** is a teacher and researcher at the Faculty of Sport Sciences of the University of Coimbra, Portugal. For decades, he has been a basketball coach at an elite level. His main research interests are in the field of youth sport, namely the factors that contribute to success in the "rocky" path specialisation in sport.

**Linda L. Griffin** is a professor at the University of Massachusetts Amherst. Her scholarly interest has been on the teaching and learning of games through a games-centred approach. She has co-authored several books and articles and has co-edited two books with colleague Joy Butler. Linda has been a speaker and presenter all over the world. She has also received several honours and awards for her work in this area.

**Joseph Gurgis** is a PhD student in the Faculty of Kinesiology and Physical Education at the University of Toronto. Joseph conducts research on pedagogical practices in sport with a specific focus on the punitive use of exercise, benching and yelling in sport, including coaches' and athletes' perspectives on the purpose and effects of such practices. He is also interested in the design, implementation and evaluation of coach education programs.

**Stephen Harvey** is an associate professor in the Department of Recreation and Sport Pedagogy at Ohio University, USA. His research is focused on advancing teaching/coaching pedagogy through the utilisation of game-centred approaches and emerging technologies in physical education/coaching. Stephen is co-author of *Advances in Rugby Coaching: An Holistic Approach*, and co-editor of *Contemporary Developments in Games Teaching*, and *Ethics in Youth Sport: Policy and Pedagogical Applications*, all published by Routledge.

**Karlene Headley-Cooper** is a lecturer in the Faculty of Kinesiology and Physical Education at the University of Toronto, Canada. She teaches fundamentals in fitness, exercise, physical activity and communication. Karlene is a recipient of a 2017 University of Toronto KPE Award of Excellence in Teaching. She was also a member of the Great Britain (GB) Women's Softball team for ten years (2005–2014) and has coached various GB national teams from u13 to Women's (2007–2016).

**Mitchell Hewitt** is the National Education Project Manager at Tennis Australia (TA). Mitch has over 25 years coaching experience, from novice to elite players, and he has been a primary and secondary physical education teacher. Mitch is a highly regarded presenter in sport pedagogy, with numerous published articles relating to teaching and coaching styles. He has a PhD in sport pedagogy, co-authored the Tennis for Primary Schools resource and is a major contributor in the development of coaching curriculum at TA.

**Gretchen Kerr** is a professor in the Faculty of Kinesiology and Physical Education at the University of Toronto. Her research focuses broadly on athlete maltreatment with a specific interest on emotional abuse within the coach–athlete relationship. Gretchen also conducts studies of coach education with a focus on advancing developmentally appropriate methods of enhancing the psychosocial health of young people in sport.

**Richard Light** is Professor of Sport Coaching in the College of Education, Health and Human Development at the University of Canterbury, Christchurch, New Zealand. He has been a prominent figure in research on and the development of game-based approaches (GBA) to teaching and coaching over the past 16 years. He was a founding member of the TGfU Task Force from 2002–2010 and has convened a range of international conferences on GBA such as TGfU and Game Sense. His most recent books on athlete-centred coaching include *Advances in Rugby Coaching: An Holistic Approach* (Light, Evans, Harvey, & Hassanin, 2015 – Routledge) and *Positive Pedagogy for Sport Coaching: Athlete-Centred Coaching for Individual Sport* (2017 – Routledge).

**Andy Lowe** is a county coach developer for the English Football Association, where his responsibilities include supporting the successful delivery of the EFA's Coaching Strategy across the National Game by supporting the development of regional coaches and coach educators. Prior to this, Andy worked as a secondary school physical education teacher for 15 years, and had worked in an academy football club for 10 years. Andy's main research interests are in differentiation strategies utilised by coaches in practice.

**Terry Magias** is an associate lecturer in physical education and sport at Flinders University, Australia. He lectures in skill acquisition and sport pedagogy. Terry is currently completing a PhD study into swim coaches' intended and enacted pedagogy.

**Andrew Marks** is the football manager at the West Adelaide Football Club. He oversees football operations, including talent identification, management and player welfare. With a history in education, over 20 years as a primary school teacher, Andrew has a keen interest in education programs for player development. He is a recipient of the Governor's Multi-Cultural Award.

**Daniel Memmert** is a professor and Executive Director of the Institute of Training and Computer Science in Sport, German Sport University Cologne, Cologne, Germany, with a visiting assistant professorship 2014 at the University of Vienna (Austria). He studied PE for high school teaching and has trainer licenses in soccer, tennis, snowboard and skiing. Daniel transfers his expertise to business companies, professional soccer clubs and football national teams.

**Dawn Penney** is a professorial research fellow in the School of Education at Edith Cowan University, Australia, and an adjunct professor of physical education and sport pedagogy at Monash University, Australia. Dawn's research pursues issues of quality and equity in exploring developments in curriculum, pedagogy and assessment in health and physical education and sport contexts. Dawn has authored many journal articles and several research-based books, including *School Health Education in Changing Times: Curriculum, Pedagogies and Partnerships* (2016).

**Rod Philpot** is a senior lecturer in health and physical education in the School of Curriculum and Pedagogy within the Faculty of Education and Social Work, at the University of Auckland, New Zealand. Rod is the current leader of the Faculty's Bachelor of Sport, Health and Physical Education. His research and teaching focus are on critical pedagogies in diverse physical education, sport and health contexts.

**Machar Reid** is the Innovation Catalyst for Tennis Australia (TA) and a pre-eminent voice in sport/coaching science and policy in international tennis. He has trained top 100 professional players, led strategic reviews for the International Tennis Federation (ITF), co-authored the ITF's coaching curriculum and received a PhD in biomechanics. He is an adjunct associate professor at Victoria University, and has contributed to books, book chapters and peer reviewed articles.

**Joanna Sheppard** is an associate professor in the Department of Kinesiology and Physical Education at the University of the Fraser Valley (UFV) in Chilliwack, B.C. Her research focuses on physical and health education, life skills, curriculum development and Teaching Games for Understanding. Joanna's passion lies in the collaborative efforts of best practices with local, national and international teaching colleagues.

**Wayne Smith** is an associate professor and deputy dean of the Faculty of Education and Social Work, at the University of Auckland, New Zealand. His research and major teaching contributions are in skill acquisition and socially critical pedagogy in physical education. Wayne has been involved in physical education teacher education for two decades, and from 2002–2009 was head of programme of the Faculty's Bachelor of Physical Education.

**Ashley Stirling** is an associate professor, Teaching Stream, in the Faculty of Kinesiology and Physical Education at the University of Toronto. Her research expertise is in the areas of athlete maltreatment in sport with a particular focus on emotional abuse, as well as strategies for athlete protection. In 2012, Ashley co-wrote a coach education module for the Coaching Association of Canada on creating positive and healthy sport experiences.

**Robert Townsend** is a PhD researcher with the Peter Harrison Centre for Disability Sport at Loughborough University. His research involves understanding coach education, learning and development across disability sport contexts, within a critical sociological framework. He has a further interest in the use and advancement of qualitative methods in coaching. In addition, he coaches in high performance disability sport.

**Adrian P. Turner** is an associate professor of sport pedagogy and coaching at Bowling Green State University in Ohio, USA. His scholarship focuses on tactical approaches to teaching games, and he has published and presented nationally and internationally on Teaching Games for Understanding (TGfU). Adrian has conducted numerous in-service workshops on games teaching for physical educators and coaches and continues to invoke a games-based approach during his coaching of youth soccer at the grass roots level.

**Chris Zehntner** is a lecturer in health and physical education at University of Tasmania, Australia. He teaches in physical education pedagogy and sports coaching. Chris is also a silver license swim coach with over 20 years of coaching experience. He has taught swimmers from their first forays into the water and has coached masters and elite age-group athletes. His research interests include coach education and athlete-centred coaching.

# INTRODUCTION

*Shane Pill*

An athlete-centred coaching approach is defined by a style of coaching that promotes athlete learning through athlete ownership, responsibility, initiative and awareness, guided by the coach. Ownership and responsibility encourage athlete accountability for his or her performance on and off the field. The coach asking questions in preference to being directive or commanding marks the athlete-centred coaching style (Kidman & Davis, 2006). Asking questions puts the onus of knowledge formation and construction on the athlete instead of placing the athlete in the role of replicator of the coach's directions and movement models, as is commonly the positioning of the athlete in a more directive approach to coaching. "In an athlete centred environment, the athlete owns the direction, is accountable for that direction and this takes responsibility for their actions and performance" (Penney & Kidman, 2014, pp. 2–3). In an athlete-centred coaching environment, athletes are encouraged to participate in decision-making and problem solving in a shared approach to knowledge and its transmission.

The contrast to an athlete-centred coach is the coach-centred or autocratic coach (Ahlberg, Mallett, & Tinning, 2008). This style of coaching is characterised as directive, commanding and prescriptive coaching, emphasising conformity and transmission of information for reproduction. The athlete is positioned as reliant on the coach to facilitate performance, particularly their competitive performance. A coach-centred approach operates in order to control players and, as such, predominantly acts to disempower athletes.

An athlete-centred approach is underpinned by a philosophy of empowerment. This empowerment is built on the provision of age and developmentally appropriate autonomy for players to make decisions, develop intrinsic motivation to improve and perform and develop goals and solutions to enhance their performance on the field and behaviour off the field. An athlete-centred approach is, however, a social process embedded in a range of complex power relations. It is not simply a choice for a coach to make, regardless of his or her coaching context.

Empowerment, decision-making, knowledge formation and culture are the common themes running through the chapters that comprise this book. They position the 'act' of coaching very differently to the more historically common description of the coaching process and coaches' practices as formed through an exercise of power that subordinates athletes' minds and bodies through the application of various pedagogical, disciplinary and discursive techniques (Denison, Mills, & Konoval, 2015). In this book, we see that athlete-centred coaching is an idea that has developed into a movement to empower athletes and foster more humanistic coaching, where athletes have more responsibility and ownership of their development and performance. What we see in the chapters comprising this book is the development of the propositions underpinning the idea of athlete-centred coaching that has occurred in recent years and their application across the participant spectrum, as well as insights into the complexities associated with coaching using the precepts of athlete-centred coaching. Greater emphasis on relational understandings that extend concern for the whole person, rather than the historically common reductionist perspective on training (and possibly controlling) the athlete's body, is evident.

This book brings together leading and innovative thinkers in the field of coaching pedagogy to provide a range of perspectives on an athlete-centred coaching approach. This book is divided into three sections. They focus on: 1) developments in theoretical perspectives, 2) research perspectives and 3) researcher-practitioner and practitioner involvement in athlete-centred coaching.

## Part I Theoretical perspectives on athlete-centred coaching

This section includes new ideas, refinements and advancements in the precepts of athlete-centred coaching. It begins with Linda Griffin and colleagues in Chapter 1 describing athlete-centred coaching as a holistic approach and explaining the practices that encompass this approach. They offer a theory and a rationale that include the explicit teaching of life skills. In Chapter 2, Gretchen Kerr and colleagues advance the concept of *thriving* and the role coaches play in developing the quality of this experience for both players and coaches. They expand the holistic notion of athlete-centred coaching by linking the concept of thriving to a model for actualising thriving in coaching settings. Chapter 3 outlines the ideas central to player development of tactical creativity, and Daniel Memmert explains the coaching dimensions that allow athletes to learn the divergent thinking that enables tactical creativity to emerge. Robert Townsend and Chris Cushion explore the complexity of athlete-centred coaching with athletes with special needs in Chapter 4. This important consideration covers a coaching dimension rarely discussed in research books on sport coaching. They introduce and apply the four models of disability – medical, social, relational and human rights – in the context of athlete-centred coaching. In Chapter 5, John P. Alder explains how the concept of empowerment is often presented too simplistically in coaching literature.

Discourses related to empowerment frequently do not give sufficient attention to the power relationships and hierarchies in sport settings. John explains how to frame a more equal relationship through the concept of sense-giving. The section concludes with Chapter 6, in which Wayne Smith and Rod Philpot draw attention to the influence of cultural and social contexts in shaping athlete development. They challenge readers to think about skillful performance through the idea of an imagination of possibilities.

## Part II  Research perspectives on athlete-centred coaching

This section contains recent research with athletes and coaches. Part II starts with Stephen Harvey investigating how athlete-centred coaching is being developed in US Field Hockey using coach interviews in Chapter 7. Sport pedagogy research continues in Chapter 8, where Shane Pill explores an Australian football coach's use of the Game Sense coaching approach for the first time. Sport pedagogies like the Game Sense approach (Australia), Teaching Games for Understanding (UK) and the Tactical Games approach (USA) are frequently associated with an athlete-centred approach. In Chapter 9, Deb Agnew and Andrew Marks explore athlete transition from elite sport to other levels of competition or retirement. This is an important dimension of a holistic consideration of the life of an athlete with little mention in contemporary games teaching and sport coaching literature. Carlos Eduardo Gonçalves and colleagues also examine the complexity of athletes in Chapter 10. They consider the biological diversity of athletes and how that may be catered for in an athlete-centred approach. Part II concludes with Adrian Turner using Windschitl's dilemmas framework to address the conceptual, cultural, pedagogical and political challenges of using an athlete-centred approach in Chapter 11. Adrian uses data from his work in community sport coaching to expose the layers of complexity when attempting to implement a learning culture based on a player-centred coaching philosophy.

## Part III  Researcher-practitioner and practitioner involvement in athlete-centred coaching

This section contains ethnographic accounts of athlete-centred coaching. Richard Light introduces Productive Pedagogies as a unique lens on athlete-centred coaching in Chapter 12. He goes on to outline the application of the productive pedagogy in his own experience of coaching swimming. In Chapter 13, Karlene Headley-Cooper provides a unique autoethnographic exploration of athlete-centred coaching from her experience as an athlete, coach and researcher. Many of the chapters in this book show that athlete-centred coaching is far from a straightforward process when attempted in the field, and Karlene's journey with athlete-centred coaching provides a distinctive perspective on the complexities of player empowerment and supportive coaching contexts. In Chapter 14, Terry Magias also provides an autoethnographic experience of his attempts to reconcile what he was learning as 'best practice' sport coaching and the coaching approach required in a learn to swim setting. Terry's attempts to apply an athlete-centred perspective were met with resistance and were challenged by the institution. Greg Forrest also provides a personal perspective in Chapter 15, offering an analysis of his experiences as a coach and coach educator in community sport through promoting an athlete-centred coaching philosophy. It is revealed that without Greg's background, as first a physical education teacher and then physical education academic, the coaching knowledge required for athlete-centred coaching is both foreign to community coaches and daunting for them to consider. Ed Cope and Andy Lowe also consider athlete-centred coaching from the perspective of coach development, but from the context of a national sport coach development role, in Chapter 16. They analyse the journey of a coach educator to athlete-centred coaching as a national sporting organisation evolves its coaching philosophy, and discuss the role of scaffolding coach development for the explicit development of athlete-centred coaching competencies. Also within the context of a national sporting organisation, Mitchell Hewitt and colleagues explain in Chapter 17 Tennis Australia's adoption of the Game Sense approach for learning to play tennis in primary school and junior sport coaching contexts. The Tennis Australia conceptual framework for athlete-centred junior tennis coaching is explained and examples of coaching activities are provided. Part III concludes with Dawn Penney and Chris Zehntner in Chapter 18 providing ethnographic insights and examples of the challenges of athlete-centred coaching in a masters' athlete swimming context. The complexities of being an athlete-centred coach coaching within a group 'squad' environment are revealed.

## Using this book

This book is intended to engage undergraduate and postgraduate students in physical education and sport coaching, practicing coaches and coach educators. The contributions, taken together or individually, provide insight, learning and opportunities to foster athlete-centred coaching ideas. Each chapter raises issues that can resonate with the sport practitioner and researcher. In this way, the chapters can assist one to make sense of their own coaching, provide deeper insight into personal conceptualisations of the athlete–coach relationship or stimulate reflections on their own coaching or the coaching contexts they are involved in. This book both summarises current thinking about athlete-centred coaching as well as providing direction for further practical, pragmatic and research consideration of the concept and its precepts.

## References

Ahlberg, M., Mallett, C., & Tinning, R. (2008). Developing autonomy supportive coaching behaviours: An action research approach to coach development. *International Journal of Coaching Science, 2*(2), 3–22.

Denison, J., Mills, J. P., & Konoval, T. (2015). Sports' disciplinary legacy and the challenge of 'coaching differently'. *Sport, Education and Society*, Published online: 8 July 2015, 1–12. Retrieved from http://dx.doi:org/10.1080/13573322.2015.1061986

Kidman, L., & Davis, W. (2006). Empowerment in coaching. In W. Davis & G. Broadhead (Eds.), *Ecological task analysis perspectives on movement* (pp. 121–140). Champaign, IL: Human Kinetics.

Penney, D., & Kidman, L. (2014). Opening call for discourse: Athlete centered coaching – a time for reflection on meanings, values and practice. *Journal of Athlete Centered Coaching*, *1*, 1–5.

**PART I**

# Theoretical perspectives on athlete-centred coaching

# 1

# ATHLETE-CENTRED COACHING

## Extending the possibilities of a holistic and process-oriented model to athlete development

*Linda L. Griffin, Joy I. Butler and Joanna Sheppard*

Sport matters to individuals (i.e., athletes, coaches and fans), teams, communities, universities, countries and beyond these more obvious categories to influence national cultures. Sport sociologists have stated that contemporary sport is a microcosm of society; in fact, it is difficult to understand contemporary society and culture without recognising the position of games and sport (Jarvie, 2012). While it is critical to examine through research the influences of sport via such aspects of society such as ecology, spirituality, ethics, democracy-in-action and social justice issues across lifestyles and alternative cultures, it is also important to consider the individual development of the athlete in light of these broader notions. To do this, we argue that the pedagogies chosen are a powerful way to influence athletes' development and sense of themselves as they develop and evolve. The purpose of this chapter is to explore and extend the possibilities of an athlete-centred coaching approach that promotes an educative and holistic process for athletes' sporting experiences (Kidman & Lombardo, 2010). First, we will outline the sporting experience (i.e., sport as a form of play), the athletes and coach. Second, we will present major aspects to consider in an athlete-centred approach (i.e., pedagogical principles, democracy in action, integration of life skills) that extend this approach. Finally, we present an Athlete-Centred Coach model (ACC) and offer our reflections and thinking about this holistic and process-oriented approach to athletes' development and sense of themselves.

## Sporting experience

In this section, we will highlight the athlete's sporting experience and present the notion of coach as educator.

## The athlete's sporting experience

Sports are games that involve combinations of physical skill and strategy (Siedentop & van der Mars, 2012). Sport is a prominent social institution with pervasiveness and impact on the individuals who participate (Frey & Stanley, 1991). Sport stems from the play instinct in human behaviour and the play element in culture. In other words, sport is a playful, participation-oriented activity (Frey & Stanley, 1991). When sport is most playful, it is most meaningful for participants. Competition lies at the heart of sport and is one of its defining characteristics, since without competition there is no game (Siedentop & van der Mars, 2012). Viewed in this playful light, sport is not professional but rather voluntary, as athletes come together to achieve their collective goals during a time period known as a season (Kidman & Lombardo, 2010). Second, individuals, as athletes, come to play sport for various reasons (i.e., competition, socialisation, enjoyment and satisfaction).

While competition is central to sport, the various reasons athletes participate provide insight into the deeper meanings of why individuals play. Competition is usually described as a rivalry, thus highlighting an economic/business argument as sport is positioned as a zero-sum game (Siedentop & van der Mars, 2012). Because of this zero-sum view of competition, the concept of competition is often misunderstood. Alternatively, competition can be as a 'coming together' that signifies an event or a celebration with particular rituals and traditions (e.g., Olympics, World Cup). The athlete is also striving to be competent (i.e., having sufficient skill, knowledge, being capable). Finally, there is rivalry, a highly valued aspect of sport to be sure; yet, when considering deeper meaning of competition, it is important to extend the types of rivalry to include team against team, athlete against athlete, athlete against record, athlete against best performance and individual against specific physical barriers. These alternatives all serve to broaden the meaning of the word 'competition'.

It is very likely that a majority of people in the United States have all seen and heard the claim by the National Collegiate Athletic Association (NCAA) indicating that more than 480,000 compete as NCAA athletes, and just a select few within each sport move on to compete at the professional or Olympic level (www.ncaa. org/). In fact, professional opportunities are extremely limited and the likelihood of a high school or even college athlete becoming a professional athlete is very low (www.ncaa.org/). This claim should serve to remind all sport enthusiasts, particularly coaches, athletes, parents and fans involved in sport, of the realities of the athlete's vulnerabilities (i.e., susceptible to harm or degradation).

We believe athletes need to develop in a way that involves a comprehensive holistic model rather than a combination of individual parts. This comprehensive holistic model provides intentional linkages among the pedagogy (i.e., coaching), culture and climate of sport and the holistic development of athletes (see Figure 1.1), as it extends aspects of the athlete-centred approach and serves as a guide for coaches.

In fact, while organised sports opportunities for youth 5–13 years old have doubled in the past 20 years (Hofferth & Sandberg, 2001), many of them are opting out in large numbers (Fidelis, 2008; Visek et al., 2015). The following list summarises the reasons young people gave for opting out of sport (Alvarez, Balaguer Sola, Castillo Fernández, & Duda, 2009; Ewing & Seefeldt, 2002; Wall & Cote, 2007):

- I lost interest
- I had no fun, and it took too much time
- The coach did not empower players
- There was too much pressure and worry
- The coach played favourites
- The sport was boring
- There was an over-emphasis on winning
- There was too much sport-specific practice and 'deliberate practice' at a young age
- The sports programs were poorly run

Crucially, when athletes are criticised for poor performance in a game, they are unlikely to make confident decisions, or decisions that involve risk. The ACC model we suggest (Figure 1.1) is a holistic approach, which takes into account these affective experiences. After all, athletes should have the opportunity to experience what Kretchmar (2005) describes as 'delight'. Moments of delight may happen infrequently in games, but they keep us coming back for more. Furthermore, we suggest that learning should not be compartmentalised into behavioural domains and neatly subdivided into the cognitive, the psychomotor and the affective, since all human systems are nested and interconnected.

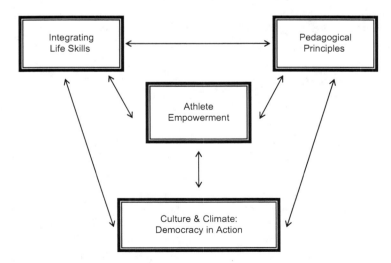

**FIGURE 1.1** Athlete-centred coach model.

## Coach as educator

Many scholars and educational professionals believe that sport is an educative process (Kidman & Lombardo, 2010; Cassidy, Jones, & Potrac, 2016). Most coaches are able to address physical and skill development, tactical and strategic knowledge in addition to fair play and good sporting behaviours. Awareness of situations that arise inside and outside the sporting setting and the people involved (e.g., athletes, other coaches and parents) can be seen as critical to success and a sense of belonging. When a coach places the people and situations at the centre of an athletes' experience, they become more holistic in their thinking and approach to coaching. This holistic (i.e., humanistic) shift provides the athletes agency to directly influence and own their own learning and sporting experiences in order to generate knowledge, understand skills and make effective, useful decisions. The athlete–centred coach creates a climate and culture of ownership and responsibility, and in this next section we will illustrate this assertion as we offer the theory and rationale of the athlete–centred approach.

## Theory and rationale of the athlete-centred coaching model

The original athlete–centred work by Kidman and Lombardo (2010) offers three primary practices that encompass this approach: (a) Teaching Games for Understanding (TGfU) (Bunker & Thorpe, 1982) or a games–centred approach, (b) questions and (c) team culture. To explain a rationale for an athlete–centred approach, first, we will offer specific pedagogical principles that can help coaches shift their leadership style. Second, we present the notion of democracy in action as a way for athletes to gain ethical understanding and life skills, tactics, skills and game play development through well-designed game-like situations and structured group processes (Butler, 2016). Finally, we introduce the explicit integration of life skills into the approach.

## Pedagogical principles for shifting coaching leadership styles

We offer four pedagogical principles that will help the coach to plan and design practices aimed to help athletes become more reflective and self-directed. These have been adapted from Thorpe, Bunker and Almond's (1986) work, and are also grounded in ecological complexity theory. From these perspectives, coaches see good game play as being fun, sustainable and packed with educational potential. Their actions and decisions can never be entirely separated from those of their athletes or from the context within which they occur. With this perspective, the coach should not only be concerned with the short-term – wins and losses during the sport season – but with the long-term learning and lifestyles that these games may inspire.

Coaches coming from this perspective focus upon emergent learning as they encourage learners to ask and consider critical questions in order to construct knowledge and meaning, and develop a sense of ownership of their own learning. Rather than fixing errors, coaches who have an ecological complexity worldview work to make sense of their athletes' interpretations and perceptions, and they offer their students opportunities to practice the critical analyses, interpretations, dispositions and attributes that they will find useful as engaged global citizens (Butler, 2016).

## Pedagogical principle 1: coaching as facilitating

Active learning is the signature pedagogy of TGfU as the coach adopts the role of facilitator. This approach aligns directly with the first pedagogical principle – *Coaching as Facilitating*. A game-centred approach shifts the pedagogy from coach-centred to athlete-centred and places responsibility and ownership on the athletes as learners. The coach facilitates the process by setting problems, goals and/or boundaries that guide tasks: students grapple with these tasks as they seek solutions. An assumption is that in order for students to become good games players, they need to become good problem solvers. In this regard, the coach becomes a connector and integrator. Athletes are then able to share perspectives and experiences, which in turn stimulates thinking, encourages explorations and makes associations. The following suggestions may help the coach adopt, design and structure practices as well as the season:

- Teach athletes their roles and responsibilities in an active learning practice. Decide what rules, routines and expectations you need to put in place so that athletes feel safe and are willing to engage. Your athletes will also need time to adjust to their new role. Be patient with them and yourself.
- Think through the organisation of space, athletes (individual, pairs or small groups) and equipment. Planning helps you to stay in the role of facilitator, and helps you be flexible and nimble. For example, Kidman and Lombardo (2010) suggest one way to organise space and athletes is to use a mini-group structure. This practice structure could be arranged by positions (e.g., guards and forwards in basketball or setters, hitters and defensive specialists in volleyball) or mixed position mini-groups to work on specific game situations. Mini-groups are a way of having players work with each other in various practice situations and keeps the coach in the role as facilitator.
- Select a game situation for the athletes to think through. Coaches will need to consider how much you actually want to say about the situation since you want athletes to grapple with it. As facilitator, the coach can ask questions that will help athletes explore possible solutions. The coach can also facilitate practice by shaping the games (i.e., simplifying or challenging game conditions) to meet the developmental needs of the learners. Athletes need to be able to (a) define the problem, (b) gather information about the problem, (c) identify the

decision-making options, (d) make the decision and (e) put the decision into action. For example, if the problem or task in basketball is to shoot when open, then the coach should consider what players need to do to make this happen (e.g., give and go, pick, screen, etc).

- Questions can be an excellent way for coaches to engage your athletes. As facilitators, coaches will need to know when to ask questions and when to provide answers. Literature on games-centred approaches has consistently emphasised the importance of high quality questions by the coach (Bunker & Thorpe, 1982; Mitchell, Oslin, & Griffin, 2013). The quality of questions should thus be a central element of the planning process. The following are six types of question stems and the possible game aspects they can cover:

  - Tactical or strategic awareness: 'What do you. . .'
  - Skill & movement execution: 'How do you. . .'
  - Time: 'When is the best time to. . .'
  - Space: 'Where is/can. . .'
  - Risk: 'Which choice. . .'
  - Rationale: 'Why are you. . .'

The number and types of questions are determined by the coach, and are based on the individual athlete's readiness. For example, during practice, the coach can have athletes process in a number of ways: (a) coach asks the full team, and a couple of athletes answer; (b) coach places athletes in think–pair–share partners to discuss solutions; and (c) coach places athletes in small walking/jogging groups to have them problem solve. These practice strategies place the athletes in the role of decision-maker, which is the essence of a sporting experience. As coaches reflect on this role as facilitator, they should consider shifting to the notion of a 'pedagogy of engagement' (Almond, 2010). Pedagogical engagement is a coaching strategy that focuses athletes' interaction, cooperation and collaboration among athletes, and the active engagement of the athletes in the learning and performance process.

## Pedagogical principle 2: tactical complexity

Tactical complexity involves the tactical concepts (i.e., scoring and preventing scoring) and movement concepts (body, space, effort and relationship) of games and the athletes' ability and skills (i.e., psychomotor, cognitive and affective) to implement these concepts (Howarth, Fisette, Sweeney, & Griffin, 2010). At the heart of tactical complexity is the games classification system (Bunker & Thorpe, 1982; Mitchell et al., 2013), which serves as an organising structure for a game-centred approach. The ultimate goal of the classification system is to provide athletes with connections that lead to transfer of concepts, strategical principles and tactics within each classification.

Sport-related games can be viewed along a continuum of tactical complexity. Here you want athletes to consider the action required (i.e., skills and movements), the conditions of the situation (e.g., out-of-bounds play) and the goal of the situation (e.g., to gain possession of the ball). Games with fewer variables are easier to adapt (i.e., shape) for athletes. Tactical complexity can be a difficult principle to deconstruct and reconstruct as you consider the developmental needs of your athletes.

### Pedagogical principle 3: modifications (representation, exaggeration and adaptation)

Proponents of a game-centred approach argue that all athletes can access and play a game if it is shaped and modified in a way that more easily facilitates meaningful play. They also believe that learning occurs in context (Ellis, 1986; Thorpe, 2001). To achieve the right context, coaches need to consider the pedagogical principle of modification through representation, exaggeration and adaption.

- *Representation*: Maintaining some contextual aspect of the game but slowing play down. Simply put, *do less to get more* play for your athletes.
- *Exaggeration*: Game or game forms that overemphasise some aspect of play to encourage a particular tactical or movement experience.
- *Adaptation*: The game is adapted to increase the challenge once an athlete has achieved success. Changes are made in relation to game constrains (e.g., space, score, rules, number of players) to ensure that the game remains competitive (Hopper, 2011).

These three concepts help coaches to simplify the complexities of the sport. Modifying a game through these three methods can slow down its pace and flow and allow coaches to focus on a particular aspect of game play. The modification principle also helps keep athletes engaged by building upon their game competence.

Modifications may be made to a simple game, one tactic/strategy or movement concept or a game situation. Modification may mean beginning with few skills, few rules and few players, thus slowing down the pace and tempo of the game. Modified games or game forms should be representative of the advanced form (i.e., regulation game) and contain the same tactical structures, played with adjustments (i.e., conditioned) to meet the developmental needs (e.g., size, age, ability) of your athletes. The following are five aspects of the game or game form that can be exaggerated or adapted to draw attention to a particular tactical problem and focus on the decision-making process.

1  *Rules*. Rules can be changed to create a specific learning emphasis;
2  *Number of players*. Small-sided games or game forms (3v3 or 2v1) slow down the tempo and flow of a game, thus limiting the tactical complexity, which, in turn, simplifies the decision-making process;
3  *Playing area*. Altering the size of the playing area or changing the size of the goal may help athletes focus on learning a particular aspect of the game. Narrowing the court restricts space and can accompany skills of drop and lob shots;
4  *Equipment*. Modifying the playing equipment makes the students feel safer, which allows for more successful execution of skills and movements. For

example, athletes are more likely to have more time to think about ball placement if the ball travels more slowly or to attempt the forearm pass or dig in the volleyball unit when trainer volleyballs are used; and

5   *Scoring or modifying the goal.* Scoring allows the game to be shaped to reinforce practice. For example, in a volleyball lesson, the final game goal might have teams earn points for containing the first pass on their side of the court.

### Pedagogical principle 4: assessment of learning outcomes

The final pedagogical principle is assessment of learning outcomes. Assessment in the act of playing games is the most authentic and meaningful way for athletes to receive formative feedback and develop skillfulness and competence as players (Corbin, 2002). Assessment should be an ongoing part of instruction so that athletes are provided with continuous feedback that helps them to reflect on and self-manage their own learning. These assessments can be based on: (a) contest or performance statistics, and (b) goals that athletes and coaches set for the individual athlete, as a team, for the specific game or for the overall season. Sport coaching is dramatically enriched through the use of assessment, particularly when that assessment is aligned with instructional objectives (Mitchell et al., 2013). There are three interacting components – the coach, the game situation and the assessment. The reciprocal aspect is indicated by the dual direction lines since the relationship or action of each one is mutual (see Figure 1.2).

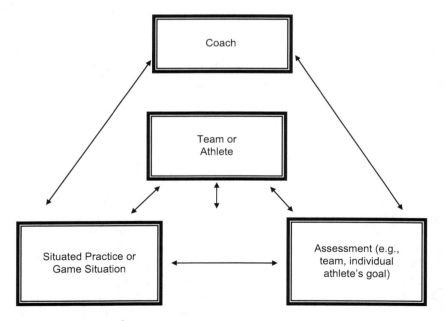

**FIGURE 1.2**   Reciprocal assessment.

(Adapted from Butler, 2016, p. 66).

A game-centred approach with an emphasis on authentic performance promotes an active in-depth learning setting for athletes. One of the primary goals of game-centred approaches is to appeal to the interest of athletes in game play so that they value the need to work toward competence (i.e., improved game knowledge and performance).

## Sport setting culture and climate: incorporating democracy in action

As coaches consider this shift to an ACC model, another aspect of the sport environment to consider is the climate and culture of their program – the foundation upon which any sport program is built. Culture develops over time and consists of values, norms, rituals and traditions and communication (Thompson, 2003; Kidman & Lombardo, 2010). In essence, culture is the temperament of the sport program. Climate, on the other hand, is the here-and-now, which has more to do with the mood of the team (i.e., what does it feel like to be a member of a particular team?). Climate is more short-term, and several interacting factors can influence it, such as the tone, athlete-to-athlete interactions and coach-to-athlete interactions and range of perspectives. As you seek to create a more holistic athlete-empowered climate, we would like you to consider the notion of democracy in action (DiA).

In sport culture, there has been an historic assumption that sport teaches personal and social responsibility. For example, in the nineteenth century, teachers, parents and administrators in private schools believed that playing games 'built character', at least for boys (Hellison & Martinek, 2006). The underlying assumption by many coaches is that participation in sport will teach athletes how to be 'good sports' in the same way that educators today assume that asking learners to work in groups will teach them about effective communication, cooperation and teamwork. As Seefeldt and Ewing (1997) pointed out, however, 'the physical act of performing sport skills will not teach moral action' (p. 7). Therefore, the premise of teaching and incorporating DiA into the climate and culture of your team is that moral action and democratic citizenship must be a planned and deliberate part of the curriculum.

As the coach, you encourage athletes to understand that a large measure of responsibility comes with freedom. For example, you and your team can create a list of individual rights stating: (a) that each member has the right to be heard by others respectfully, and (b) a group has the responsibility to include all members in group discussions and decisions and to respect an individual's right not to be involved (Butler, 2016). The notion of 'democracy in action' counteracts the common assumption that 'ethics' comprises a set of a priori principles. Rather, it suggests that principles, skills and aptitudes emerge in authentic situations in a participatory, adaptive learning culture. For the purposes of this chapter, these include: (a) group process; (b) personal and social responsibility; (c) free inquiry; (d) decision-making; and (e) social justice.

*Group process*: Sports have a team structure which requires coaching and learning skills to help athletes to negotiate, decide upon and adhere to group structures (e.g., reaching consensus; listening to minority viewpoints) and to explore ways of working together and resolving conflicts. Tuckman (2001) described the ways in which groups (i.e., team) usually move through stages such as 'forming', 'storming', 'norming' and 'performing'.

- *Forming*: The team starts to *orientate* themselves to the season; they begin with fresh energy and enthusiasm and believe that anything seems possible. Also, athletes are checking out the ways that they relate to one another, thoughtfully or not.
- *Storming*: Potential time of immense growth as athletes start to come together as performers and teammates. Storming can also be a time of conflict and struggle as athletes struggle for power.
- *Norming*: Moments of aporia (stuckness – impasse – anger) can render a team unable to proceed, and here, policy and co-created rules come in useful, so that trust can be built.
- *Performing*: The bonding achieved in the previous stages allows the team to work more closely. Cohesion is witnessed at the various competitions.

We advocate that teams that work through these stages effectively usually move onto making good and quick decisions on and off the field, court or pitch.

*Personal and social responsibility in groups*: All games are social, and thus involve athletes in complex relationships with both coach and teammates. Learning how to negotiate relationships is a critical part of this holistic process; it plunges athletes into collective processes that are no different from the real-life situations they will face. All collective processes strike a balance between the needs and desires of the individual athlete and the needs and momentum of the team, and consider questions such as: How much should an individual give up for the good of the majority? How much should the majority take the needs of a minority group into account? Is it okay not to contribute to every decision? What should one do if one totally disagrees? How much should one speak, and how much should one listen? How do members of a team support each other? What does it mean to be a good team player?

*Free inquiry*: Without free inquiry, there can be no democracy. Coaches coming from an athlete-centred perspective believe that knowledge is not an entity that is fixed and 'out there' but rather constructed and reconstructed on a daily basis, through the 'debate of ideas' (Wallion, 2005). These coaches want lively discussions, not simply drill for skill. As in real life, communication will fail, tempers will fray and differences will seem irreconcilable. Coaches should view these moments as opportunities for athletes to become more articulate, practice active listening and learn to accept that not all situations can be resolved. Sometimes we have to settle for a compromise, trust others or delay a final decision until we see how things turn out.

*Decision-making*: As athletes ask questions about their actions – such as 'Shall I pass or retain the ball?' – they exercise attributes such as social conscience, critical thinking and commitment (Goodlad, Mantle-Bromley & Goodlad, 2004). All athletes should be involved in decision-making through tactical awareness so that they will gain understanding and meaning and become more engaged in the game (Bunker & Thorpe, 1982, 1986). Decision-making is at the heart and soul of sport, and athletes will learn whether their decisions are sound, feasible or, at times, messy and convoluted.

*Social justice*: Informed by an athlete-centred philosophy, coaches and athletes should cultivate a sport climate that is fair and attentive to issues of power, privilege and difference. By implementing DiA, we ultimately are advocating the replacement of a hierarchical approach with a culture and climate in which information is shared with all, and athletes exercise independence in their thoughts and actions by establishing well-articulated boundaries. These boundaries result in teams that will be able to self-manage.

## Integrating life skills into an athlete-centred approach

Sport, like all educational experiences, has a social dimension that we believe should be addressed explicitly in an athlete-centred model. The social dimension of education addresses interpersonal relationships and the development of the social skills that will support athletes throughout their lives. In this section, we present skills and knowledge athletes need to develop the social dimensions for their future work, life and citizenship, such as critical thinking and problem, communication and collaboration.

The Partnership for 21st Century Learning (www.p21.org/our-work/p21-framework) provides a comprehensive framework for thinking about life skills. We advocate that coaches focus on integrating the following major concepts: (a) critical thinking and problem solving; (b) communication and collaboration; (c) flexibility and adaptability; (d) initiative and self-direction; and (e) social and cross-cultural skills. Table 1.1, which was adapted from the original Partnership for 21st Century Learning framework, breaks down each of the major concepts into defined critical elements to help you integrate these into your sport program. For example, consider the critical elements of communication: (a) articulate thoughts and ideas effectively using oral and nonverbal communication skills in a variety of situations; (b) listen effectively to translate meaning, including knowledge, values, attitudes and intentions; and (c) communicate effectively in diverse environments. Integrating life skill concepts into the ACC model encourages an autonomy-supportive style into athletes' sporting experience (Deci & Ryan, 2002; Mandigo, Holt, Anderson, & Shephard, 2008). Coaches can be intentional about designing opportunities for athletes to work on their communication with each other as a team, with coaches, with their fans and with their families.

**TABLE 1.1** Life skill concepts to integrate into athlete–centred coaching

| | LIFE SKILL CONCEPTS | | | | |
| --- | --- | --- | --- | --- | --- |
| | CRITICAL THINKING & PROBLEM SOLVING | FLEXIBILITY & ADAPTABILITY | INITIATIVE & SELF-DIRECTION | SOCIAL & CROSS-CULTURAL SKILLS | COMMUNICATION & COLLABORATION |
| **CRITICAL ELEMENTS** | ***Reason Effectively***<br>Use various types of reasoning (inductive, deductive, etc.) as appropriate to the situation<br><br>***Use Systems Thinking***<br>Analyse how parts of a whole interact with each other to produce overall outcomes in complex systems | ***Adapt to Change***<br>Adapt to varied roles, responsibilities, schedules and contexts<br>Work effectively when there is ambiguity and change<br><br>***Be Flexible***<br>Incorporate feedback effectively<br>Deal positively with praise, setbacks and criticism<br>Understand, negotiate and balance diverse views and beliefs to reach workable solutions | ***Manage Goals and Time***<br>Incorporate short- and long-term goal setting<br>Utilise time and manage workload<br><br>***Work Independently***<br>Monitor, define, prioritise and complete tasks without direct oversight | ***Interact Effectively with Others***<br>Know when it is appropriate to listen and when to speak<br>Conduct themselves in a respectable manner<br><br>***Work Effectively in Diverse Teammates***<br>Respect cultural differences and work effectively with teammates from a range of social and cultural backgrounds<br>Respond open-mindedly to different ideas and values | ***Communicate Clearly***<br>Articulate thoughts and ideas effectively using oral and nonverbal communication skills in a variety of situations<br>Listen effectively to translate meaning, including knowledge, values, attitudes and intentions<br>Communicate effectively in diverse environments<br><br>***Collaborate with Others***<br>Demonstrate ability to work effectively and respectfully with diverse teammates<br>Exercise flexibility and willingness to be helpful in making necessary compromises to accomplish a common goal |

*Make Judgments and Decisions*

Effectively analyse and evaluate evidence, arguments, claims and beliefs

Reflect critically on learning experiences and processes

*Solve Problems*

Solve different kinds of problems in both conventional and innovative ways

Identify and ask significant questions that clarify various points of view and lead to better solutions

*Be Self-directed Learners*

Demonstrate initiative to advance skill levels

Demonstrate commitment to learning as a lifelong process

Reflect critically on past experiences in order to inform future progress

Adapted from Partnership for 21st Century Learning (www.p21.org/our-work/p21-framework)

## Athlete-centred model: our reflecting and thinking

Our intention has been to extend the notion of an athlete-centred approach to coaching to empower athletes and throughout their various sport experiences. Athletes are a vulnerable population, particularly in an economic view of sport, which opens possibilities for inequitable distribution of power, exploitation and unfair and dangerous demands in terms of health and emotional well-being. We offer a model as a way of thinking about an ACC which integrates the major ideas we have discussed in the chapter – pedagogical principles, democracy in action and integration of life skills (see Figure 1.1). Each aspect is significant to creating a holistic experience for athletes. We believe each major aspect of this triangle of the ACC model leads to athletes who are healthy, skilful and empowered. Empowering athletes is a way of investing in their growth and development and entrusting them with ownership and responsibility for themselves, the team and their season. We believe that if sport is an educative process then it should support the social system. This social system should support athletes' collective ethics, values and goals as well as encourage them to examine ways they can help improve society.

## References

Almond, L. (2010). Revisiting the TGfU brand. In J. I. Butler & L. L. Griffin (Eds.), *more Teaching Games for Understanding: Moving globally* (pp. VII–X). Champaign, IL: Human Kinetics.

Alvarez, M. S., Balaguer Sola, I., Castillo Fernández, I., & Duda, J. (2009). Coach autonomy support and quality of sport engagement in young soccer players. *The Spanish Journal of Psychology, 12*(1), 138–148.

Bunker, D., & Thorpe, R. (1982). A model for the teaching of games in secondary schools. *Bulletin of Physical Education, 10*(1), 9–16.

Bunker, D., & Thorpe, R. (1986). The curriculum model. In R. Thorpe, D. Bunker, & L. Almond (Eds.), *Rethinking Games Teaching* (pp. 11–14) Loughborough, UK: Loughborough University of Technology.

Butler, J. I. (2016). *Playing fair: Using student-invented games to prevent bullying, teach democracy, and promote social justice.* Champaign, IL: Human Kinetics.

Cassidy, T., Jones, R. L., & Potrac, P. (2016). *Understanding sports coaching: The pedagogical, social and cultural foundations of coaching practice* (3rd ed.). New York: Routledge.

Corbin, C. B. (2002). Physical activity for everyone: What every physical educator should know about promoting lifelong physical activity. *Journal of Teaching in Physical Education, 21*(2), 128–144.

Deci, E. L., & Ryan, R. M. (2002). *Handbook of self-determination research.* Rochester, NY: University of Rochester Press.

Ellis, M. (1986). Making and shaping games. In R. Thorpe, D. Bunker, & L. Almond (Eds.), *Rethinking games teaching* (pp. 61–65). Loughborough: Department of Physical Education and Sport Science, Loughborough University of Technology.

Ewing, M., & Seefeldt, V. (2002). Patterns of participation and attrition in American agency-sponsored youth sports. In F. L. Smoll & R. E. Smith (Eds.), *Children and youth in sport: A biopsychosocial perspective* (pp. 39–56). Dubuque: Kendall/Hunt.

Fidelis, I. (2008). *Sport participation in Canada, 2005, culture, tourism and the center for education statistics.* Statistics Canada. Retrieved from www.statcan.ca/english/research/81-595-MIE/81-595-MIE2008060.pdf

Frey, J. H., & Eitzen, D. S. (1991, August 1). Sport and society. *Annual Review of Sociology*, *17*(1), 503–522.

Goodlad, J. L., Mantle-Bromley, C., & Goodlad, S. J. (2004). *Education for everyone: Agenda for education in a democracy*. San Francisco, CA: Jossey-Bass.

Hellison, D., & Martinek, T. (2006). Social and individual responsibility programs. In D. Kirk, D. McDonald, & M. Sullivan (Eds.), *The handbook of physical education* (pp. 610–626), Thousand Oaks, CA: Sage.

Hofferth, S. L., & Sandberg, J. F. (2001). How American children spend their time. *Journal of Marriage and Family*, *63*(2), 295–308.

Hopper, T. (2011). Game-as-teacher: Modification by adaptation in learning through game-play. *Asia-Pacific Journal of Health, Sport and Physical Education*, *2*(2), 3–21.

Howarth, K., Fisette, J., Sweeney, S., & Griffin, L. L. (2010). Unpacking tactical problems in invasion games: Integrating movement concepts into games education. In J. I. Butler & L. L. Griffin (Eds.), *More Teaching Games for Understanding: Moving globally* (pp. 245–256). Champaign, IL: Human Kinetics.

Jarvie, G. (2012). *Sport, culture and society: An introduction*. New York: Routledge.

Kidman, L., & Lombardo, B. J. (2010). *Athlete-centered coaching: Developing decision makers* (2nd ed.). Worcester: IPC Press Resources.

Kretchmar, S. (2005). Teaching Games for Understanding and the delights of human activity. In L. L. Griffin & J. I. Butler (Eds.), *Teaching Games for Understanding: Theory, research and practice* (pp. 199–212). Champaign, IL: Human Kinetics.

Mandigo, J. L., Holt, N., Anderson, A., & Sheppard, J. (2008). Children's motivational experiences following autonomy-supportive games lessons. *European Physical Education Review*, *14*(3), 407–425.

Mitchell, S. A., Olsin, J. L., & Griffin, L. L. (2013). *Teaching sport concepts and skills: A tactical games approach for ages 7 to 18* (3rd ed.). Champaign, IL: Human Kinetics.

National Collegiate Athletic Association. (n.d.). Retrieved from www.ncaa.org/

Partnership for 21st Century Skills. (n.d.). Retrieved from www.nea.org/home/34888.htm

Seefeldt, V. D., & Ewing, M. E. (1997). Youth sports in America: An overview. *Physical Activity and Fitness Research Digest*, *2*, 1–11.

Siedentop, D., & van der Mars, H. (2012). *Introduction to physical education, fitness and sport* (8th ed.). New York: McGraw Hill.

Thompson, J. D. (2003). *Organizations in action: Social science bases of administrative theory*. New Brunswick, NJ: Transaction Publishers.

Thorpe, R. (2001). Rod Thorpe on Teaching Games for Understanding. In L. Kidman (Ed.), *Developing decision makers: An empowerment approach to coaching* (pp. 22–36). Worcester: IPC Print Resources.

Thorpe, R., Bunker, D., & Almond, L. (1986). *Rethinking games teaching* (pp. 25–34). Loughborough: Department of Physical Education and Sports Science, Loughborough University of Technology.

Tuckerman, B. W. (2001). Developmental sequence in small groups. *Group Facilitation*, *3*, 66–81.

Visek, A. J., Achrati, S. M., Manning, H., McDonnell, K., Harris, B. S., & DiPietro, L. (2015). The fun integration theory: Towards sustaining children and adolescents sport participation. *Journal of Physical Activity and Health*, *12*(3), 424–433.

Wall, M., & Cote, J. (2007). Development activities that lead to dropout and investment in sport. *Physical Education and Sport Pedagogy*, *12*(1), 77–87.

Wallion, N. (2005). *Assessing learning as an understanding: Towards a semioconstructivist approach in ball games*. Paper presented at the meeting of the International Teaching Games for Understanding Conference, Hong Kong.

# 2

# AN ATHLETE-CENTRED APPROACH TO ENHANCE *THRIVING* WITHIN ATHLETES AND COACHES

*Gretchen Kerr, Ashley Stirling and Joseph Gurgis*

Sport is a context often cited for its ability to foster development. Every year across westernised countries, millions of parents enrol their children in sport programs because they believe sport participation, in addition to enhancing their child's physical development, will foster self-esteem, skills of teamwork and collaboration, perseverance, and frustration tolerance. Researchers of youth sport participation have provided support for many of these assumptions (Donaldson & Ronan, 2006; Holt, 2013). However, researchers have also shown that sport participation may be associated with distressing experiences and outcomes such as a poor sense of self and negative peer interactions (Hansen, Larson, & Dworkin, 2003; Kendellen & Camiré, 2015), thus demonstrating that sport experiences are not inherently developmentally helpful.

Coaches are key stakeholders in sport and are important influencers over the nature and quality of sport experiences for athletes. While there is a substantial body of literature that addresses qualities and competencies of effective coaches (Lawley & Linder-Pelz, 2016), little attention has been devoted to the quality of the experiences for coaches and the ways in which they may develop personally and professionally through their coaching experiences.

In this chapter, we explore the ways in which an athlete-centred approach to the design and delivery of sport programs can contribute to thriving for both athlete participants and coaches. We will begin with a description of the concept of thriving and will then demonstrate the ways in which the tenets of athlete-centred sport are aligned with the development of thriving. Finally, through the use of examples, we will show how sport programs designed and delivered according to athlete-centred tenets can foster thriving for coaches and sport participants.

## What is thriving?

Thriving has been defined as an active process of observable growth along an upward developmental trajectory towards fulfilling one's potential (Benson &

Scales, 2009). Stemming from positive psychology and notions of self-actualisation, thriving includes personal fulfillment and realisation of individual potentials. Thriving also draws upon developmental systems theories, which emphasise the role of external influences in the pursuit of individual actualisation (Bronfenbrenner & Morris, 1998). As such, there is a bi-directional relationship between the individual and his or her context in which positive development occurs, with mutual benefit occurring for both the person and the environment (Lerner, Brentano, Dowling, & Anderson, 2002). Bundick and colleagues (2010) have defined thriving as a "dynamic and purposeful process of individual-context interactions over time, through which the person and his/her environment are mutually enhanced" (p. 891). Similarly, Easterbrooks and colleagues (2013) conceived thriving as "positive and healthy functioning that occurs when the strengths and potentials of an individual are combined with the resources in his or her environment" (p. 103).

While the construct of thriving is similar to self-actualisation, positive development, flourishing, and positive growth, it may be differentiated by its emphasis on embeddedness within social contexts, the bi-directional influences between the individual and contexts, and the positive contributions thriving makes to oneself, as well as one's family, community, and society. A synthesis of the literature on thriving indicates a number of distinguishing features that interact with one another. Each is described below.

## Thriving as a general upward trajectory

Thriving is a developmental construct that involves a general pattern of relatively consistent development along an upward trajectory in which individually and socially valued behaviours, such as confidence and caring, develop (Bundick et al., 2010). Theories of thriving refer to movement towards attainment of 'idealised personhood', including positive contributions to self, family, community, and civil society (Lerner, 2006). Given that thriving is a process, the term 'thriving-oriented' is generally used.

Critical to this feature is the dynamic, non-linear nature of this trajectory. In other words, those who are thriving are not always happy, functioning well, or experiencing smooth life experiences; instead, they face challenges, hardships, failures, and life crises but emerge and grow from these experiences with greater self-awareness and understanding and strength. Further, thriving individuals "accept the struggle" (Colby & Damon, 1992, p. 66) associated with the normal 'ups and downs' of life, and demonstrate adaptability to adversity and challenge and embrace these experiences. In this way, thriving goes beyond adapting to life's twists and turns in order to function adequately, and instead implies a journey towards optimal development.

## Thriving as mutual enhancement of the individual and the context

Thriving refers to the dynamic and bi-directional nature of relations between the individual and his or her context, through which both are mutually enhanced

(Lerner et al., 2002, 2011). Not only do people and environments influence the ways in which people develop, but the individual also influences others and the context in which she or he interacts. With respect to young people, Benson and Scales (2009, p. 94) write:

> one of the major dynamics involved in the thriving process is the embeddedness of the young person in relationships (teachers, parents, coaches, mentors, youth workers, youth ministers, neighbors) and developmental settings (schools, families, congregations, youth programs, neighborhoods) that affirm their talents and interests (and, in some cases, actually help a young person discover them), provide one-on-one encouragement and guidance, celebrate movement and growth, provide appropriate demands and expectations, and provide opportunities (or connect the young person to other opportunities within one's community) for expressing their core passions.

According to several authors (e.g. Ford & Smith, 2007; Lerner, Dowling, & Anderson, 2003), a thriving orientation involves contributing to social wellbeing at the levels of the family, friends, community, and broader society, which, in turn, enhances the achievement of individual actualisation.

### Thriving as the active pursuit of full potentials

Thriving entails the pursuit of optimal development across all life domains, beyond the achievement of developmental tasks. It also pertains to the pursuit of one's full potentials, including unique talents, interests, and/or aspirations (Bundick et al., 2010). A thriving-oriented individual has self-awareness of his or her own uniqueness and actively engages in the process of realising one's potential, including seeking of opportunities, people, and resources to purposefully manifest potential (Bundick et al., 2010). Central to the theory of thriving is the role of the individual as "both the active producer and the product of his or her ontogeny" (Brandtstädter 1998, p. 800), thus highlighting the significance of individual agency.

### Dimensions of thriving

Huffington, in her 2014 book entitled *Thrive*, proposes that individuals thrive when they experience wellbeing, wisdom, wonder, and giving. Wellbeing is achieved through such behaviours as adequate sleep and nutrition, exercise, mindfulness and meditation, and disconnecting from technology. Through experimentation with various experiences, connections, and relationships, and taking time to process these, Huffington proposes that wisdom is built. Wonder may occur through opportunities for creation, curiosity, uni-tasking and flow, or transcendence experiences. Giving represents the serving of others, caring, empathy, and compassion. We propose the addition of a dimension of achievement given the significance of achievements for one's sense of self and the upward trajectory of growth and development towards self-actualisation. We also suggest that an athlete-centred approach to sport is well suited to thriving through the provision of opportunities to experience wellbeing, wisdom, wonder, giving, and achievement. In the following section, we elaborate on the ways in which athlete-centred sport can promote thriving.

## Athlete-centred sport as a vehicle for thriving for athletes and coaches

Athlete-centred is both a philosophy of sport as well as a specific approach to the design and delivery of sport programs. The foundation of an athlete-centred approach is that sport is to be used as a vehicle that contributes to the athlete's overall performance and personal development (Clarke, Smith, & Thibault, 1994). Athlete-centredness espouses a value-based approach and recognises the athlete "as the focal point, and, as such, the organisational structure, sport infrastructure and decision-making process have been adapted to support and respond to the needs, values, and objectives of athletes" (Kihl, Kikulis, & Thibault, 2007, p. 2). In this way, the holistic health and wellbeing of the athlete takes precedence over performance outcomes and is the priority focus for policies, procedures, and programs (Kerr & Stirling, 2008). The goal of athlete-centred approaches is to enhance the athletes' development of personal and life skills, and to encourage ethical conduct and citizenship, thus contributing to individual as well as athletic development. Proponents of athlete-centredness advocate that athletic performance emerges from a focus on personal development (Miller & Kerr, 2002). To date, the vast majority of the research on athlete-centred sport identifies a broad range of benefits for athletes while neglecting potential benefits for coaches.

To date, thriving has not been addressed in the sport literature. Thriving shares similarities with other concepts that have been applied to sport, such as positive youth development, post-traumatic growth, and resilience in terms of attention to positive developmental trajectories, fulfillment of potentials, and constructive responses to adversity. However, thriving differs from these concepts by virtue of the emphases on individual agency in one's growth and the bi-directional benefits to the individual and his or her environment. We propose that an athlete-centred approach to sport holds significant potential for the promotion of thriving amongst both athletes and coaches. In Figure 2.1, we propose a theoretical model of the ways in which the various tenets of athlete-centred sport are conceptually linked with the dimensions of thriving.

The following section outlines the main tenets of athlete-centred sport and illustrates the ways in which athlete-centred approaches to sport may enhance thriving for both athletes and coaches.

### *Enhancement of holistic health and wellbeing*

With athlete-centred approaches, the athletes' rights and developmental needs drive the design and delivery of sport programs (Clarke et al., 1994), and, as such, the

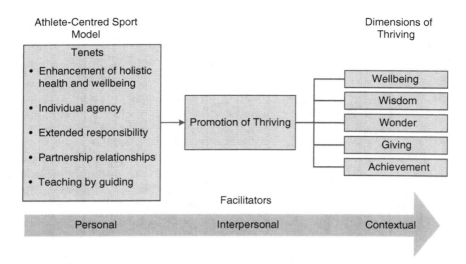

**FIGURE 2.1** Conceptual model of athlete-centred sport as a vehicle for thriving. (Adapted from Huffington, 2014).

athlete's holistic health and wellbeing are prioritised. For example, thriving depends upon embeddedness within relationships and developmental settings that help individuals identify, nurture, express, and celebrate individual interests, competencies, and passions. This is congruent with the athlete-centred tenet of designing and delivering sport programs based upon individual needs and strengths. With an athlete-centred approach, sport is viewed as the vehicle by which athletes are provided with opportunities and the guidance necessary to develop such transferable life skills as respect, trust, independence, responsibility, and accountability. With such a focus on transferable skills and competencies, sport has the potential to contribute in positive ways to the athlete's development outside of the sport context.

An athlete-centred approach challenges the assumption that striving for personal development precludes athletic excellence or that athletic excellence is viable only through personal sacrifices (Miller & Kerr, 2002). Instead, a core assumption of an athlete-centred model of sport is that performance excellence is facilitated by personal growth rather than achieved at its expense. By providing opportunities to individuals to "develop the talents that interest them, spark a sense of passion and purpose in their lives" (Scales, Benson, & Roehlkepartain, 2011, p. 275), thriving is promoted.

Although the majority of the athlete-centred sport literature focuses on development of the athlete, we suggest that athlete-centred approaches also have the potential to enhance the holistic health and wellbeing of sport coaches. The commitment to holistically developing athletes through an empowering and cultivating coaching style may positively influence the growth and wellbeing of coaches. For example, an athlete-centred approach to sport assists athletes to develop citizenship, sportsmanship, and ethical conduct (Clarke et al., 1994). While the expression of these positive behaviours reflects the personal, holistic growth of athletes, this may in turn influence the growth of coaches, who may be more likely to respond in constructive ways to the positive behaviour expressed by athletes and to develop meaningful relationships with athletes who are perceived to be respectful and responsible. This bi-directional nature of thriving enables coaches to experience personal growth in response to athletes' thriving from athlete-centred coaching.

## Importance of individual agency

Athlete-centred coaching refers to a process in which "athletes gain and take ownership of knowledge, development and decision-making that will help them to maximise their performance and their enjoyment" (Kidman & Lombardo, 2010, p. 13). Promoting individual agency of athletes is a process by which coaches balance, in a developmentally appropriate manner, the provision of structure, or "contouring individual dispositions and behavior along socially prescribed lines" with athlete autonomy, or "the capacity of individual actors to choose their behavior regardless of structural influences" (Cockerham, 2005, p. 51). This process requires a gradual shift of power from the coach to the athlete, similar to the 'power-to' style of coaching within an athlete-centred program which sees coaches actively sharing power with their athletes, granting them the freedom, or agency, to make responsible decisions for the betterment of the team and their individual development (Tomlinson & Strachan, 1996). Through the process of developing autonomy and agency, athletes have opportunities to contribute to the nature of their experiences, experiment, exercise curiosity and creativity, test their skills and competencies, and develop self-awareness, all of which are important contributors to thriving.

The sharing of power between coach and athlete presents growth opportunities for the coach as well. Throughout this process, coaches may experience rewards as well as trials and tribulations in response to the choices made by young athletes, who are learning to accept increased responsibility and are developing decision-making skills. By balancing the best interests of the team with the provision of opportunities for athlete agency, coaches may gain self-insight, develop a higher moral purpose, and portray a commitment to learning, all of which are reflective of a thriving individual.

## Extended responsibility

Inherent to an athlete-centred approach is a focus on the long-term health and wellbeing of the athlete and a recognition that the sport experiences of athletes today affect their development long after their sport involvement has ended. The long-term commitment of holistic development within an athlete-centred program inspires athletes to become lifelong participants, equipped with the life skills to thrive within and outside of sport.

Researchers (Weiss & Sisley, 1984) have shown that coaches value the social (co-operation among teammates and sportsmanship), psychological (self-control, self-confidence, and positive attitudes), and physical (skill development and physical fitness) outcomes of sport. When coaches feel motivated, supported, and efficacious, they find coaching to be a pleasurable and enlightening experience (Kidman & Hanrahan, 2011). Further, significant intrinsic rewards are gleaned when coaches see long-term benefits resulting from their roles and contributions in their athlete's development as athletes and individuals after the sport involvement has ceased.

## Partnership relationships

Athlete-centred coaches create partnership relationships with their athletes. The athletes are empowered and included in some of the planning, decision-making, and evaluation processes in a developmentally and situationally appropriate manner. Moreover, for coaches to experience success, they must be open and considerate of external perspectives, such as those proposed by their athletes, which will facilitate individual actualisation (Denison, Mills, & Konoval, 2015). In creating this partnership relationship, athlete-centred coaches are generally more oriented to being democratic and humanistic than autocratic when coaching (Philippe & Seiler, 2006).

The mutually interdependent relationship established within an athlete-centred program grants coaches and athletes the opportunity to concurrently meet team and performance objectives, and collaboratively address problems and challenges (Clarke et al., 1994). A partnership relationship is thought to enhance such transferable skills in athletes as communication, problem-solving, and conflict management (Kidman, 2005; Light & Harvey, 2017). Coaches are also thought to benefit developmentally from this partnership and from deepened relationships with their athletes (Philippe & Seiler, 2006). Positive relationships between athletes and coaches provide reinforcement to both parties that their behaviours and interpersonal conduct are appropriate and constructive. Schreiner (2010) suggested that thriving can occur only in the context of meaningful relationships or interpersonal thriving.

## Teaching by guiding

The democratic style of leadership upheld in an athlete-centred approach allows coaches to lead athletes by example, by modelling behaviour that depicts integrity and openness, while also providing athletes significant opportunities to express themselves (Clarke et al., 1994). When coaches accept the philosophy and responsibility of empowering athletes to become free agents within a sporting program, rather than the object of one (Clarke et al., 1994), then the coach is more likely to abandon autocratic teaching styles in favour of more democratic teaching styles.

With such coaching approaches, athletes are encouraged to develop the ability to make informed decisions for the purpose of achieving their goals and personal improvement (Clarke et al., 1994; Miller & Kerr, 2002). Coaches, in turn, thrive from the gratification of knowing that their guidance has contributed towards athletes' development of informed decision-making skills. It is an invigorating experience for coaches to witness their athletes make considered and deliberate choices for the betterment of themselves and the team.

## Facilitators of thriving within an athlete-centred sport model

In this final section, we will suggest ways in which an athlete-centred sport model may enhance thriving for both athletes and coaches. Facilitators of thriving may exist at the personal, interpersonal, and contextual level. Within an athlete-centred sport model, personal facilitators may pertain to behaviours or qualities of the coach or athlete; interpersonal facilitators can include the nature and quality of the coach–athlete relationship, amongst others; and the contextual facilitators may refer to the sport organisation or actual sport environment. In Table 2.1, we provide examples of ways in which the dimensions of thriving, as adapted from Huffington (2014), may be facilitated with an athlete-centred sport model. Given the focus of this chapter on thriving for both athletes and coaches, and the bi-directional influences of one on another, the examples listed pertain to coaches and/or athletes.

**TABLE 2.1** Facilitating thriving in athletes and coaches

| *Facilitator* | *Example* |
| --- | --- |
| **Wellbeing** | |
| • Prioritise appropriate sleep, nutrition, for both athletes and coaches<br>• Incorporate mindfulness for athletes and coaches into daily training<br>• Disconnect from technology before training to enable appropriate preparation, and after training to enable time for processing and reflection (for both athletes and coaches)<br>• Apply a long-term vision for wellbeing | • Set and share goals on each of these dimensions<br>• Set time for mindfulness during warm-up or cool down<br>• Collect all phones in a common space before training<br>• Be guided by the question: "How are the activities and behaviours we are engaging in today going to affect our wellbeing, individually and collectively, in the future?" |
| **Wisdom** | |
| • Re-define what success means by prioritizing wellbeing and personal development for both coaches and athletes; performance successes will emerge as byproducts<br>• Change habits and social conventions: shift dialogue about high stress levels, lack of sleep and time as 'badges of honour' to experiences that are not rewarded or reinforced. Alternatively, reward adequate sleep and strong time and stress management skills.<br>• Incorporate time and space for reflection within training for both athletes and coaches | • Set and share goals for health (e.g. sleep, nutrition, stress and time management), relationships (e.g. teamwork, communications), creativity (experimentation), and caring (e.g. looking after others, empathy)<br>• Celebrate success in achieving the goals identified above<br>• Post-practice, ask: "What went well about today's training? What do you wish had been different about today's training? What will you do tomorrow to make a difference?"<br>• Provide opportunities for professional development (e.g. coach education for senior athletes) |

*(Continued)*

**TABLE 2.1** (Continued)

| Facilitator | Example |
|---|---|
| | • Invite guest speakers on training topics (e.g. technique, drills, nutrition, strength and conditioning) for coaches and athletes to learn together<br>• Sharing about the 'why' of training strategies amongst the team<br>• Opportunities for both coaches and athletes to suggest topics in need of further information |

### Wonder

| | |
|---|---|
| • Create situations that are conducive to exploration, creativity, and curiosity without judgment<br>• Enable activities that call for total absorption of one's attention and focus to promote transcendent experiences | • Ask athletes: "How many different ways can they work with teammates to move a soccer ball down the field? How many different ways can they get over the vaulting horse in gymnastics?" For coaches, explore benefits of various coaching styles, such as remaining highly interactive or silent during game situations.<br>• Encourage athletes to focus on feeling the water against the skin in swimming, or notice the sound of feet as they prepare for the take-off in long jump. For coaches: focus on minute movements of athletes |

### Giving

| | |
|---|---|
| • Engage athletes in peer instruction and feedback<br>• Engage coaches in mentorship programs<br>• Engage athletes and coaches in the broader community through volunteer or service contributions<br>• Encourage athletes to give back to the sport upon their retirement | • After teaching a skill, have athletes give feedback to one another<br>• Mentor new, developing coaches; mentor senior athletes into coaching<br>• Deliver sport-specific workshops or playing time to youth in marginalised communities<br>• Facilitate opportunities for retired athletes to contribute to coaching, officiating, volunteering |

### Achievement

| | |
|---|---|
| • Set and support individual and collective goals regarding wellbeing, wisdom, wonder, and giving<br>• Ensure opportunities for challenge, success, and failure for athletes and coaches<br>• Provide opportunities for athletes to give feedback on coaches and vice versa | • As a team, athletes and coaches engage in setting a goal for cumulative sleep that includes a minimum of 7 hours per night per individual. Celebrate coaches who prioritise the holistic health and wellbeing of athletes and who have positive appraisals from athletes and parents<br>• Arrange for exhibition games with more successful teams and make time to reflect |

| Facilitator | Example |
|---|---|
| • Recognise and reward individual and collective goals regarding wellbeing, wisdom, wonder, and giving<br>• Recognise, reward, and celebrate process and outcomes goals | • Offer athletes constructive feedback on behaviour and performance and provide them an opportunity to share their views on your coaching methods<br>• Provide positive feedback on improvements made on sport-related goals (e.g. sport skill acquisition, managing performance anxiety).<br>• Recognise athletic accomplishments<br>• Implement team celebrations |

Adapted from Huffington (2014).

## Conclusion

In this chapter, we propose that youth sport, when delivered according to the tenets of athlete-centred sport, has the potential to promote thriving amongst both athletes and coaches. Thriving refers to a general upward trajectory of growth and development towards the fulfillment of one's potential; through this process the individual and her or his environment are mutually enhanced. As a result of the bi-directional relationship between individual and context, athlete-centred sport has the potential to advance thriving amongst athletes as well as coaches. To date, little attention has been devoted to the benefits of athlete-centred sport models on the growth and fulfillment of coaches. Given the significant role of coaches in determining the nature and quality of the sport experience for athletes, we suggest that a focus on thriving of coaches is needed to enhance their experiences as well as those of the athletes. Further consideration of the facilitators of thriving is an important direction for future research and applied work.

## References

Benson, P. L., & Scales, P. C. (2009). The definition and preliminary measurement of thriving in adolescence. *Journal of Positive Psychology, 4*(1), 85–104.

Brandtstädter, J. (1998). Action perspectives on human development. In W. Damon & R. M. Lerner (Eds.), *Handbook of child psychology, Vol. 1: Theoretical models of human development* (pp. 807–863). New York: John Wiley & Sons.

Bronfenbrenner, U., & Morris, P. A. (1998). The ecology of developmental processes. In W. Damon & R. M. Lerner (Eds.), *Handbook of child psychology, Vol. 1: Theoretical models of human development* (pp. 993–1023). New York: John Wiley & Sons.

Bundick, M. J., Yeager, D. S., King, P. E., & Damon, W. (2010). Thriving across the life span. In W. F. Overton & R. M. Lerner (Eds.), *The handbook of life-span development, Vol. 1: Cognition, biology, and methods* (pp. 882–923). Hoboken, NJ: John Wiley & Sons.

Clarke, H., Smith, D., & Thibault, G. (1994). *Athlete-centred sport: A discussion paper*. Federal/Provincial/Territorial Sport Police Steering Committee, Sport Canada, Ottawa, Canada.

Cockerham, W. C. (2005). Health lifestyle theory and the convergence of agency and structure. *Journal of Health and Social Behavior, 46*(1), 51–67.

Colby, A., & Damon, W. (1992). *Some do care: Contemporary lives of moral commitment*. New York: Free Press.

Denison, J., Mills, J. P., & Konoval, T. (2015). Sports' disciplinary legacy and the challenge of 'coaching differently'. *Sport, Education and Society, 22*(6), 772–783. Published online: 8 July 2015, 1–12.

Donaldson, S. J., & Ronan, K. R. (2006). The effects of sports participation on young adolescents' emotional well-being. *Adolescence, 41*(162), 369–389.

Easterbrooks, M. A., Ginsberg, K., & Lerner, R. M. (2013, Fall). Resilience among military youth. *The Future of Children, 23*(2), 99–120. Retrieved from futureofchildren.org/futureofchildren/publications/docs/Chapter%205.pdf

Ford, M. E., & Smith, P. R. (2007). Thriving with social purpose: An integrative approach to the development of optimal human functioning. *Educational Psychologist, 42*(3), 153–171.

Hansen, D. M., Larson, R. W., & Dworkin, J. B. (2003). What adolescents learn in organized youth activities: A survey of self-reported developmental experiences. *Journal of Research on Adolescence, 13*, 25–55.

Holt, N. (2013). *Positive youth development through sport* (2nd ed.). London: Routledge.

Huffington, A. (2014). *Thrive: The third metric to redefining success and creating a happier life*. London: Random House.

Kendellen, K., & Camiré, M. (2015). Examining former athletes' developmental experiences in high school sport. *SAGE Open, 5*(4), 1–10.

Kerr, G., & Stirling, A. (2008). Child protection in sport: Implications of an athlete-centered philosophy. *Quest, 60*(2), 307–323.

Kidman, L. (2005). *Athlete-centred coaching: Developing inspired and inspiring people*. Christchurch, NZ: IPC Print Resources.

Kidman, L., & Hanrahan, S. J. (2011). *The coaching process: A practical guide to becoming an effective sports coach* (3rd ed.). London: Routledge.

Kidman, L., & Lombardo, B. (2010). *Athlete-centered coaching: Developing decision makers* (2nd ed.). Worcester: Innovative Print Communications Ltd.

Kihl, L. A., Kikulis, L. M., & Thibault, L. (2007). A deliberative democratic approach to athlete-centred sport: The dynamics of administrative and communicative power. *European Sport Management Quarterly, 7*(1), 1–30.

Lawley, J., & Linder-Pelz, S. (2016). Evidence of competency: Exploring coach, coachee and expert evaluations of coaching. *Coaching: An International Journal of Theory, Research and Practice, 9*(2), 110–128.

Lerner, R. M. (2006). Developmental science, developmental systems, and contemporary theories of human development. In R. M. Lerner (Ed.), *Theoretical models of human development: Volume 1 of handbook of child psychology* (pp. 1–17). Hoboken, NJ: Wiley-Blackwell.

Lerner, R. M., Brentano, C., Dowling, E. M., & Anderson, P. M. (2002). Positive youth development: Thriving as a basis of personhood and civil society. In C. S. Taylor, R. M. Lerner, & A. von Eye (Eds.), *New directions for youth development: Theory, practice and research: Pathways to positive youth development among gang and non-gang youth* (pp. 11–34). San Francisco, CA: Jossey-Bass.

Lerner, R. M., Dowling, E. M., & Anderson, P. M. (2003). Positive youth development: Thriving as the basis of personhood and civil society. *Applied Developmental Science, 7*(3), 172–180.

Lerner, R. M., Lerner, J. V., von Eye, A., Bowers, E. P., & Lewin-Bizan, S. (2011). Individual and contextual bases of thriving in adolescence: A view of the issues. *Journal of Adolescence, 34*(6), 1107–1114.

Light, R. L., & Harvey, S. (2017). Positive pedagogy for sport coaching. *Sport, Education and Society, 22*(2), 271–287.

Miller, P. S., & Kerr, G. A. (2002). Conceptualizing excellence: Past, present, and future. *Journal of Applied Sport Psychology, 14*, 140–153.

Philippe, R. A., & Seiler, R. (2006). Closeness, co-orientation and complementarity in coach athlete relationships: What male swimmers say about their male coaches. *Psychology of Sport and Exercise, 7*, 159–171.

Scales, P., Benson, P., & Roehlkepartain, E. (2011). Adolescent thriving: The role of sparks, relationships, and empowerment. *Journal of Youth and Adolescence, 40*(3), 263–277.

Schreiner, L. A. (2010). The "thriving quotient": A new vision for student success. *About Campus, 15*(2), 2–10.

Tomlinson, P., & Strachan, D. (1996). *Power and ethics in coaching.* Gloucester, Canada: National Coaching Certification Program. Retrieved from www.coach.ca/eng/products/documents/Power-Ethics.pdf

Weiss, M. R., & Sisley, B. L. (1984). Where have all the coaches gone? *Sociology of Sport Journal, 1*, 332–347.

# 3

# COACHING TACTICAL CREATIVITY IN TEAM SPORTS

*Daniel Memmert*

For more than 35 years, athlete-centred coaching models have been developed around the world on how to introduce invasion games in schools or sport clubs. The Teaching Games for Understanding approach (TGfU) (Bunker & Thorpe, 1982), the Tactical Games Model (Mitchell, Oslin, & Griffin, 2006; Metzler, 2000), Game Sense (den Duyn, 1997; Light, 2004), Invasion Games Competence Model (Tallir, Lenior, Valcke, & Musch, 2007), Games Concept Approach (Rossi, Fry, McNeill, & Tan, 2007), and the Tactical-Decision Learning Model (Grehaigne, Wallian, & God-bout, 2005) are well-established models for teaching and coaching. They offer children and students pathways of learning both tactical and technical skills in many invasion games (e.g., basketball, netball, soccer, etc.). These models put emphasis on the improvement of an understanding of the tactical dimensions (i.e., what to do) of game play before the teacher/instructor concentrates on the improvement of the students' technical (i.e., how to do) skills associated with the game (cf. Grehaigne, Godbout, & Bouthier, 1999). The main aim of many of these athlete-centred coaching models is to teach tactical problem solving in different types of invasion games (Memmert, 2015a). Thus, decision-making (e.g., game sense, game playing ability, or even game performance) and skill development with decision-making contexts are of importance. I will focus on the development of tactical creativity. After defining and exposing the relevance of tactical creativity in invasion games, the main attention is on sport activities, coaching, and training environments to foster tactical creativity in youth sports. Here, the tactical creativity approach (TCA, Memmert, 2015) will be introduced, which is based on extensive research and can be seen as the groundwork for the development of tactical creativity.

## Definition of creativity and of tactical creativity

Since Guilford's work (1967), creativity has been an inherent part of scientific research and has provided considerable patterns of findings in numerous contexts, such as science, literature, music, religion, politics, and sports (for a review, see Milgram, 1990; Sternberg, 1999; Sternberg & Lubart, 1999; Runco, 2007; Memmert, 2013, 2015). As a result, an enhanced need for evaluation has started worldwide to examine the effects of education and school (for a review, see Scott, Leritz, & Mumford, 2004), and physical education, unfortunately, just occasionally, on the improvement of general, area-unspecific creativity (e.g., Garaigordobil & Berrueco, 2011; Haddon & Lytton, 1968; Olive, 1972; Tuckman & Hinkle, 1986: for a review, Memmert, 2015).

The difference between expert decision-making and creativity may be based on the theoretical distinction between 'divergent thinking' and 'convergent thinking' (Guilford, 1967), which have been integrated as well into invasion games (Roth, 2005). For invasion games, in recent years, the two tactical thinking processes − tactical intelligence (e.g., game sense) and tactical creativity − have been derived from these theoretical distinctions (cf. Roth, 2005; Memmert & Roth, 2007), which can be defined in the following way (Memmert, 2015):

- *Tactical intelligence (convergent tactical thinking)*: In team and racket sports, tactical game intelligence is understood as the production of the best solution for specific individual, group, or team tactic match situations.
- *Tactical creativity (divergent tactical thinking)*: In team and racket sports, tactical creativity is understood as the generation of a variety of solutions in specific individual, group, and team tactic situations which are surprising, infrequent, and/or original.

Empirical evidence from the World Cup 2010 and 2014 and the European Cup 2016 demonstrated that the closer actions took place to the goal, the more tactically creative they were evaluated (Kempe & Memmert, in preparation).

## The tactical creativity approach in invasion games

The tactical creativity approach (TCA) by Memmert (2015) is based on extensive research and can be seen as the groundwork for the development of tactical creativity in invasion games. The TCA discriminates between a micro (process) level and a macro (content) level (see also Memmert, 2015b). The former points towards the mechanism and psychological processes in the training units (micro rules) that lead to the generation of creative ideas, and the latter towards the organisable environmental training conditions that can be used by teachers and coaches (macro rules). The TCA focuses on seven methodological principles that foster tactical creativity in team sports. All of these seven principles (one-dimension games, diversification, deliberate practice, deliberate play, deliberate coaching, deliberate memory, deliberate motivation) (Figure 3.1) are discussed now on the basis of an empirical background.

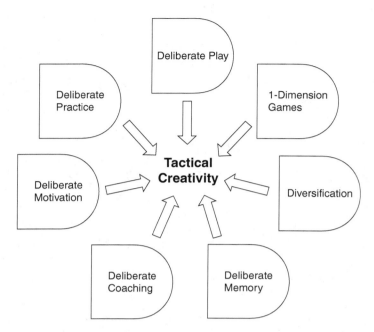

**FIGURE 3.1**  Theoretical framework of the tactical creativity approach (TCA): The 7 Ds fostering tactical creativity in team and racket sports. The order of the seven principles indicates a chronological order from children and youth training to adolescent and adult training. While the first five principles are more suitable for younger age groups, all principles are useful for groups at an older age and should be integrated in training units.

(Adapted from Memmert, 2010c, 2011, 2015).

## The 7 Ds of promoting tactical creativity in invasion games

### Deliberate play

The non-instructed and preferably free experimentation in practical and unstructured situations ('deliberate play') seems to be an important characteristic for promoting tactical creativity in childhood (Baker, Côté, & Abernethy, 2003). Studies concerning movement experiences indicate that deliberate play in youth has influenced the creativity of current national team and top league players (Memmert, Baker, & Bertsch, 2010). For the composition of physical education classes and sport coaching, this implies that trying out highly diverse variations of response has to be encouraged in tactical tasks.

### One-dimension games

The term 'small-sided games' has become more and more popular (Hill-Haas, Dawson, Impellizzeri, & Coutts, 2011; Clemente, Couceiro, Martins, & Mendes,

2012). Small-sided games are well-defined as adaptations of real matches, reducing the game complexity into small parts; e.g., being played on reduced pitch areas, using modified rules, and involving a smaller number of players (e.g., Clemente et al., 2012; Hill-Haas et al., 2011; Rampinini et al., 2007). These modified games are used by trainers to develop technical skills or aerobic fitness components (Gabbett, 2006; Gabbett, Jenkins, & Abernethy, 2009) and are often utilised in soccer or basketball (Hill-Haas, Coutts, Rowsell, & Dawson, 2008; Hill-Haas, Dawson, Coutts, & Rowsell, 2009). Meanwhile, the consensus prevails in invasion games literature that general and sports-specific (tactical) skills are also gained in small-sided games (e.g., Memmert & Harvey, 2010; Mitchel et al., 2006).

Similar to small-sided games for the training of technical skills or fitness components, so-called one-dimension games, were developed for fostering divergent thinking skills in tactical situations. Due to a large number of always repeating, similar situational conditions in these one-dimension games, various specific or sports-specific tactical solutions can be developed in invasion games (Memmert, 2015). The idea is that a fixed number of players, as well as defined rules and environmental constraints, exist in basic tactical constellations, and the players are provoked to produce adequate and creative solutions. The opportunities for diagnostics and assessment of divergent tactical creativity in these one-dimension games are published in various places (Memmert, 2007; 2010a, b).

## Diversification

Direct environmental influences, like diversification on the development of tactical creativity in invasion games, were proved in numerous investigations (Abernethy, Baker, & Côté, 2005; Baker et al., 2003; for a review, see Memmert, 2015). Experimental field-based studies (Memmert & Roth, 2007) showed that the perception of many different situations in various invasion games can have a positive influence on the development of multi-variant solutions. Thus, positive tactical transfer is evident and can foster tactical creative solutions in invasion games. Tactical creativity can especially develop if children and youth act with various motor skills in one-dimension games. For the teacher/coach, this implies letting a game be played with hands, with feet, or with an implement. For example, the one-dimension games seen in Figure 3.2 evokes tactical behaviour in the identification of gaps in recurring comparable situations (Memmert, 2015). Strikers 1, 2, 6, and 7 have the task of playing the ball past defenders 3, 4, and 5, and below the upper boundary into the opposite field. The players' aim is to find gaps and pass the ball through them. To stress diversification, the players should use different motor skills: left and right foot, hands, and implements.

## Deliberate memory

In the centre of conscious information processing lies the working memory, in which a limited amount of information can be processed that is relevant for the current activity (see Baddeley, 2007). The capacity and the general function of the

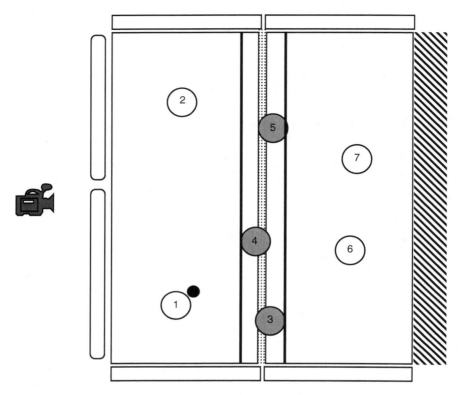

**FIGURE 3.2** One-dimension game evokes tactical behaviour in the identification of gaps. (Adapted from Memmert & Roth, 2007; Memmert, 2015).

working memory (Furley & Memmert, 2010) are of special importance for tactical creativity training in invasion games. Even though an athlete's individual capacity of working memory does not seem to have an influence on divergent performance in invasion games (Furley & Memmert, 2015). Nevertheless, it is advisable that a coach does not deliver too much information simultaneously during tactical orders, instructions, or team meetings due to the limited working capacity (Cowan, 2005). The fact that information in the working memory is worked on, manipulated, and structured on short notice (Conway, Jarrold, Kane, Miyake, & Towse, 2007), has important effects for training in invasion games.

Furley and Memmert (2013) demonstrated that the activated contents of the working memory guide an athlete's focus by biasing attention towards objects in the visual field that are related to the recent contents of working memory. In addition, working memory has been shown to be predictive of controlling attention in a goal-directed way and avoiding interference amongst athletes (Furley & Memmert, 2012). Thus, on a positive occasion this implies that instructions from the trainer can guide the children's attentional focus and thus make tactical decisions easier. On a negative occasion, children come back more and more to irrelevant information from the teacher, which prevents them from making optimal decisions through unfavourable attention control in a specific situation.

## Deliberate coaching

Especially by the use of particular possibilities of instruction and through giving external (implicit) hints, the attentional focus in invasion games can be controlled specifically (Memmert, 2015c). In a series of experiments concerning cognitive–tactical decision behaviour, it was shown that attentional focus is targeted by the simplest variations of instructions ('inattentional blindness') and that this has an immediate influence on the quality of tactical performances (Furley, Memmert, & Heller, 2010). It is the pivotal result of field studies (Memmert, 2007) that through a wide attentional focus, unexpected and potentially better versions of a solution can be perceived, deployed, and, therefore, be learned. This means, for the teacher/coach, that no hints need to be used in one-dimension games that diminish children's attentional focus.

## Deliberate motivation

The latest theoretical models and empirical evidence from social psychology point to the fact that creative performances can be influenced by the simplest instructions, which manipulate, for example, the test person's emotional states (Friedman & Förster, 2000, 2001; Hirt, Levine, McDonald, Melton, & Martin, 1997; Isen, 2000; Isen, Daubman, & Nowicki, 1987). As the distinct result patterns show, a promotion focus – defined as feeling pleasure when receiving positive action outcomes and sorrow when such positive outcomes are absent (cf. Higgins, 1997) – facilitates the generation of creative solutions more easily than having a prevention focus – defined as feeling successful when avoiding inconvenient, negative results and feeling sorrow when such negative results occur. In a study by Memmert, Hüttermann, and Orliczek (2013), it was demonstrated that tactical creativity in invasion games benefits from a promotion focus. In the 'promotion' condition, the athletes generated more creative and flexible solutions than 'prevention'-manipulated athletes. Thus, in a 5:2 game, the teachers would rather say, "It is your aim to find as many spaces as possible" instead of, "You must find as many spaces as possible".

## Deliberate practice

There is a great amount of research showing that sport-specific experiences over a long time (the 10-year rule of Ericsson, Krampe, & Tesch-Römer, 1993) are necessary for the attainment of expertise (e.g., Helsen, Starkes, & Hodges, 1998; Kalinowski, 1985; Monsaas, 1985). The term deliberate practice offers a task-centred training program based on specific instructions and training environments. Memmert et al. (2010) showed that, especially for top team players in the highest national league or even in the national team, the number of hours of training activities also makes the difference between more creative and less creative team sport players. National league players started their specific sport significantly later than players in the next highest level of competition. Thus, in adolescence and adult training programs, deliberate practice is useful and should be integrated in training units.

## Summary

This chapter gave an overview of literature on tactical creativity in invasion games. In summary, in invasion games, contrary to so-called best solutions (game sense, game playing ability), tactical creativity is defined as the surprising, original, and flexible production of tactical solutions (Memmert & Roth, 2007). The TCA by Memmert (2015) contains the seven Ds for fostering tactical creativity (see Figure 3.1). Empirical evidence suggests that all Ds can be useful methods to foster infrequent and flexible solutions in invasion games. These seven key principles of developing tactical divergent thinking in invasion games are described in Table 3.1 and may be considered as first recommendations for sport lessons and training units.

These principles stand partly in contrast to recent coaching behaviour in youth soccer. Partington, Cushion, and Harvey (2014) revealed that the coaches of younger aged soccer groups currently give more instructions than coaches of the older age groups. However, as Kidman and Lombardo (2010) noted, "The game is the teacher" (p. 23). This way, all forms of play and practice that have been developed so far, accounting for age adaptations, can be applied to the development of

**TABLE 3.1** The 7 Ds of the TCA fostering tactical creativity

| | |
|---|---|
| **D**eliberate play: | Uninstructed play without instructions or feedback can lead to trying out a multitude of different solutions. |
| 1-**D**imension-Games: | By means of multiple repetitions of similar situations, structured game forms can improve basic tactical skills across different sports with an amount of creative solutions. |
| **D**iversification: | Use of different motor skills in 1-**D**imension-Games can support the development of original solutions. |
| **D**eliberate memory | Quantity and quality of information should be considered in tactical instructions, in order to 'fill' the working memory with useful information. |
| **D**eliberate coaching: | In 1-**D**imension-Games, no instructions shall be given that narrow the focus of the acting players' attention. |
| **D**eliberate motivation: | For 1-**D**imension-Games, promotion instructions are to be given to enlarge the generation of extraordinary solutions. |
| **D**eliberate practice: | In more advanced games, task-centred practice can lead to repetition and exploration of infrequent but adequate solutions. |

(Adapted from Memmert, 2015).

tactical creativity in children. It will be the role of clubs and schools to try to create learning environments that allow the implementation of these methods (Memmert, 2015).

The measures invoked in Table 3.1 serve as a first starting point for the development of divergent tactical brainpower in school. Naturally, in the educational context an evaluation of these opportunities is necessary in order to create the conditions for physical education classes. For this, concrete school interventions have to be planned, which consider especially the peculiarities of the sports game classes next to contextual premises (attention, motivation). An enhanced integration of other research disciplines, like sports education and sports didactics, is essential to this to be able to deduce still more concrete statements for the teaching/coaching practice. Similar to the Game Sense approach, more contextual and ecological research of athlete-centred coaching is necessary (see the literature review by Oslin & Mitchell, 2006). Additionally, more manipulation checks, improved assessment tools, longitudinal research designs, and longer intervention programs are needed for athlete-centred coaching models (Harvey & Jarrett, 2013).

## References

Abernethy, B., Baker, J., & Côté, J. (2005). Transfer of pattern recall skills may contribute to the development of sport expertise. *Applied Cognitive Psychology, 19*, 705–718.

Baddeley, A. D. (2007). *Working memory, thought, and action.* Oxford: Oxford. University Press. doi:10.1093/acprof:oso/9780198528012.001.0001

Baker, J., Côté, J., & Abernethy, B. (2003). Sport specific training, deliberate practice and the development of expertise in team ball sports. *Journal of Applied Sport Psychology, 15*, 12–25.

Bunker, D., & Thorpe, R. (1982). A model for the teaching of games in secondary schools. *Bulletin of Physical Education, 18*(1), 5–8.

Clemente, F., Couceiro, M., Martins, F. M. L., & Mendes, R. (2012). The usefulness of small-sided games on soccer training. *Journal of Physical Education and Sport, 12*, 93–102.

Conway, A. R. A., Jarrold, C., Kane, M. J., Miyake, A., & Towse, J. N. (2007). *Variation in working memory.* New York: Oxford University Press.

Cowan, N. (2005). *Working memory capacity.* Hove, East Sussex: Psychology Press.

Den Duyn, N. (1997). *Game sense: Developing thinking players.* Belconnen, ACT: Australian Sports Commission.

Ericsson, K. A., Krampe, R., & Tesch-Römer, C. (1993). The role of deliberate practice in the acquisition of expert performance. *Psychological Review, 100*, 363–406.

Friedman, R. S., & Förster, J. (2000). The effects of approach and avoidance motor actions on the elements of creative insight. *Journal of Personality and Social Psychology, 79*(4), 477.

Friedman, R. S., & Förster, J. (2001). The effects of promotion and prevention cues on creativity. *Journal of Personality and Social Psychology, 81*(6), 1001.

Furley, P., & Memmert, D. (2010). The role of working memory in sports. *International Review of Sport and Exercise Psychology, 3*, 171–194.

Furley, P., & Memmert, D. (2012). Working memory capacity as controlled attention in tactical decision making. *Journal of Sport and Exercise Psychology, 34*, 322–344.

Furley, P., & Memmert, D. (2013). "Whom should I pass to?" The more options the more attentional guidance from working. *PLOS ONE, 8*(5), e62278. doi:10.1371/journal.pone.0062278

Furley, P., & Memmert, D. (2015). Creativity and working memory capacity in sports: working memory capacity is not a limiting factor in creative decision making amongst skilled performers. *Frontiers in Psychology*. doi: 10.3389/fpsyg.2015.00115

Furley, P., Memmert, D., & Heller, C. (2010). The dark side of visual awareness in sport – inattentional blindness in a real-world basketball task. *Attention, Perception, & Psychophysics*, *72*, 1327–1337.

Gabbett, T. (2006). Skill-based conditioning games as an alternative to traditional conditioning for rugby league players. *Journal of Strength Conditioning Research*, *20*, 309–315.

Gabbett, T., Jenkins, D., & Abernethy, B. (2009). Game-based training for improving skill and physical fitness in team sport athletes. *International Journal of Sports Science Coaching*, *4*, 273–283.

Garaigordobil, M., & Berrueco, L. (2011). Effects of a play program on creative thinking of preschool children. *Spanish Journal of Psychology*, *14*(2), 608–618.

Grehaigne, J. F., Godbout, P., & Bouthier, D. (1999). The foundations of tactics and strategy in team sports. *Journal of Teaching in Physical Education*, *18*, 159–174.

Grehaigne, J. F., Wallian, N., & Godbout, P. (2005). Tactical-decision learning model and students' practices. *Physical Education & Sport Pedagogy*, *10*(3), 255–269.

Guilford, J. P. (1967). *The nature of human intelligence*. New York: McGraw Hill.

Haddon, F. A., & Lytton, H. (1968). Teaching approach and the development of divergent thinking abilities in primary schools. *British Journal of Educational Psychology*, *38*(2), 171–180.

Harvey, S., & Jarrett, K. (2013). A review of the game-centred approaches to teaching and coaching literature since 2006. *Physical Education and Sport Pedagogy*. Published online: 21 January 2013. doi:10.1080/17408989.2012.754005

Helsen, W. F., Starkes, J. L., & Hodges, N. J. (1998). Team sports and the theory of deliberate practice. *Journal of Sport & Exercise Psychology*, *20*, 12–34.

Higgins, E. T. (1997). Beyond pleasure and pain. *American Psychologist*, *52*, 1280–1013.

Hill-Haas, S. V., Coutts, A., Rowsell, G., & Dawson, B. (2008). Variability of acute physiological responses and performance profiles of youth soccer players in small-sided games. *Journal of Science and Medicine in Sport*, *11*, 487–490.

Hill-Haas, S. V., Dawson, B. T., Coutts, A. J., & Rowsell, G. J. (2009). Physiological responses and time-motion characteristics of various small-sided soccer games in youth players. *Journal of Sports Sciences*, *27*, 1–8.

Hill-Haas, S. V., Dawson, B., Impellizzeri, F. M., & Coutts, A. J. (2011). Physiology of small-sided games training in football. A systematic review. *Sports Medicine*, *41*, 199–220.

Hirt, E. R., Levine, G. M., McDonald, H. E., Melton, R. J., & Martin, L. L. (1997). The role of mood in quantitative and qualitative aspects of performance: Single or multiple mechanisms? *Journal of Experimental Social Psychology*, *33*, 602–629.

Isen, A. M. (2000). Positive affect and decision making. In M. Lewis & J. Haviland-Jones (Eds.), *Handbook of emotions* (2nd ed., pp. 417–435). New York: Guilford.

Isen, A. M., Daubman, K. A., & Nowicki, G. P. (1987). Positive affect facilitates creative problem solving. *Journal of Personality and Social Psychology*, *52*, 1122–1131.

Kalinowski, A. G. (1985). The development of Olympic swimmers. In B. S. Bloom (Ed.), *Developing talent in young people* (pp. 139–192). New York: Ballantine.

Kempe, M., & Memmert, D. (in preparation). *Good, better, creative! The relevance of tactical creativity in world class soccer*.

Kidman, L., & Lombardo, B. J. (2010). TGfU and humanistic coaching. In J. I. Butler & L. L. Griffin (Eds.), *More Teaching Games for Understanding: Moving globally* (pp. 171–186). Champaign, IL: Human Kinetics.

Light, R. (2004). Coaches' experiences of games sense: Opportunities and challenges. *Physical Education & Sport Pedagogy*, *9*, 115–131.

Memmert, D. (2007). Can creativity be improved by an attention-broadening training program? An exploratory study focusing on team sports. *Creativity Research Journal*, *19*, 1–12.

Memmert, D. (2010a). Creativity, expertise, and attention: Exploring their development and their relationships. *Journal of Sport Science*, *29*, 93–104.

Memmert, D. (2010b). Testing of tactical performance in youth elite soccer. *Journal of Sports Science and Medicine*, *9*, 199–205.

Memmert, D. (2010c). Development of creativity in the scope of the TGfU approach. In J. I. Butler & L. L. Griffin (Eds.), *Teaching Games for Understanding: Theory, research and practice* (2nd ed., pp. 231–244). Champaign, IL: Human Kinetics.

Memmert, D. (2011). Sports and creativity. In M. A. Runco & S. R. Pritzker (Eds.), *Encyclopedia of creativity* (2nd ed., pp. 373–378). San Diego, CA: Academic Press.

Memmert, D. (2013). Tactical creativity. In T. McGarry, P. O'Donoghue, & J. Sampaio (Eds.), *Routledge handbook of sports performance analysis* (pp. 297–308). Abingdon: Routledge.

Memmert, D. (2015a). *Teaching tactical creativity in sport: Research and practice*. Abingdon: Routledge.

Memmert, D. (2015b). Development of Tactical Creativity in Sports. In J. Baker & D. Farrow (Eds.), *The Handbook of Sport Expertise* (pp. 363–372). Abingdon: Routledge.

Memmert, D. (2015c). Visual Attention in Sports. In J. Fawcett, E. F. Risko, & A. Kingstone (Eds.), *The Handbook of Attention* (pp. 643–662). Cambridge: MIT Press.

Memmert, D., Baker, J., & Bertsch, C. (2010). Play and practice in the development of sport-specific creativity in team ball sports. *High Ability Studies*, *21*, 3–18.

Memmert, D., & Harvey, S. (2010). Identification of non-specific tactical problems in invasion games. *Physical Education and Sport Pedagogy*, *15*, 287–305.

Memmert, D., Hüttermann, S., & Orliczek, J. (2013). Decide like Lionel Messi! The impact of regulatory focus on divergent thinking in sports. *Journal of Applied Social Psychology*, *43*(10), 2163–2167.

Memmert, D., & Roth, K. (2007). The effects of non-specific and specific concepts on tactical creativity in team ball sports. *Journal of Sport Science*, *25*, 1423–1432.

Metzler, M. W. (2000). *Instructional models for physical education*. Boston, MA: Allyn & Bacon.

Milgram, R. M. (1990). Creativity: An idea whose time has come and gone. In M. A. Runco & R. S. Albert (Eds.), *Theory of creativity* (pp. 215–233). Newbury Park: Sage.

Mitchell, S. A., Oslin, J. L., & Griffin, L. L. (2006). *Teaching sport concepts and skills: A tactical games approach* (2nd ed.). Champaign, IL: Human Kinetics.

Monsaas, J. A. (1985). Learning to be a world – class tennis player. In B. S. Bloom (Ed.), *Developing talent in young people* (pp. 139–192). New York: Ballantine.

Olive, H. (1972). The relationship of divergent thinking to intelligence, social class, and achievement in high-school students. *The Journal of Genetic Psychology*, *121*, 179–186.

Oslin, J., & Mitchell, S. (2006). Game-centred approaches to teaching physical education. In D. Kirk, D. MacDonald, & M. O'Sullivan (Eds.), *The handbook of physical education* (pp. 627–651). London: Sage.

Partington, M., Cushion, C. J., & Harvey, S. (2014). An investigation of the effect of athletes' age on the coaching behaviours of professional top-level youth soccer coaches. *Journal of Sports Sciences*, *32*(5), 403–414.

Rampinini, E., Impellizzeri, F. M., Castagna, C., Abt, G., Chamari, K., Sassi, A., & Marcora, S. M. (2007). Factors influencing physiological responses to small-sided soccer games. *Journal of Sports Sciences*, *25*, 659–666.

Rossi, T., Fry, J. M., McNeill, M., & Tan, C. W. K. (2007). The Games Concept Approach (GCA) as a mandated practice: Views of Singaporean teachers. *Sport, Education and Society*, *12*, 93–111.

Roth, K. (2005). Taktiktraining [training of tactics]. In A. Hohmann, M. Kolb, & K. Roth (Hrsg.), *Handbuch sportspiel [Handbook of sport games]* (S. 342–349). Schorndorf: Hofmann.

Runco, M. A. (2007). *Creativity – theories and themes: Research, development, and practice.* Burlington: Elsevier Academic Press.

Scott, G., Leritz, L. E., & Mumford, M. D. (2004). The effectiveness of creativity training: A quantitative review. *Creativity Research Journal, 16*(4), 361–388.

Sternberg, R. J. (Ed.) (1999). *Handbook of creativity.* Cambridge: Cambridge University Press.

Sternberg, R. J., & Lubart, T. I. (1999). The concept of creativity: Prospects and paradigms. In R. J. Sternberg (Ed.), *Handbook of creativity* (pp. 3–15). Cambridge: Cambridge University Press.

Tallir, I. B., Lenoir, M., Valcke, M., & Musch, E. (2007). Do alternative instructional approaches result in different game performance learning outcomes? Authentic assessment in varying game conditions. *International Journal of Sport Psychology, 38*, 263–282.

Tuckman, B. W., & Hinkle, J. S. (1986). An experimental study of the physical and psychological effects of aerobic exercise on schoolchildren. *Health Psychology: Official Journal of the Division of Health Psychology, American Psychological Association, 5*(3), 197.

# 4

# ATHLETE-CENTRED COACHING IN DISABILITY SPORT

## A critical perspective

*Robert Townsend and Christopher Cushion*

'Athlete-centred' discourses continue to gain prominence in coaching, where such an approach is assumed to better facilitate athlete learning and, therefore, optimise performance (Cassidy, Jones, & Potrac, 2009; Kidman, 2005). However, in reality it is more likely a discourse that legitimises the power-dominated means of developing athletes that are 'empowered' and able to make decisions. It is well established that coaching is situation- and context-dependent, and as such disability sport provides an interesting and useful lens to challenge and extend our understanding of 'athlete-centred' coaching. Connecting the two is not an easy task. An athlete-centred coaching approach is a complex construct that currently lacks theoretical depth or application in research, and in practice is often housed in conservative coaching platitudes. It is often subsumed under a broad 'athlete-centred' coaching 'philosophy', conflated into a prescriptive set of coaching behaviours and 'styles' or used as an underpinning pedagogical approach to designing coaching practice. In turn, coaching in disability sport is an emerging field that is characterised by a normative focus that often forces disability into the background of coaching (cf. Townsend, Smith, & Cushion, 2016).

It is in the consideration of 'disability' that there is some common ground between coaching and athlete-centred ideologies. As Lyle (2010) argued, by athlete-centred, if we mean that the athletes' needs should be paramount, then the premise is appealing; however, we must avoid producing research in which there is a danger of a lack of domain and context specificity. Therefore, if we are to develop a greater understanding of what is meant by 'athlete-centred' coaching, we believe that much greater conceptual and theoretical clarity is needed (Nelson, Potrac, & Marshall, 2010). Thus, in order to add some theoretical substance to athlete-centred coaching in disability sport, we propose connecting with critical disability studies, and the models of disability, to help to provide an understanding as a basis for both coaching practice and coach education that is firmly grounded ontologically and epistemologically. Engaging with disability discourses is important as it helps to make clear coaches' assumptions about the athletes with whom they work, recognising the social and cultural constructions that influence practice, which in turn frames notions of 'athlete-centred'.

## 'Athlete-centred' discourses in coaching and disability sport

While interest in disability sport continues growing, there is limited research on disability coaching (Townsend et al., 2016). This is an important oversight. Disability sport provides a context that may influence the social understanding of disability significantly. This, in part, may be due to its disruptive potential, generated from the visibility of people with disabilities (DePauw, 1997) and the perceived tension between cultural perceptions of disability and the practices of elite sport, of which coaching is a central and defining part (Brittain, 2010; DePauw, 1997; Silva & Howe, 2012). The disabled *athlete*, then, is at the very centre of the coaching process in disability sport.

Currently, coaches are not trained in the specific circumstances of many disability contexts (Bush & Silk, 2012; Tawse, Bloom, Sabiston, & Reid, 2012). As identified by Bush and Silk (2012), often disability coach education in its various modalities occupies a separate and distinct 'space' from traditional coach education pathways, and therefore coaches face a lack of structured, disability specific coach education (McMaster, Culver, & Werthner, 2012; Taylor et al., 2014). The findings of these early forays into disability coaching are somewhat troubling and, consistent with findings from the coaching literature, coaching knowledge and practices broadly, are derived overwhelmingly from informal and non-formal sources (e.g. Cushion, Armour, & Jones, 2003; Nelson, Cushion, & Potrac, 2006; Lemyre, Trudel, & Durand-Bush, 2007). Coaches are left to draw upon knowledge generated outside of disability sport to apply to specific contexts (MacDonald et al., 2015) that can place demands beyond coaches' existing skills and knowledge (Burkett, 2013). Such a position is concerning as coaches are left to take knowledge generated outside of disability contexts and ground their understanding in material and experiential conditions through a process of 'trial and error' (Taylor et al., 2014).

In heavily stratified social conditions such as coaching, socialisation has a powerful structuring effect on the knowledge and practices of coaches. This can lead to the uncritical adoption and reproduction (Piggott, 2015) of coaching discourses that are often subsumed under 'inclusive' and 'athlete-centred' axioms (e.g. 'coach the athlete, not the disability'). Therefore, received wisdom argues that athlete-centred approaches are 'best', but without theoretical or empirical substance this concept remains an assemblage of meanings and practices, that is, a dominant system of meanings: an ideology. While appearing as an instrument of accepted coaching knowledge – that is, to coach the 'athlete' and reject the complexity of disability in favour of a more functional and normative coaching framework – it can also become an instrument of domination. Particularly when coaches decide what is athlete-centred and what that should look like. Such messages, when applied uncritically within a powerful normalising framework, can divert critical attention away from the impact that impairment has on the lives of people with a disability (Feely, 2016). Indeed, to impose such 'athlete-centred' discourses on athletes can be just as rigid and oppressive as more authoritarian approaches (Nelson et al., 2014), and could arguably lead to an ideology of 'person-centredness' that is based on coaches' preconceptions and assumptions about disability. The agency of disabled athlete then is downplayed in an oppressive coaching structure that privileges ableist norms and uncritical knowledge about disability.

Specifically, by imposing judgements about coaching and athletes under an 'athlete-centred' banner, coaches can be "inadvertently imposing an ideology and value on the athlete rather than providing that which will best meet the athlete's individual needs, compatible with their individual learning" (Nelson et al., 2014, p. 527). By adopting an unconsidered and supposed 'athlete-centred' approach to coaching, coaches risk imposing a definition of the world most congruent with their particular interests; this results in a wide-ranging definition of athlete-centred which is in fact the arbitrary and culturally derived nature of their practice (cf. Cushion & Partington, 2016). Coaches rationalise their actions as being in the best interest of athletes but are paradoxically agents of a selective tradition and cultural incorporation, where normative, ableist practices become legitimised. Indeed, such a focus blurs the structural and systemic causes of disability (Grue, 2016) and can contribute to an ideological position where athletes are forced to showcase their 'superhuman' athletic ability and, in so doing, distance themselves from devalued, disabled identities (Bundon & Clarke, 2015; Bush, Silk, Porter, & Howe, 2013; Purdue & Howe, 2012).

This situation can – in part – be attributed to a lack of informed resources to support coach development (Fairhurst, Bloom, & Harvey, 2017; Tawse et al., 2012). However, 'athlete-centred' discourses can be enabling as well as constraining. This is especially the case in coaching, where coaches are positioned as central and defining figures in shaping the sporting experience for people with disabilities. To do so requires coaches and researchers to engage with critical disability studies. In this chapter, we suggest that an understanding of the cultural frameworks that support the delivery of coaching within the wider social context can advance an athlete-centred agenda that is geared towards social change, inclusion and empowerment without recourse to a dominance of humanistic platitudes that are common in this field.

## Models of disability

Within disability studies there are linguistic struggles that seek to foreground legitimate understandings of what disability 'is'. In disability coaching, due to the lack of coach education in this area, it is imperative to examine critically how disability is explained and understood in coaching contexts. As Smith and Bundon (2016) argue, having a grasp on how disability is explained and understood is vital for individuals working with disabled people in any context, as practice is fundamentally shaped by our working understanding of disability (DePauw, 2000). These understandings can be captured through theoretical models of disability that – it should be remembered – are not static definitions but bound up in the ways that they are used, their interrelations and their effects (Wacquant, 2008). Each model brings with it a set of assumptions about constructs such as impairment, disability, disablism and oppression that we argue are fundamental to the construction of an athlete-centred approach in disability sport. This chapter considers four models of disability – from the medical and social model, through to a more contemporary social relational understanding, and finally the human rights model of disability. To contextualise the models, and show their applicability in developing athlete-centred coaching environments, we briefly describe and outline the key assumptions within each model and how they connect to coaching.

## *Medical model*

The medical model has historically been dominant in understanding disability and positioning research (Smith & Perrier, 2014). This perspective, emerging from clinical practice, places the body under intense scrutiny. The central focus of the medical model lies in its link to impairment as the *cause* of disability (Swain, French, & Cameron, 2003) and therefore the defining feature of the disability experience (Fitzgerald, 2012). Underpinning this model is an individualist position shaped by powerful medical discourses that assumes a normative perspective on disability, creating a 'normal/abnormal' dichotomy and overlooking the apparent social construction of 'disability' and 'normality'. As Quinn, Degener, and Bruce (2002) claimed, the medical model "encapsulates a broader and deeper social attitude" (p. 14) in which a tendency to problematise people with an impairment and view them as an object for intervention is entrenched. The lived experience of disability is also ignored. Furthermore, the social environment and culture are treated as unproblematic, and people with impairments are instead viewed as disadvantaged by their own bodies (Oliver, 1996). The medical model frames disability as an individual problem, a phenomenon located outside of culture, a "significant bodily and/or cognitive variation from those who meet the cultural expectation of embodied normality" (Thomas, 2004, p. 28). In so doing, the medical model reinforces dominant ableist (i.e. normal) ideals and values conformity (Swain et al., 2003).

Coach education in disability sport – reflective of discourses in the wider coaching field – remains largely informed by medical discourses. Applied to coach education, the medical model perpetuates a segregated model of education, whereby to work with disabled people coaches are assumed to have, and need, 'specialist' knowledge (Bush & Silk, 2012). Coaching knowledge that is underpinned by a medical model is disciplinary rather than integrated, and often directed toward athletic achievement and performance enhancement where disability is reduced and individualised to biological processes and mechanisms. As a result, coach education that follows a medical model is commonly categorised according to different impairment 'types', where the pedagogical focus of coaching is on the athlete and their impairment as 'problematic' and judged in relation to ableist conceptions of 'ability' (DePauw, 2000). Such a normative coaching agenda embraces a technocratic consciousness where all problems are instrumental or technical problems to be solved (e.g. Cregan, Bloom, & Reid, 2007), with technical procedure and given 'facts' providing sequence and direction while disabled athletes are viewed as biological objects (DePauw, 2000) for intervention under a dominating 'performance' pedagogy.

However, when used in an informed way to underpin aspects of coaching practice, the medical model has useful implications, particularly when dealing with individual athletic needs, specialised prostheses and equipment or classificatory competition demands (Burkett, 2013; Cregan et al., 2007). Furthermore, medical models applied to coach education can be useful in development impairment specific knowledge that has been suggested to be important in ensuring coaching success (Wareham, Burkett, Innes, & Lovell, 2017; Tawse et al., 2012). It is important therefore not to write the body out of our theorising (Hughes & Paterson, 1997), but to also view the wider social environment that influences disability sport. Therefore, an athlete-centred coaching approach that considers the individual complexity of impairment in relation to the sporting context can be considered progressive and an informed basis around which to construct coaching practice (Townsend et al., 2016).

## Social model

The social model[1] was developed by disabled activists from the Union of the Physically Impaired Against Segregation (UPIAS), who attempted to reclaim the term 'disability' from medical discourse. The social model breaks the causal link between impairment and disability (Oliver & Barnes, 2010; Smith & Bundon, 2016) to reconstruct disability as *entirely* socially constructed (Thomas, 2014). This radical constructionist position turns a critical gaze towards society and is based on the premise that disability is the product of a complex collection of structural barriers that create disadvantages, exclusions and restrictions for people with impairments (Thomas, 2014). Importantly, the social model delineates *impairment*, as in the medical model, as a physical characteristic (Swain et al., 2003), but reconceptualises *disability* based on the notion that it is socially constructed and an act of exclusion and oppression:

> In our view, it is society which disables physically impaired people. Disability is something imposed on top of our impairments by the way we are unnecessarily isolated and excluded from full participation in society. Disabled people are therefore an oppressed group in society.
>
> *(Union of the Physically Impaired Against Segregation*
> *[UPIAS], 1976, cited in Oliver, 1996, p. 33)*

Engaging with a social model demands that the social barriers – both actual and ideological, individual and collective – in coaching require recognition and scrutiny. Research in coaching disabled athletes, for example, points to coaches managing a multitude of pragmatic and contextual constraints such as limited financial support, fewer coaching and support staff, a lack of coaching and training resources and equipment and a smaller talent pool (Taylor et al., 2014). Furthermore, coaches may need to communicate with athletes' families, support workers and caregivers, and reflect upon the accessibility of facilities and transportation (Cregan et al., 2007). Indeed, combined with these, access to facilities, a lack of information, equipment costs and a lack of professional training for coaches directly impact upon the sporting opportunities disabled people can enjoy (Bush & Silk, 2012; Smith & Sparkes, 2012). Using the social model can help coaches to reflect on coaching in such a way that considers the athlete, their impairment and the coaching environment in relation to exclusion. The focus is then on the coach and coaching – not the 'problem' of impairment – to adapt in relation to the individual athlete to create and maintain an athlete-centred coaching environment.

The social model as a reflective tool, however, is limited in that it fails to address an important reality for many people – that of dysfunction, illness or bodily pain (Martin, 2013). As Hughes and Paterson (1997) argued, the social model of disability proposes an "untenable separation" (p. 326) between body and culture, and impairment and disability. As a result, the social model fails to explain the role that impairments have upon individuals and their embodied, lived experiences (Shakespeare, 2006), and that even in 'inclusive' and 'athlete-centred' coaching environments impairments can impact on sporting participation in various ways.

## Bringing back the 'relational'

A problem with conceptualising disability in reductive terms (i.e. medical and social models) is essentially the dichotomising of 'disability' and 'impairment'. To this end, Thomas (1999, 2007) sought to rework the social model toward a more *relational* perspective that understands disability as a manifestation of social relationships (Smith & Bundon, 2016; Smith & Perrier, 2014). This means that the interplay of impairment and social barriers can be understood in terms of *disablism*:

> Disablism is a form of social oppression involving the social imposition of restrictions of activity on people with impairments *and* the socially engendered undermining of their psycho-emotional well-being.
>
> *(Thomas, 2007, p. 73)*

Thomas (2007) extended the social relational understanding of disability by addressing the structural causes of disability, *and* how individuals position themselves *in relation to* disability. The distinction this model presents is, according to Reindal (2008), in the ability to distinguish between personal experiences of social restrictions due to the effects of impairment in a social setting, on the one hand, but also the *imposed social restrictions* in social settings, on the other hand. A social relational perspective recognises the enabling and disabling practices within sport – at both structural and individual levels – and, when applied to 'athlete-centred' coaching and coach education, it asks coaches to consider the interaction of impairment, disablism and individual experience in constructing coaching practice.

## Human rights (meta) model

The human rights model was drawn from the United Nations Convention on the Rights of Persons with Disabilities (CRPD). This international treaty was the first to address the rights of disabled people, recognising both equality *and* diversity (Ollerton & Horsfall, 2013). Underpinned by a strong activist ideology, the human rights model builds on the foundations of the social model of disability, and places people with disabilities as subject to the disabling practices of society (Harpur, 2012). Under the banner of the human rights model, participation in disability sport is a fundamental human right. Article 30 of the CRPD, which addressed 'Participation in Cultural Life, Recreation, Leisure and Sport', clearly outlined how people with disabilities are entitled to participate in sport on an equal basis with others (Hassan, McConkey, & Dowling, 2014). This model highlighted the need to provide policies and practices that support the involvement of people with disabilities in sport. Such measures include appropriate training and education for coaches to create more inclusive and high-quality coaching environments.

For coaching researchers, the human rights model can be conceptualised as a meta-model for framing research into disability sport. We have proposed the medical, social and social relational models in order to explain the ontological basis of disability, but a meta-model provides a powerful rationale for researching disability sport in order to uncover and address inequality in sport. Despite its potential to engage with people of all ages and abilities, sport can indeed reaffirm and reproduce feelings of marginalisation (Hassan et al., 2014) and regularly does marginalise disabled bodies (Bundon & Clarke, 2015; Hassan, Dowling, McConkey, & Menke, 2012). As Bundon and Clarke (2015) argued, in the case of disability sport, whilst it is possible for athletes with disabilities to be included in mainstream sport, some athletes may still be excluded by attitudes, practices and policies that privilege able-bodied athletes and reproduce ableism within the structure of coaching. The adoption of a human rights model into coaching identifies and challenges exclusion under a powerful, athlete-centred and socially just perspective.

## Conclusion

If there is a genuine desire within coaching in disability sport to promote an 'athlete-centred' approach, then it is crucial to develop a critical understanding of disability by extending beyond our field and engaging with concepts from outside of our discipline. To advance 'athlete-centred' coaching, coaches need to re-examine how they coach and challenge their assumptions so that they can begin to understand how they have been influenced by dominant discourses about disability that in turn influence beliefs about coaching disabled athletes (Denison, 2010). To engage with disability models is to promote a view of coaching that is athlete-centred; that is, it helps coaches to understand the needs of their athletes, without recourse to generalising and superficial statements about coaching athletes with a disability (e.g. 'coach the athlete, not the disability') and to understand coaches' assumptions about the athletes that they coach.

In considering coaching through the models of disability it is important to demonstrate the ideological dimensions of ideas that are routinely embedded and 'enshrined' in professional coaching discourse (Nelson et al., 2014). This prevents ideals of 'athlete-centred' coaching from simply "sliding into an unproblematised focus" on performance (Nelson et al., 2014, p. 523). Arguably, to practice athlete-centred coaching in disability sport is to not only challenge the conditions in coaching that produce disablement, but to theorise and challenge the conditions of communities that are traditionally marginalised in sport (cf. Goodley & Lawthom, 2005). To this end, we argue that connecting with disability studies in coaching and coach education is a fundamental starting point for the development of true athlete-centred approaches in disability sport.

## Note

1 The social model is neither a social theory in its own right (Oliver, 1996; Thomas, 2007) nor, strictly speaking, a model. It is perhaps closer to a conceptual tool. Because it is commonly called a 'model' in the literature, this term will be used throughout the paper.

## References

Brittain, I. (2010). *The Paralympic Games explained*. London: Routledge.

Bundon, A., & Clarke, L. H. (2015). Honey or vinegar? Athletes with disabilities discuss strategies for advocacy within the Paralympic movement. *Journal of Sport and Social Issues, 39*, 351–370.

Burkett, B. (2013). Coaching athletes with a disability. In P. Potrac, W. Gilbert, & J. Denison (Eds.), *Routledge handbook of sports coaching* (pp. 196–209). New York: Routledge.

Bush, A. J., & Silk, M. L. (2012). Politics, power & the podium: Coaching for Paralympic performance. *Reflective Practice: International and Multidisciplinary Perspectives, 13*, 471–482.

Bush, A. J., Silk, M. L., Porter, J., & Howe, P. D. (2013). Disability [sport] and discourse: Stories within the Paralympic legacy. *Reflective Practice: International and Multidisciplinary Perspectives, 14*, 632–647.

Cassidy, T., Jones, R., & Potrac, P. (2009). *Understanding sports coaching: The social, cultural and pedagogical foundations of coaching practice*. London: Routledge.

Cregan, K., Bloom, G. A., & Reid, G. (2007). Career evolution and knowledge of elite coaches of swimmers with a physical disability. *Research Quarterly for Exercise and Sport, 78*(4), 339–350.

Cushion, C. J., & Partington, M. (2016). A critical analysis of the conceptualisation of 'coaching philosophy'. *Sport, Education and Society, 21*(6), 851–867.

Cushion, C. J., Armour, K. M., & Jones, R. L. (2003). Coach education and continuing professional development: Experience and learning to coach. *Quest, 55*, 215–230.

Denison, J. (2010). Holism in sports coaching: Beyond humanistic psychology. A commentary. *International Journal of Sports Science & Coaching, 5*(4), 489–491.

DePauw, K. P. (1997). The (in)visibility of disability: Cultural contexts and sporting bodies. *Quest, 49,* 416–430.

DePauw, K. P. (2000). Social-cultural context of disability: Implications for scientific inquiry and professional preparation. *Quest, 52,* 358–368.

Fairhurst, K. E., Bloom, G. A., & Harvey, W. J. (2017). The learning and mentoring experiences of Paralympic coaches. *Disability and Health Journal, 10*(2), 240–246.

Feely, M. (2016). Disability studies after the ontological turn: a return to the material world and material bodies without a return to essentialism. *Disability & Society, 31*(7), 863–883.

Fitzgerald, H. (2012). Paralympic athletes and "knowing disability". *International Journal of Disability, Development and Education, 59,* 243–255.

Goodley, D., & Lawthom, R. (2005). Epistemological journeys in participatory action research: Alliances between community psychology and disability studies. *Disability & Society, 20*(2), 135–151.

Grue, J. (2016). The problem with inspiration porn: A tentative definition and a provisional critique. *Disability & Society, 31*(6), 838–849.

Harpur, P. (2012). Embracing the new disability rights paradigm: The importance of the convention on the rights of persons with disabilities. *Disability & Society, 27*(1), 1–14.

Hassan, D., Dowling, S., McConkey, R., & Menke, S. (2012). The inclusion of people with intellectual disabilities in team sports: Lesson from the youth unified sports programme of Special Olympics. *Sport in Society, 15,* 1275–1290.

Hassan, D., McConkey, R., & Dowling, S. (2014). Understanding sport and intellectual disability: An introduction. In D. Hassan, S. Dowling, & R. McConkey (Eds.), *Sport, coaching and intellectual disability* (pp. 1–10). London: Routledge.

Hughes, B., & Paterson, K. (1997). The social model of disability and the disappearing body: Towards a sociology of impairment. *Disability & Society, 12,* 325–340.

Kidman, L. (2005). *Athlete-centred coaching: Developing inspired and inspiring people.* Christchurch, NZ: Innovative Print Communications Ltd.

Lemyre, F., Trudel, P., & Durand-Bush, N. (2007). How youth-sport coaches learn to coach. *The Sport Psychologist, 21,* 191–209.

Lyle, J. (2010). Holism in sports coaching: Beyond humanistic psychology. A commentary. *International Journal of Sports Science & Coaching, 5*(4), 449–452.

MacDonald, D. J., Beck, K., Erickson, K., & Côté, J. (2015). Understanding sources of knowledge for coaches of athletes with intellectual disabilities. *Journal of Applied Research in Intellectual Disabilities, 29*(3), 242–249.

Martin, J.J. (2013). Benefits and barriers to physical activity for individuals with disabilities: a social-relational model of disability perspective. *Disability and Rehabilitation, 35*(24), 2030–2037.

McMaster, S., Culver, D., & Werthner, P. (2012). Coaches of athletes with a physical disability: A look at their learning experiences. *Qualitative Research in Sport, Exercise and Health, 4,* 226–243.

Nelson, L. J., Cushion, C. J., & Potrac, P. (2006). Formal, nonformal and informal coach learning. *International Journal of Sport Science and Coaching, 1*(3), 247–259.

Nelson, L., Cushion, C. J., Potrac, P., & Groom, R. (2014). Carl Rogers, learning and educational practice: Critical considerations and applications in sports coaching. *Sport, Education and Society, 19*(5), 513–531.

Nelson, L., Potrac, P., & Marshall, P. (2010). Holism in sports coaching: Beyond humanistic psychology. A commentary. *International Journal of Sports Science & Coaching, 5*(4), 465–468.

Oliver, M. (1996). *Understanding disability: From theory to practice*. London: Macmillan Press.

Oliver, M., & Barnes, C. (2010). Disability studies, disabled people and the struggle for inclusion. *British Journal of Sociology of Education, 31*, 547–560.

Ollerton, J., & Horsfall, D. (2013). Rights to research: Utilising the convention on the rights of persons with disabilities as an inclusive participatory action research tool. *Disability & Society, 28*, 616–630.

Piggott, D. (2015). The open society and coach education: A philosophical agenda for policy reform and future sociological research. *Physical Education and Sport Pedagogy, 20*, 283–298.

Purdue, D. E. J., & Howe, P. D. (2012). See the sport, not the disability: Exploring the Paralympic paradox. *Qualitative Research in Sport, Exercise and Health, 4*, 189–205.

Quinn, G., Degener, T., & Bruce, A. (2002). *Human rights and disability: The current use and future potential of United Nations human rights instruments in the context of disability*. New York: United Nations Publications.

Reindal, S. M. (2008). A social relational model of disability: A theoretical framework for special needs education? *European Journal of Special Needs Education, 23*(2), 135–146.

Shakespeare, T. (2006). *Disability rights and wrongs*. Abingdon: Routledge.

Silva, C. F., & Howe, P. D. (2012). The (in)validity of supercrip representation of Paralympian athletes. *Journal of Sport and Social Issues, 36*(2), 174–194.

Smith, B., & Bundon, A. (2016). Disability models: Explaining and understanding disability sport. In I. Brittain (Ed.), *Palgrave handbook of Paralympic studies*. Basingstoke: Palgrave Macmillan.

Smith, B. M., & Perrier, M. J. (2014). Disability, sport, and impaired bodies: A critical approach. In R. Schinke & K. R. McGannon (Eds.), *The psychology of sub-culture in sport and physical activity: A critical approach*. London: Psychology Press.

Smith, B. M., & Sparkes, A. (2012). Disability, sport and physical activity: A critical review. In N. Watson, A. Roulstone, & C. Thomas (Eds.), *Routledge handbook of disability studies* (pp. 336–347). London: Routledge.

Swain, J., French, S., & Cameron, C. (Eds.) (2003). *Controversial issues in a disabling society*. Berkshire: Open University Press.

Tawse, H., Bloom, G. A., Sabiston, C. M., & Reid, G. (2012). The role of coaches of wheelchair rugby in the development of athletes with a spinal cord injury. *Qualitative Research in Sport, Exercise and Health, 4*(2), 206–225.

Taylor, S. L., Werthner, P., & Culver, D. M. (2014). A case study of a parasport coach and a life of learning. *International Sport Coaching Journal, 1*, 127–138.

Thomas, C. (1999). *Female forms: Experiencing and understanding disability*. Buckingham, UK: Open University Press.

Thomas, C. (2004). Rescuing a social relational understanding of disability. *Scandinavian Journal of Disability Research, 6*, 22–36.

Thomas, C. (2007). *Sociologies of disability and illness*. London: Palgrave Macmillan.

Thomas, C. (2014). Disability and impairment. In J. Swain, S. French, C. Barnes & C. Thomas (Eds.), *Disabling barriers – enabling environments*, 3rd ed. (pp. 9–16), London: Sage.

Townsend, R. C., Smith, B., & Cushion, C. J. (2016). Disability sports coaching: Towards a critical understanding. *Sports Coaching Review, 4*(2), 80–98.

Wacquant, L. (2008). Pierre Bourdieu. In R. Stones (Ed.), *Key contemporary thinkers* (pp. 261–277). New York: Palgrave Macmillan.

Wareham, Y., Burkett, B., Innes, P., & Lovell, G. P. (2017). Coaching athletes with disability: Preconceptions and reality. *Sport in Society*, Online First, 1–18. doi:10.1080/17430437.2016.1269084

# 5

# TEAM CULTURE AND ATHLETE-CENTRED COACHING

*John P. Alder*

Establishing a quality team culture forms a prominent feature of the athlete-centred coaching approach (Kidman & Lombardo, 2010). Firmly established in the coaching lexicon, team culture is a concept valued by coaches (Kidman & Lombardo, 2010) and has been associated with not only positive learning environments (Johnson, Martin, Palmer, Watson, & Ramsey, 2011; Kidman, 2005) but also on-field success (Kerr, 2013; Schroeder, 2010). Indeed, in the media, teams such as the San Antonio Spurs (Blinebury, 2016) and the much celebrated New Zealand All Blacks (Kerr, 2013) have been lauded for their team culture, which reportedly acts as the competitive advantage behind their success. Conversely, culture has also been linked with negative player experiences (Cresswell & Eklund, 2006) and cited as underpinning a number of undesirable 'off-field' incidents (Bluestone Edge Ltd, 2013).

Given the reported link between culture and performance enhancement, it has become increasing unlikely to find coaches (and managers) who are not concerned with the development, maintenance or change of culture (Cruickshank, Collins, & Minten, 2014). Despite its prominence in the coaching rhetoric, little research has examined the symbolic or interpretative elements of teams or coaching (Schroeder, 2010), and while discussions of athlete-centred coaching have focused upon practices and methods, they have been detached from theory (Nelson, Cushion, Potrac, & Groom, 2014). Authors have commented on team culture in sport and its elements (Cruickshank, Collins, & Minten, 2013; Kidman, 2005; Yukelson, 1997), and despite some similarities in authors' descriptions and depictions, an empirically founded framework on which to base understanding and practice of team culture is lacking, particularly in the context of athlete-centred coaching.

Media narratives and limited empirical research have resulted in the indiscriminate use of the term *culture*. The popular narrative provides both the researcher and practitioner with little clarity about team culture in coaching beyond buzzwords and ethereal descriptions or euphemisms for gaining a winning edge.

Consequentially, the word *culture* requires careful handling to avoid amorphousness and drifting into romantic but superficial narratives of team culture and success. As Alvesson and Sveningsson (2008, p. 35) argued,

> the potential value of the culture concept easily disappears behind rather thin and superficial descriptions . . . characterisations are often used as slogans, wishful thinking and fantasies, rather than a way of gaining a deeper understanding of organisational life.

These issues are directly linked to the central theme of this chapter: team culture and athlete-centred coaching. In the absence of empirical research, it is necessary to turn to other disciplines where culture has received more attention. This chapter seeks to synthesise perspectives from sociology, organisation science and existing coaching research, to establish some landmark, sensitising concepts that provide for a more grounded dialogue of team culture in athlete-centred coaching.

## Defining team culture: a social construct

The term 'team culture' has been used to refer to the psychosocial factors that influence team chemistry and group synergy (Yukelson, 1997) and is described as the "social architecture that nurtures the team psyche" (Martens, 2012, p. 40). Kidman (2005, p. 270) importantly foregrounded the impact of social processes, describing team culture as "the environment that the athletes, coach and manager create . . . it is based on the standards and values that direct how things are done". The team culture that emerges from such social interactions will influence levels of trust, respect, attitudes, values and care for and between team members, and influences day-to-day practices around the team environment (Kidman, 2005). More recently, Cruickshank and Collins (2012, p. 340) conceptualised team culture in the following definition: "the shared values, beliefs, expectations, and practices across the members and generations of a defined group".

The positioning of team culture as the product of a complex series of social interactions influencing team beliefs and subsequent behaviour firmly situates the construct of team culture as both anthropological and sociological in origin. While there is no universally accepted definition of culture in the social sciences, most converge on the idea that culture is concerned with the way people make sense of their experience and the world through the existence of shared meanings (Barker, 2008). Culture forms as people search for and construct meaning from their lived experiences and social interactions (Berger & Luckmann, 1967). The social interactions that take place within sports teams shape the formation of these often 'taken for granted' meanings that act to guide expectations, beliefs and behaviour (Fine, 1979). Of particular importance to athlete-centred coaching is the idea that shared meaning is constructed and sustained from a *shared understanding of the same experience* (Weick, 1995). There is also consistency across the definitions that culture is historically determined, imbued with and characterised by anthropological concepts such as ritual, myth and symbol.

The focus upon interpretive and symbolic elements of teams coupled with the perspective that culture exists as a complex system of shared understanding that emerges from and through social interaction is a significant departure from the sports literature, which has traditionally examined the dynamics of groups and teams through a sport psychology and largely positivist paradigm. This paradigm uses popular concepts such as group cohesion and team building exercises. Encouragingly, a handful of scholars have begun to address the shortfall by offering interpretive analyses of team culture in sport (Cruickshank et al., 2013; Kidman, 2005; Schroeder, 2010).

## 'A team culture' or 'the team culture'?

Although 'a team culture' and 'the team culture' are often used indiscriminately, there exists a key difference between the use of 'team' as an adjective or noun that requires elucidating to avoid conflation and misrepresentation. Cultural research views 'culture' as either a variable (team as an adjective) or a metaphor (team as a noun) (Scott, Mannion, Davies, & Marshall, 2003). Through a 'variable' lens, culture becomes an attribute, something an organisation *has*, often a desired state, for example, a 'performance culture' or a 'family culture'. This perspective positions culture as a tangible outcome or goal that can be achieved, often through conscientious leadership actions: something done *to* people. When team culture is reduced to a function and managerial technique, it becomes easy to misinterpret or misunderstand the nature and influence of power, conflict and cooperation in cultural settings, like sports teams. This largely deterministic perspective has permeated the organisational culture literature and become popular largely due to the central agency afforded to leaders and an accompanying optimism of causal relationships that lead to culture creation and change (Alvesson & Sveningsson, 2008).

Conversely, 'the team culture' adopts the 'metaphor' perspective, viewing culture as something an organisation *is*: a complex system of social relationships, interactions and co-constructed meaning. Culture acts as a lens through which to understand the highly networked, fluid, tacit and tribal nature of groups and teams. In this chapter, I recommend the latter of these two uses of the term 'team culture'. Instead of a destination or goal, culture becomes represented to and by us in meaningful ways through a system of language, signs, material objects, beliefs and rituals. This distinction is of importance to athlete-centred coaching as a humanistic discourse that acknowledges "athletes' voice and dignity in their participation experience" (Kidman & Penney, 2014, p. 1). Furthermore, viewing team culture as a lens through which coaches can better understand individuals and their needs goes some way to avoiding athlete-centred coaching being reduced to functional ways of thinking (Kidman & Penney, 2014). Before exploring what team culture means for athlete-centred coaching, it is necessary to introduce some theories that can offer clarity in our understanding of team culture.

## Helpful theories in making sense of team culture

As renowned organisational psychologist Kurt Lewin argued, "There's nothing more practical than a good theory" (Lewin, 1952, p. 169). Lewin's paragon of generating theories that exist in mutuality between helping understand human nature and providing frames of reference for action to maximise it is at the heart of this chapter. The application of theory will help make sense of team culture in athlete-centred coaching and offer an explanation as to why things happen in the way they do. The plethora of relevant cultural theories across the disciplines encourages the adoption of a multi-theoretical approach. Some of the useful theories in conceptualising and understanding team culture in coaching include social construction, sense-making and sense-giving, structure and agency, idiocultures, organisational culture and levels of culture. Table 5.1 summarises these relevant theories to team culture and relates them to coaching.

**TABLE 5.1** Useful theories for conceptualising team culture in athlete-centred coaching

| Theory | Premise for Team Culture | Implications for Coaching |
|---|---|---|
| Social construction (Berger & Luckmann, 1967) | Team culture is socially constructed and reconstructed by actors (athletes, coaches and practitioners) within the group. | As the product of a unique group of individuals bound by time and context, every team culture is complex, dynamic, in a constant state of (re)creation but therefore changeable. |
| Sense-making (Weick, 1995) and sense-giving (Maitlis & Christianson, 2013) | The processes through which athletes and coaches construct meaning and trigger meaning making amongst others in response to shared (and often ambiguous) experience. | All behaviours and actions by the coach (and athletes) are sensitive to filtering and meaning attribution and this will consequently shape the team's culture. Thus, every coaching action and interaction matters. |
| Duality of structure & agency (Giddens, 1984) | Social structure (the team culture) is both the medium and the outcome of social action by agents (coaches *and* athletes). | All voices in the culture matter and have influence and power flows in all directions. People own what they create. |
| Idiocultures (Fine, 1979) | Every sports team or group has to some extent a culture of its own or an 'idioculture', rich with beliefs, symbols and expressions, known only to insiders and used to separate insiders from outsiders and employed as the basis of interaction. | Every team culture is different despite often having similar goals and aspirations; what worked there *will not* transpose directly here. The construct of an 'idioculture' makes the culture concept useful by focusing on observable interpersonal and group social interactions as the fulcrum of cultural creation. |

| Theory | Premise for Team Culture | Implications for Coaching |
|---|---|---|
| Organisational Culture (Alvesson & Sveningsson, 2008) | A process of sensemaking and subsequent meaning construction, where culture is expressed in terms of language, stories, social practices or rituals and collective experience. | The language, stories, social practice and shared experiences both convey and create the culture of a team. Coaches should be sensitive to these and utilise them to help meet athletes' needs. |
| Levels of Culture (Schein, 2004) | Team culture consists of three interrelated levels: **artefacts** (the most superficial level of culture refers to tangible cultural elements which one can see, hear or feel and are often made public, **espoused values** (norms that provide the day-to-day operating principles that guide group behaviour) and **basic underlying assumptions** (tacit beliefs that act as mental maps that govern group behaviour). | All aspects of a team's culture tell a story about what matters to individuals (athletes and coaches) and the team. However, coaches should be wary of artefacts as they can be superficial and misleading. |

As people seek to make sense and meaning from ambiguous experience, sports teams can clearly be a primary site for expression, group cohesion and nurturing of identity through shared experience (Vallée & Bloom, 2016). Popular views of culture assume social order is centred on value consensus and common values (the general agreement on and patterning of the fundamental beliefs of a group) and point toward a harmonious portrayal of team culture in sport where unity and behavioural uniformity is revered and regarded as crucial to team effectiveness (Vallée & Bloom, 2016; Yukelson, 1997). However, for athlete-centred coaching, a discipline with humanism and social justice in its philosophical fabric, a critical lens reveals culture, values, consensus and the coach's role in this as not so straightforward.

## Problematising team culture: a critical view

Values consensus is underpinned by the concept of cultural hegemony (Gramsci, 1971), the spontaneous (and often subconscious) consent of the masses to the direction imposed on social life by the dominant group. Therefore, a sport team's culture and values are inherently political, where ideologies can be used to influence the way people think through shared values and beliefs. In problematising team culture, it becomes apparent that dialectical tensions exist between individual and team identity and empowerment and disempowerment. These tensions present several philosophical and ethical challenges to the athlete-centred coach.

## Team vs individual identity

Values by their nature exist at a conceptual level. They are abstract and largely idiosyncratic concepts, since everyone has different prior experience. As a culture and its values are socially created, they are also context bound and often transient. Individuals can hold many different values that evolve and (re)prioritise over a lifetime, bringing into question whether absolute consensus to a set of team values is even possible (Weick, 1995). Therefore, while team culture can act as both a source of identity and harmony, in the 'teaching' or 'creation of shared values', team culture can also act as a medium for compliance, conformity and uniformity (Ogbor, 2001). The process of subordinating one's values and norms to those of the team comes at the expense, or at least a reconciling, of the individual's identity (Ogbor, 2001). This process can be driven by implicit fears of not being seen as 'a team player', and acts as a form of emotional control, creating behavioural scripts that repress the very diversity that athlete-centred coaching is said to promote, cater for and celebrate. While players may align themselves to behave in accordance with the expressed values, this is just as likely to be a product of self-preservation as it is an embodiment and belief in any espoused values.

## Empowerment and disempowerment

The importance of the process in which athletes (and other coaches and staff) are actively encouraged or empowered to take responsibility for establishing and maintaining a direction for the team's culture is "a major philosophical underpinning in athlete-centred coaching" (Kidman, 2005, p. 20). The promise of emancipation from power relations and athletes being given voice through empowerment is an attractive proposition for humanistic coaching (Cassidy, Jones, & Potrac, 2009; Kidman, 2005; Vallée & Bloom, 2016). However, it is argued that the very nature of leader facilitated cultural hegemony in a team *is* a form of disempowerment, as members are required to conform, comply and subjugate their existing beliefs (Ogbor, 2001).

Subsequently, it is argued that the praxis of empowerment has been promoted too simplistically (Denison, Mills, & Konoval, 2015; Nelson et al., 2014) and needs to recognise the uneasy coexistence between athletes who may or may not want power and coaches who may or may not want to devolve power (Cassidy et al., 2009). The dominant hierarchy of responsibility in sports raises the question that if true accountability always sits with the coach, to what extent are athletes truly empowered when coaches can regain power when desired (Jones, Potrac, Cushion, & Ronglan, 2011). Research has revealed that the values, standards and practices of a sports team are at all times sensitive to exploitation by privileged stakeholders (Cruickshank et al., 2013, 2014). The term 'buy-in', popular in the team culture rhetoric, reveals a subtext, where for one to 'buy' another must 'sell', implying coercion, and is in direct conflict with the genuine shared construction, ownership or autonomous embracing of values or beliefs that underpins athlete-centred coaching (Kidman, 2005). Coaches have been reported as presenting a semblance of empowerment to manufacture 'buy-in' to their agenda (Cruickshank & Collins, 2015), where power is not given but loaned to athletes until sharing no longer benefits the coach (Nelson et al., 2014).

While a coach conceding his power to encourage athletes to create and police their team's culture may give the impression of cultural ownership, it should be noted that empowerment is never equal. An argument can be made that by declaring values is to publish a language of power that, once explicit, is open to politicking and disingenuousness by cultural members (Cha & Edmondson, 2006). While empowerment forms a cornerstone of the team culture rhetoric, authors are sceptical about the extent to which the neo-liberal practices celebrated in research actually cross the threshold into coaching practice (Denison et al., 2015; Nelson et al., 2014). The coach case study below documents the story of how Bill (pseudonym), a professional basketball coach from Australia, navigated the idea of empowerment in team culture.

A team's culture is no doubt influenced by the beliefs, actions and behaviours of the coach. However, it is how the coach positions him or herself within the culture, and how they reconcile with the inevitable dialectic tensions, that will determine whether they are embodying an athlete-centred philosophy or not.

## Coach case study

### "Feels like you're giving up control" – wrestling with empowerment

*Bill, Professional Basketball Coach, Australia*
I guess when we first introduced it to the team we sat down with the whole group and I just spoke about this is who we are and these are the values by which we want to live by [sic]. Obviously give the opportunity for those guys to have their input, ask questions and give their opinions on it . . . But it was still a top down approach. It was like "This is how you will live and this is how you will conduct yourself". But players can then choose to buy in or not to buy in and particularly when things get stressed and times are tough, that's when you're more likely to go "Well, I've had nothing to do with this, I've had no input".

The big eye opener for me was the first time we went with [leadership company] . . . He goes around the room, "How many games experience have you got in this league? 70. You? 100. You're a 300 game veteran. So, you guys have 1000-games of experience and you're asking me how this team is supposed to work?"

I guess the light went on and from that moment we have continued with a constant process of the players coming up with their own values system of who they want to be, how they want to be perceived within the community, how they want be perceived by their peers, their opposition and, more importantly, how internally are we going to function and how are we going to deal with each other . . . So now everybody within the team has had input into the process and therefore there's accountability because everyone's had the opportunity to say "This is bulls***. I agree with that. This is how we should operate". Now with everybody having had that input there is shared accountability. As a coach, it's no longer a top down approach, I guess it's a unified approach. It's not me saying "We need to do this", you guys have said you wanted to do it, so go ahead do it. So, as the coach now, it's much more my responsibility to continue to provide that environment where we can address it and we talk about it . . . But I think from a coaching perspective that's one of the hardest places to get to because it feels like you're giving up control, that you're starting to let the lunatics run the asylum, but I guess I don't think that anymore. I find that's the most powerful way, is to empower the players, the guys who are actually out there, facing the challenges and dealing with all the issues that are happening on court and to give them the power to deal with it and have the input and come up with a solution.

## 'Thinking culturally': the necessary skills for the athlete-centred coach

Sharing leadership and decision-making so that athletes themselves create a vision, governing principles (or values) and associated expectations results in a sense of belonging and commitment because athletes take ownership of the vision and values, live according to them and take responsibility for monitoring teammates (Johnson et al., 2011; Kidman & Lombardo, 2010; Vallée & Bloom, 2016). While visions and values are central to the culture rhetoric and have been argued to be a critical part of a healthy team culture (Kidman & Lombardo, 2010; Schein, 2004; Schroeder, 2010), they require careful handling to avoid the tensions described earlier.

As a cultural initiative, the 'values whiteboard session' (the process by which all players sit down and establish what the team's values are or should be) is one common approach for coaches to promote an athlete-centred team culture (Kidman, 2005). There is considerable merit in sensitising a group of athletes to explore and articulate what is valued in their team; this brings the whole idea of culture, purpose, beliefs and identity into the team discourse. Equally, the motives for creating team values are often well intended – to sanctify ideals and beliefs so that individual players can become a whole as part of a shared identity. However, as a result of deterministic and functionalist world views, they have the tendency to manifest in mission statements, handbooks or slogans or posters displayed around clubrooms and organisational buildings (Kidman & Lombardo, 2010). In the materialistic sense values are limiting, offering simplistic interpretations of a team's culture that are quickly reduced to false totems by the way of values, posters, slogans and rhetoric (Weick, 1995). When viewed as materialistic and tangible, values "are less valuable than most people seem to think in understanding and influencing culture", forming a ruse that can misrepresent culture, diverting leader and member attention from what really matters (Alvesson & Sveningsson, 2008, p. 182).

For coaches to cultivate meaningful shared experiences for athletes that better meet their needs as individuals and collectives, cultural, social and interpersonal skills and knowledge, or 'cultural literacy', become of central importance. Cultural literacy is the ability to navigate and meaningfully work through cultural concepts, such as meaning, narrative, language, symbols and rituals, to enhance the athlete experience. An alternative to the problematic concept of 'values' is to abandon the term altogether and instead embrace the idea of meaning and shared experience (Weick, 1995). As meaning is inextricably linked with culture, and culture shapes behaviour, for coaches to uncover the near tacit, shared assumptions that shape team culture, it is necessary to go beyond surface issues and constructs and look at athletes' (and coaches') sense-making (Weick, 1995). In other words, how they draw on cues to interpret their experiences and how experiences come to be viewed as important or meaningful. By acknowledging that at the bedrock of culture is a shared meaning emergent from shared understanding of the same experience (Weick, 1995), perhaps the most important implication is that athlete-centred coaching practices need to meaningfully engage and involve all agents in the culture. Culturally literate coaches are able to facilitate and utilise shared experience and encourage sustained, sincere and meaningful shared reflection for local re-interpretation (co-construction) of meaning amongst members.

To 'think culturally', athlete-centred coaches should endeavour to adopt an ethnographic lens and anthropological perspective to focus upon the meanings, symbols and social constructions of a team. Such a position will allow the coach to become continually sensitive to their athletes and context (cultural, historical, political and local) and to acknowledge their impact on the culture. Thus, coaches will come to notice new and rich data across a plethora of sources to construct a 'thick' cultural interpretation of what is going on. This approach seeks to answer *why* people behave in a particular way rather than merely label *what* they do, and in doing so acknowledges the human experience and gives voice and agency to athletes.

Coaches require sensitising not only to their own personal sense-making (understanding the culture) but the ongoing, reciprocal process with their sense-giving (where their decisions and behaviours act as a frame of reference for athletes to make sense of their team's culture) (Maitlis & Christianson, 2013). A culturally literate coach acknowledges and respects their critical role as a cultural sense-giver. Sense-giving triggers can include the things which coaches pay attention to, measure and control, role model or reward, and how they recruit, select, promote and excommunicate (Schein,

2004). The stable frames of reference provided by consistent coach leadership ('walking the talk') helps players make meaning from ambiguity. Inconsistency in coach behaviour and decisions heightens ambiguity and results in a confusing cultural template as players try to decipher the meaning behind a coach's behaviour. Equally, consistency of sense-giving by a coach also creates the psychological safety required for athletes to construct and learn new meanings and assumptions (Schein, 2004). If cultural meaning is communicated consistently, the same understanding from the same experience becomes patterned, leading to a shared belief system, or team culture. This perspective positions the role of the athlete-centred coach as a crafter and custodian of the team's culture and not the author or enforcer, where coaches can promote collective sense-making by prioritising meaning and talking about it.

With the acknowledgement of team culture as socially constructed and therefore unknowable and unpredictable, for the coach, team culture cannot be viewed as something with a 'magic formula' but is instead rooted in complexity. To 'think culturally' is to put matters of culture and shared meaning as a priority coaching praxis while acknowledging team culture is not a product with a fixed or static endpoint but a complex, dynamic and ever-changing problem with no 'one size fits all' solution. The view of cultural literacy as a core coaching skill moves practice away from mechanical or deterministic models of 'best practice', linear steps or recipes for success, and sensitises coaches to the subtle and non-objectifiable features of team dynamics (dialogue, language and meaning).

## Future issues and trends in team culture in athlete-centred coaching

More research is required to further understand the socio-cultural and political processes through which culture is (re)constructed and embodied by members of a team. To move beyond the rhetoric, team culture research should be practice-centric and context specific, proceeding from constructivist and interpretivist paradigms, and most importantly should investigate coaching practise as it happens.

Team culture is a 'living thing' and best understood in its natural habitat. Therefore, naturalistic, ecological and ethnographic approaches are needed to enhance our understanding beyond retrospective accounts of successful cultures and superficial descriptions. There is much to be learned by moving away from retrospective accounts of culture (*what happened*), and by interrogating the discourse that emerges from participants' interactions in a particular space and time (*what is happening now*). It can then be established how coaches and athletes' actions are contextually and situationally constructed, and in turn influence and are influenced by team culture. Furthermore, action-oriented scholarship holds great promise for understanding how coaches wrestle with sense-making, power and collaborative practices to develop meaningful and contextually sensitive culture initiatives. Considering the knowledge, skills and behaviours required by a coach to 'think culturally', an interesting avenue of scholarship would be to explore how coach development practitioners can use models, frameworks and thinking tools to help coaches become sensitised to not only their role in facilitating team culture but also their sense-making and sense-giving.

## Conclusion

The chapter began with providing a context to team culture in coaching and how it has come to be viewed by the academy and practitioners. Key definitions, concepts and theories were introduced; specifically, the view of team culture as socially constructed and dependent upon sense-making, participants' interpreting meaningfully what is going on around them. Elements of organisation science and sociology were integrated to understand how cultures are (co)created in sports settings, and team culture was situated as complex, ambiguous and unpredictable. The distinction between team culture viewed as a variable or metaphor was also highlighted. Table 5.1 summarised the theories considered to be relevant in understanding team culture.

Team culture was then problematised to foreground the inevitable dialectic tensions at play in this integral aspect of the athlete-centred coaching perspective. Coaches must wrestle with these tensions, however; if a coach truly values athlete-centred coaching as a guiding philosophy, then their cultural practices, approaches and leadership need to reflect this. Finally, the role of the coach in cultivating team culture was detailed, noting that from an athlete-centred coaching perspective, culture becomes not something done *to* people; but the product *of* people – their shared experiences, actions, interactions and introspections of athletes, coaches and support staff. The athlete-centred coach was positioned as a key custodian rather than creator of a team's culture and therefore needs to be sensitive to not only the voices, perceptions and social constructions of all members of the team, but their behaviour and decisions as a key 'sense-giver'. The ability to 'think culturally' is recommended as a central tenet of athlete-centred coaching.

## References

Alvesson, M., & Sveningsson, S. (2008). *Changing organisational culture: Cultural change work in progress*. New York: Routledge.

Barker, C. (2008). *Cultural studies: Theory & practice* (3rd ed.). London: Sage.

Berger, P. L., & Luckmann, T. (1967). *The social construction of reality: A treatise in the sociology of knowledge*. New York: Anchor Books.

Blinebury, F. (2016, February 9). Popovich sets 'gold standard of consistency' in volatile era. *NBA.com*.

Bluestone Edge Ltd. (2013). *The bluestone report: A review of culture and leadership in Australian Olympic Swimming*. Retrieved from http://bluestoneedge.com/bluestone-edge-news/bluestone-edge-culture-review-into-australian-olympic-swimming/

Cassidy, T., Jones, R., & Potrac, P. (2009). *Understanding sports coaching: The social, cultural and pedagogical foundations of coaching practice* (2nd ed.). Abingdon: Routledge.

Cha, S. E., & Edmondson, A. C. (2006). When values backfire: Leadership, attribution, and disenchantment in a values-driven organization. *The Leadership Quarterly*, *17*(1), 57–78.

Cresswell, S. L., & Eklund, R. C. (2006). The nature of player burnout in rugby: Key characteristics and attributions. *Journal of Applied Sport Psychology, 18*(3), 219–239.

Cruickshank, A., & Collins, D. (2012). Culture change in elite sport performance teams: Examining and advancing effectiveness in the new era. *Journal of Applied Sport Psychology, 24*(3), 338–355.

Cruickshank, A., & Collins, D. (2015). Illuminating and applying "the dark side": Insights from elite team leaders. *Journal of Applied Sport Psychology, 27*(3), 249–267.

Cruickshank, A., Collins, D., & Minten, S. (2013). Culture change in a professional sports team: Shaping environmental contexts and regulating power. *International Journal of Sports Science & Coaching, 8*(2), 271–290.

Cruickshank, A., Collins, D., & Minten, S. (2014). Driving and sustaining culture change in olympic sport performance teams: A first exploration and grounded theory. *Journal of Sport & Exercise Psychology, 36*, 107–120.

Denison, J., Mills, J. P., & Konoval, T. (2015). Sports' disciplinary legacy and the challenge of 'coaching differently'. *Sport, Education and Society, 22*, 1–12.

Fine, G. A. (1979). Small groups and culture creation: The idioculture of little league baseball teams. *American Sociological Review, 44*(5), 733–745.

Giddens, A. (1984). *The constitution of society: Outline of the theory of structuration.* Berkeley, CA: University of California Press.

Gramsci, A. (1971). *Selections from the prison notebooks.* New York: International Publishers Company.

Johnson, T., Martin, A. J., Palmer, F. R., Watson, G., & Ramsey, P. L. (2011). Collective leadership: A case study of the All Blacks. *Asia-Pacific Management and Business Application, 1*(1), 53–67.

Jones, R. L., Potrac, P., Cushion, C., & Ronglan, L. T. (2011). *The sociology of sports coaching.* London: Routledge.

Kerr, J. (2013). *Legacy: 15 lessons in leadership: What the all blacks can teach us about the business of life.* London: Constable.

Kidman, L. (2005). *Athlete-centred coaching: Developing inspired and inspiring people.* Christchurch, NZ: Innovative Print Communications Ltd.

Kidman, L., & Lombardo, B. J. (2010). *Athlete centred coaching: Developing decision makers* (2nd ed.). Auckland: IPC Print Resources Ltd.

Kidman, L., & Penney, D. (2014). Athlete centred coaching: A time for reflection on values, meanings and practice. *Journal of Athlete Centred Coaching, 1*(1), 2–5.

Lewin, K. (1952). *Field theory in social science: Selected theoretical papers by Kurt Lewin.* London: Tavistock.

Maitlis, S., & Christianson, M. (2013). Sensemaking in organizations: Taking stock and moving forward. *The Academy of Management Annals, 8*(1), 57–125.

Martens, R. (2012). *Successful coaching.* Champaign, IL: Human Kinetics.

Nelson, L., Cushion, C. J., Potrac, P., & Groom, R. (2014). Carl Rogers, learning and educational practice: Critical considerations and applications in sports coaching. *Sport, Education and Society, 19*(5), 513–531.

Ogbor, J. O. (2001). Critical theory and the hegemony of corporate culture. *Journal of Organizational Change Management, 14*(6), 590–608.

Schein, E. H. (2004). *Organisational culture and leadership* (3rd ed.). San Francisco, CA: Jossey-Bass.

Schroeder, P. J. (2010). Changing team culture: The perspectives of ten successful head coaches. *Journal of Sport Behavior, 32*(4), 63–88.

Scott, T., Mannion, R., Davies, H. T. O., & Marshall, M. N. (2003). Implementing culture change in health care: Theory and practice. *International Journal for Quality in Health Care, 15*, 111–118.

Vallée, C. N., & Bloom, G. A. (2016). Four keys to building a championship culture. *International Sport Coaching Journal, 3*(2), 170–177.

Weick, K. E. (1995). *Sensemaking in organizations.* Thousand Oaks, CA: Sage.

Yukelson, D. (1997). Principles of effective team building interventions in sport: A direct services approach at Penn State University. *Journal of Applied Sport Psychology, 9*(1), 73–96.

# 6

# THE IMPORTANCE OF CONTEXT IN ATHLETE-CENTRED COACHING

*Wayne Smith and Rod Philpot*

Although we argue that skillful performance is determined by culturally and socially governed contexts, we do not dismiss the importance of learning the essential physical dimensions of motor coordination. However, the cultural and social learning contexts are particularly important when learning to be skillful at the formative stages of development. As it is used here, 'cultural context' refers to the broad cultural values of a society or sectors of society. In the context of coaching, these sectors may be skiers, surfers or rugby players. Social values refer more specifically to the socially accepted norms of a particular group functioning within the cultural constraints of society. For example, the social context may refer to the commonly held beliefs, dispositions and actions of one's peers, family, or social group, such as those we find in sports clubs.

Learning to be skillful begins with exploration and experimentation, the imitation of experts and the building of an imagination of possibilities (Vygotsky, 1962, 1978), that is, the building of an inherent practical consciousness (Giddens, 1979; Bourdieu, 1990) of skill in action. Context is key to this building of an imagination of possibilities as it shapes what one perceives to be skillful. Before, we learn how to perform, we have to learn 'what to perform', that is, what skill is. We most often do this when we are young by observing and imitating those around us who we perceive to be skillful. For example, this is what happens through the eyes of a young child at a skateboard park as he or she watches the more skillful moves of youth as they perform their ollies, kickflips or grinds, or by 'a-young-would-be-surfer' watching older siblings or skillful surfers performing. In their own play, the young (and not so young) fluctuate between observation and the kinaesthetic learning associated with imitation. During their play, they imagine themselves in the context of their own actions. In this way, their imagination of skill becomes engrained within them as enduring dispositions (Bourdieu, 1990). Learners develop inspiration through observation and imagination (a picture of the mind, not a patterned response, but an imagination of self, performing in the immediate context that presents itself) through imitation and thereby the feel for what it is to be skillful.

## The limitations and strengths of enduring contextual constraints

We often see different nationally developed imaginations in action through the cultural differences in the way national teams play sport. For example, we can see this in the contrasting styles of South American and European footballers or Canadian and European hockey players. These contrasts reflect the early imaginative process of what it is to be skillful in these different cultural and social learning contexts. In New Zealand, children learn to become skillful rugby players, first and foremost, by observing and imitating the country's culturally constructed heroes, the All Blacks. The haka, off loads, quick hands, continuity of play, and the rapid transitioning from defence to attack are all part of what it means to be a skillful rugby player in New Zealand. Young, developing, imaginative minds carry this culturally constructed understanding of skillfulness into their future learning and development as players. As athlete-centred coaches, we must recognise the importance of this form of enculturation and should not ignore that our athletes' imagination of skillfulness is socially determined.

Indirectly, Newell (1986) attempted to differentiate the cultural and social context from other variables via his introduction of three different types of constraints. He classified them as being those constraints that are particular to the individual, those that refer to the task at hand, and those that relate to the environment. Although useful, these three categories present a rather simplistic picture of skillfulness in context. Given our emphasis on the importance of context, we would argue that skill is to be found in the dynamic relationship between these categories and that such categorisation does not necessarily capture the essence of skillfulness. Athlete-centred coaches must recognise that the individual, and in most cases a team, has embodied the culturally and socially significant environment in which they are embedded and that they subconsciously connect this directly with a task. When performing skillful actions, athletes draw on the dynamic relationship between all three of Newell's categories.

Our foregrounding of context is reinforced by an ecological stance that supports a relational understanding of skillfulness, as we try to de-centre the athlete and re-centre skillfulness as the central focus. Viewed this way, skill is a relational quality performed by the athlete and/or athletes in particularised contexts. Skill is simply not attributed to a single athlete acting alone and, therefore, we argue that athlete-centred coaches must focus on the more holistic contextual constraints that 'afford' (Gibson, 1979) one to become skillful in culturally defining ways. Within this, it is understood that contextual constraints imposed during the formative stages of learning have an enduring impact on future learning, and ultimately performance, because learning occurs over long periods of time with implicit outcomes. Coaches and athletes must therefore recognise both the limitations and strengths of these enduring contextual constraints.

The importance of giving due recognition to the cultural and social context and, in particular, recognition of the relationship between the athlete and environment (social and physical) is supported by many social and learning theories. For example, the social theory of Pierre Bourdieu (Bourdieu, 1977, 1990, 2000) informs our view that athlete-centred coaches would be wise to recognise that an athlete is an embodied individual, and in turn embodies a social learning context via what he referred to as the 'habitus'. This is a sub-conscious, but not unconscious practical sense of what to do and what not to do without needing to know why. According to Bourdieu (1990), the embodiment of social practice is why individuals, and in this case athletes, perform in particular ways and not others. With reference to sport, Bourdieu referred to this as the development of a sub-conscious 'feel for the game'. It is an enculturated way of performing without fully discursively knowing 'why'. Over time, the social conditioning becomes habitually 'the way we play the game'. This way of playing is not particular to just one individual but often to a whole community of players. This is why we see the same sport being played differently in different parts of the world or even in the same country by different regional communities. The point is that the *relationship between context and the athlete*, and not just the athlete alone, is important in athlete-centred coaching.

## Practical consciousness

The concept of practical consciousness crosses different epistemological boundaries. The most commonly considered is that of a practical awareness of what to do and when to do it without the need for conscious deliberation. This is typically recognised in phenomenological theorising. For example, existential phenomenologist, Merleau-Ponty, foregrounded the important relationship between learning and context. Herbert Dreyfus (2002), a proponent of Merleau-Ponty's *Phenomenology of Perception* (Merleau-Ponty, 1962), explains the relationship between learning and skillful action through Merleau-Ponty's notion of 'the intentional arc', which Dreyfus described as being 'the tight connection between body and world, such that, as the active body acquires skills, those skills are "stored", not as representations in the mind, but as dispositions to respond to the solicitations of situations in the world' (p. 367). Dreyfus (2002) proposed that 'many of our skills are acquired at an early age by trial and error or by "imitation" and as the performer gains experience, situational discriminations trigger associated intuitive responses without the need for reasoned thought processes' (p. 368).

Similarly, ecological psychologist James Gibson argued that the indirect perception of functional affordances in the environment elicit conditioned responses. Gibson (1979) argued that the individual and environment are directly connected in a meaningful coupling and, as such, the environment is not just something to be observed and interpreted internally, but rather it exists as meaningful information to the performer. Drawing on his theorising, we argue that through their early practice, performers develop direct perceptual-action couplings at the level of the individual-environment interface. The situational or social and physical game environment offers particular possibilities for action and restricts others. These are what Gibson called affordances. An example might be when, in the dynamics of open play in a team game, a gap between two defenders opens up that affords an attacking player the opportunity to pass or run through it, but only if he or she is capable of doing so. The affordance is the relationship between the individual's inherent capabilities and what the environment affords him or her to do. Importantly, in this case, the inherent capabilities of the individual performer are what he or she perceives is functionally possible at a subconscious level. This subconscious functional capability is built up over time through practice in a physical and social context that affords her or him to connect capability with context.

## *The use of imagination as an affordance*

Another theorist, Lev Vygotsky, is the most important theorist we draw on in the context of seeking to foreground the social conditioning of perceptions of skillfulness. Vygotsky (1933, cited in Smolucha & Smolucha, 1986), a prominent educational theorist, adds the very important message of the need to build an 'imagination of possibilities'. He argued that individuals, and, we add, 'athletes', need to build '*an imagination of possibilities*' through their early play to enable them to become skillful in the dynamics of play. Vygotsky highlighted for us the importance of children's play in developing imagination, and we add to this that when it comes to sporting performance, the 'imitative play' of cultural heroes is critical in developing the array of possibilities for action. Vygotsky argued that imagination is the internalisation of children's play and, like all functions of consciousness, it arises in action. Children's play is determined through collective cultural and social interactions and, in the case of athletic skill, draws on the imitation of experts. Presenting a psycho–social perspective, Vygotsky argued that play eventually becomes internalised in imagination and serves as a means of directing one's thoughts and actions. As an internal mental function, it directs the thought processes and ultimately a convergence between imagination and thinking in concepts occurs. During adolescence, this convergence matures into the creative thinking of the adult (Smolucha & Smolucha, 1986). We draw on this to support our position that this progressive development of an imagination of possibilities via the subconscious social conditioning of imitative play eventually becomes what Vygotsky calls creative thinking (or in the case of athletic skillfulness, creative action), and argue that this is an absolute necessity for meaningful, goal-directed, skillful action.

Imagine a player in the temporal and spatial 'white-hot environment' of a dynamic game, and you can envisage the absolute necessity for the player to be imagining the very immanent future in the absolute present and inherently seeing him or herself dynamically functioning in that future given the unfolding environmental situation of the moment. This imagination of possibilities should not be confused with mental rehearsal, which occurs at a more discursively conscious level. This 'in-action' imagination is just that, an embodied 'imagination of possibilities while live in the moment of action', and we argue that this creative imagination is an essential, defining internal element of skill. It is a culturally conditioned imagination and a critical internal affordance of skillful action. This use of imagination as an affordance both embraces James Gibson's notion of affordances and takes it a step further by recognising not just the affording properties of the external environment but also those of the creative imagination developed through embodied culturally and socially significant experiences.

### Authentic learning conditions

At a more functional practice level, education learning theorists have been emphasising the importance of the learning context and the need for authentic learning conditions for some decades now. For example, Brown, Collins and Duguid (1989) emphasised the need for participation over abstract learning. They argued the need for learners to engage in active perception over the teaching of concepts and representations. Their research showed a gradual acquisition of knowledge and skills as novices learn from experts in the context of their everyday activities. Likewise, in their 'theory of situated learning', Lave and Wenger (1990) argued that knowledge (and we add skill) needs to be presented in an authentic context (i.e., settings and applications that would normally involve that knowledge).

## Conclusion

The call for athlete-centred coaches to focus on both the athlete and the athlete's learning context is not new, but the fear is that in a book entitled *Athlete-Centred Coaching* we may lose sight of the essentialness of the relational dynamics between athlete and the cultural and social context if we do not address this in this text.

In our experience and reading, research about coaching, performance and, in particular, skill acquisition, most often draws on a circular body of literature that focuses on the physical dimensions of learning and biophysical components of skill development in what is most often thought to be a physical environment. The danger is that we may not fully recognise the impact of the cultural and social environmental dynamics that are so essential unless we foreground these aspects. This is why we have sought to address these in this chapter.

The early work of James Gibson (1979), with his introduction of affordances and direct perceptual-action couplings, has received the most support within the field of skill acquisition in recent years. Over time, Gibson's theorising has provided a basis for the now more readily recognised 'constraints theory' of Newell (1986), and led to the development of Davids, Button and Bennet's (2008) promotion of non-linear pedagogy. These two contributions have been most helpful in encouraging coaches to adopt an ecological approach to coaching and athlete learning. However, we see the need to take this a step further by placing greater emphasis on the social and learning theories more commonly adopted by educators and social commentators.

Within education, Vygotsky is readily recognised for his social constructivist theory of learning and his advocacy for the importance of the social interaction between learner and a significant mentor (teacher or coach) for enhancing learning, but here we find his theory of imagination to be most helpful for understanding how athletes learn the essential creative elements of skillfulness. The building of different collective imaginations of possibilities through imitation of experts provides the cultural differences that determine the different ways different countries, and communities within them, play the game. We hope that this will help coaches to also acknowledge the absolute necessity of building an imagination of possibilities in their own athletes.

## References

Bourdieu, P. (1977). *Outline of a theory of practice*. Cambridge: Cambridge University Press.

Bourdieu, P. (1990). *The logic of practice*. Cambridge: Polity Press.

Bourdieu, P. (2000). *Pascalian meditations*. Cambridge: Polity Press.

Brown, J. S., Collins, A., & Duguid, S. (1989). Situated cognition and the culture of learning. *Educational Researcher, 18*(1), 32–42.

Davids, K., Button, K., & Bennett, C. (2008). *Dynamics of skill acquisition: A constraints-led approach*. Champaign, IL: Human Kinetics.

Dreyfus, H. L. (2002). Intelligence without representation – Merleau-Ponty's critique of mental representation the relevance of phenomenology to scientific explanation. *Phenomenology and the Cognitive Sciences, 1*(4), 367–383.

Gibson, J. J. (1979). *The ecological approach to visual perception*. Boston, MA: Houghton Mifflin.

Giddens, A. (1979). *Central problems in social theory: Action, structure and contradiction in social analysis*. London: MacMillan Press.

Lave, J., & Wenger, E. (1990). *Situated learning: Legitimate peripheral participation*. Cambridge: Cambridge University Press.

Merleau-Ponty, M. (1962). *Phenomenology of perception*. London, New York: Routledge & Kegan Paul.

Newell, K. (1986). Constraints on the development of coordination. In M. G. Wade & H. T. A. Whiting (Eds.), *Motor development in children: Aspects of coordination and control* (pp. 342–360). Dordrecht: Martinus Nijhoff.

Smolucha, L., & Smolucha, F. C. (1986, August 22–26). *LS Vygotsky's theory of creative imagination*. Paper presented at the Annual Convention of the American Psychological Association (94th, Washington, DC).

Vygotsky, L. S. (1962). *Thought and language*. Cambridge, MA: MIT Press.

Vygotsky, L. S. (1978). *Mind in society*. Cambridge, MA: Harvard University Press.

# PART II

# Research perspectives on athlete-centred coaching

# 7

# DEVELOPING ATHLETE-CENTRED COACHING IN HIGH PERFORMANCE FIELD HOCKEY

*Stephen Harvey*

In contrast to a behaviouristic/reductionist worldview, a social constructivist views coaching as messy, complex, unpredictable and non-linear (Potrac, Jones, & Armour, 2002). Social constructivist theories have been employed to increase sociological and pedagogical theorising in coaching to answer research questions related to the construction of the coach–athlete relationship, and the factors that influence this (i.e., how coaches structure their learning environment and the pedagogies the coach utilises and what this means for the learners). It has been suggested that athlete-centred coaching is reflective of a move away from behaviouristic notions of coaching to one that is holistic and empowering for athletes. Research has suggested the existence of three main components of athlete-centred coaching: a) Teaching Games for Understanding (TGfU); b) questioning; and c) team culture (Kidman, 2005).

The utilisation of athlete-centred coaching can have a profound effect on the ways in which coaches shape the learning environment for their players (Light & Harvey, 2017), for example, developing a positive team culture where players are empowered to take on leadership roles and the coach is a co-participant in learning (Light, Harvey, & Mouchet, 2014). The positive affective experiences generated when a coach uses athlete-centred coaching has been outlined as synonymous to Positive Pedagogy (Light, 2017). Positive Pedagogy has three core pedagogical features (Light, 2017). These are:

a)   Engagement with the physical learning environment or experience;
b)   The coach asks questions to create dialogue, discussion and debate with players rather them telling them what to do;
c)   An inquiry-based approach to provide opportunities for players to formulate and test solutions to problems supported by a positive social–moral environment.

These features are inextricably linked to the three components of an athlete-centred coaching inquiry-based approach where questioning, dialogue, debate, reflection and empowerment are critical to player development. The athlete-centred coaching focused coach therefore utilises the pedagogical features of Positive Pedagogy to promote a learning environment where making mistakes is accepted as a central part of learning, focusing on what a player *can* do and what resources they can draw on to meet the new challenges. This is especially appropriate in elite sport, which can be a highly stressful environment (Light & Harvey, 2017). Moreover, using the pedagogical features of Positive Pedagogy aims to promote a learning environment in which deep learning occurs (Light & Harvey, 2017). This deep learning occurs due to learning being embodied and acting at a level of consciousness below that of the conscious mind. Deep learning moves beyond the replication of skills, but situates this learning in a wider socio-cultural context, where coaches and their players develop personal meaning from these embodied experiences (Light, 2017). For example, an athlete-centred coaching focused coach will use TGfU to help them design games which enable players to learn holistically and understand the team's culture and playing style (macro level), as well as the tactics (meso level) and skills/decisions required to enact this style in the emergent game situation (micro level) (Light et al., 2014). This view of learning is underpinned by a constructivist epistemology where learning is perceived "as being constructed and shaped by convention, human perception and social experience" (Light, 2017, p. 34). The macro (social, cultural) as well as meso (team) and micro (practice) aspects of coaching are aligned, further promoting the social, moral and personal development of players.

Focusing on Positive Pedagogy helps redress concerns of the imbalance between perspectives that emphasise the worst aspects of coaching (e.g., setting unattainable goals, focusing on winning, ignoring the importance of peer-to-peer player–coach relationships, etc.) and encourage a focus on positive aspects (e.g., mastery learning climate, development of positive interpersonal relations with peers and coaches, etc.) (Light, 2017). Positive pedagogies such as athlete-centred coaching and its three components therefore require coaches to move away from coach-centred environments focused on 'fixing' mistakes, to one where coaches focus on building their players' assets.

Light and Harvey (2017) explain the pedagogical features of Positive Pedagogy, which in turn encompass the three components of an athlete-centred coaching, through the lens of Antonovsky's salutogenic theory (1979, 1987). Antonovsky's theory includes three elements that promote conditions for positive experiences in learning: a) comprehensibility, b) manageability and c) meaningfulness. Light and Harvey (2017) define each of these elements (pp. 275–276):

a)   *Comprehensibility* is developed through experience and refers to the extent to which things make sense for the individual in that event, and situations are ordered and consistent. In an athlete-centred coaching this occurs when players understand not just what, but how and where knowledge can be applied in different contextual circumstances (at competition events, in completion and practice matches, as well as in training and team or leadership group meetings).

b) *Manageability* is the extent to which an individual feels s/he can manage stress and challenge by having the resources at hand. Resources can be objects such as tools and equipment, skills, intellectual ability, social and cultural capital and so on. This includes the resources players draw on to be able to solve problems set by the coach in practice, or by the competition situation they are faced with.

c) *Meaningfulness* refers to how much the individual feels that life makes sense and that its challenges are worthy of commitment. This occurs when players are engaged physically and intellectually, as well as emotionally and socially. The utilisation of TGfU is postulated as encouraging this notion of embodied cognitions as it is theorised that players engage at these levels due to it being a holistic approach to learning (Light et al., 2014).

Consequently, the purpose of this current chapter is to investigate how two high performance field hockey coaches have developed an athlete-centred coaching approach, as well as some of the challenges associated with this transition. The chapter focuses on two case studies with USA Field Hockey's Head Women's and Men's National Team coaches through the Rio 2016 Olympic Games Cycle. These narratives are explored with reference to Antonovsky's salutogenic theory and Sense of Coherence (SoC) model. I consider how these coaches moved toward an athlete-centred coaching approach, and challenges faced in delivering such an approach.

From here, this chapter is structured in three major sections. First, I briefly describe the methods utilised to generate the data employed in this current study, and the coaching contexts within which each coach worked. Second, I present the results generated from the thematic analysis of the interviews. Within this section, I will highlight common themes I identified from their narratives with respect to each of the three main components of an athlete-centred coaching approach. I finish the chapter with a brief discussion of the findings, in relation to the three components of Antonovsky's salutogenic theory and SoC model.

## Study methods

### Research design

This study employed a naturalistic case study design (Lincoln & Guba, 1985). Case studies are an appropriate methodological approach when the purpose of the research is to gain an in-depth understanding of human experience and practice within a specific socio-cultural context (Stake, 2000). It has been suggested that the value of a case study lies in its distinctiveness (Janesick, 1998). When using case studies, there is no concern with generalising to the wider, external population. Nonetheless, internal or naturalistic generalisation can be achieved as readers recognise similarities and differences in their own experiences and gain an "empathetic understanding of individual experience" (Purdy & Potrac, 2016, p. 780).

## Context of field hockey in the United States

Field hockey is traditionally a female sport in the USA with limited popular support and participation. It is mainly played by girls and women due to it being a National Collegiate Athletic Association (NCAA) sport for women, but not men. Field hockey has pockets of 'participation' across the country, mainly in the northeastern USA for women. Recreation teams also compete in a showcase event once per year held on grass fields, as the main facilities that have artificial-turf fields are NCAA colleges. At the high school level, field hockey is played on turf fields (usually where soccer and football are played), and is not necessarily conducive to player development. That said, young players participate in a futures program held in various regional centres. Futures camps are also held in the summer months, from which junior international teams are selected. Junior international teams exist at the U17, U19 and U21 for women and U21 for the men.

Field hockey is supported by the United States Olympic Committee (USOC), which means there are Olympic teams for both men and women, albeit the men have not qualified for the Olympic Games since the 1996 Olympic Games in Atlanta. Since 2013, the women's team moved to a centralised program that is housed out of a facility in Pennsylvania (PA), USA. Prior to this move, they were based out of the Olympic Training Center in Chula Vista, San Diego, Southern California (CA), but athletes were dispersed around the USA with coaching centres in different areas of the country. The women's team finished fifth at Rio and are currently ranked sixth in the Federation of International Hockey (FIH) rankings. Their only Olympic medal was Bronze in Atlanta in 1996. The men are currently ranked twenty-sixth in the FIH rankings. The men operate on a non-centralised system, although their main training base is still at the Chula Vista Olympic Training Center in San Diego due to many players based in Southern CA or in overseas domestic leagues, such as in England or Germany. Since the 2016 Rio Olympics, the men have moved to having two main centres, one on the east coast in Pennsylvania (PA) and one on the west coast in CA.

From a coaching education standpoint, USA field hockey (the main National Governing Body who receive funding from the USOC) have just re-developed their Level 1 and 2 awards to integrate more contemporary coaching methods and practice, where one key focus is TGfU. An advanced coach award is under construction. However, coaching is somewhat underdeveloped due to a historical lack of coach education courses, and this impacts coaches' knowledge of the sport, in turn influencing the quality of coaching delivery in high schools as well as futures program sessions. That said, the recent success of the US Women's National Team (USWNT), the US Men's National Team (USMNT) fifth place finish at the 2015 Pan American Games, alongside improvements to the coaching structure and investment from USA Field Hockey National Governing Body all bode well for the future of field hockey in the USA.

## Coaches' biographies

Craig Parnham and Chris Clements were the women's and men's head USA field hockey coaches through the Rio Olympic Games cycle for USA, respectively. Craig was originally from Great Britain and Chris from New Zealand. Prior to taking up their respective roles, Craig was Assistant Coach with the Great Britain women's team that won a bronze medal at the 2012 London Olympics, while Chris was Associate Head Coach of a premier women's college program in the USA (Boston College).

Craig was also an international player representing Great Britain at two Olympic Games, 2000 and 2004. While playing, he was Director of Hockey at a private school in the Midlands in England, where he coached a range of age groups from preschool to U19 during drill-based exercises. On finishing playing he moved to be an assistant coach with Scotland Hockey and Head Coach of the Scottish U21 men's team, moving back to England Hockey in May 2007, where he was an assistant coach to the Great Britain women's team at the 2008 Olympics, and continued to 2012. During his time in Scotland he worked with players individually and ran a program which provided him with a "huge experience and opportunity and exposure to managing of staff", and where the manager of the West of Scotland Institute of Sport where Craig was based provided him with a "really great environment for me to explore, to try, to play around with ideas". After returning to England, he was involved in completing his Level 4 coaching qualification (he'd previously done his first 3 levels early on in his career), which paralleled him completing a Postgraduate Diploma in Coaching at an English university. These combined experiences exposed Craig to coaches from other sports and a range of experts, both coaches and academics, and stimulated an already eager coach to explore contemporary ideas and methods with his players. Many of these ideas were trialled with the women's U21 program, as he was Head Coach there while Assistant to the senior team. After exiting the Great Britain set up, Craig was able to lead his own senior program in the USA, leading them to, and at, Rio 2016, and enjoying various successes along the way. Craig's most notable successes were gold medals at the 2015 Pan American Games and 2014 Champions Challenge. He stepped down after Rio and is now USA Field Hockey's Director of Coach Learning and Development.

Chris played representative field hockey for New Zealand but not at the Senior level. He graduated with a Bachelor of Education/Graduate Diploma in Teaching and Learning, specialising in Physical Education, from a notable school in New Zealand before moving into a teaching and coaching role at a school local to the university he graduated from; he also gained experience coaching at New Zealand National Junior Hockey international selection camps. Subsequently, he moved to Holland to play in their premier league (hoofdklasse), during which he spent his time not playing and as a technical 'trainer' and coach. Chris reflected that this experience was "where my tactical and technical knowledge got really expanded", and he was able to build on coaching awards gained in New Zealand. Following his time in Holland, he moved to the USA to take up a position as Assistant Coach at Boston College in the USA, where he moved onto become an associate head coach. During his time in the USA, he took his Level 2 and 3 accreditations and started a FIH high performance coaching course; he spent time coaching high performance groups for USA field hockey, and then worked with the women's international program before becoming a permanent assistant coach on some of the junior teams and the senior men's team. This led to him being asked to take the USA Senior Men's Head Coach role in 2011, which he held until the end of 2016, clinching a berth into Hockey World League Round 2 just before he stepped down. During this time, he completed the FIH elite coach's award.

## Data generation

After obtaining Institutional Review Board approval and informed consent from a large mid-western university in the USA, the participants' data collection was conducted. I followed interview protocols highlighted by Kidman (2005), which asked participants to describe and explain their: a) philosophy; b) development as a coach; c) establishment of a team culture; d) use of questioning; e) use of TGfU; f) implementation of an athlete-centred coaching; g) process of empowering athletes; h) challenges associated with athlete-centred coaching; and i) plans for the future. Note that participants also consented to their original names being utilised. They reviewed the final version of this chapter and agreed it was an accurate representation of the interviews that were conducted.

## Data analysis

To support a naturalistic mode of inquiry, an abductive content analysis was used to analyse the data (Partington, Cushion, Cope, & Harvey, 2015), which was conducted in three phases. The first phase began with unitising the data, where I conducted a line-by-line analysis of each of the three interviews. This unitising process led to initial data reduction by "separating [data] along their boundaries and identifying them for subsequent analysis" (Lincoln & Guba, 1985, p. 203). In phase two, I categorised the data by grouping related text segments into sub-categories. This process became more focused through repetitive and comparative text examination. The objective of these first two sub-processes was to organise and interpret the unstructured qualitative data generated (Glaser & Strauss, 1967). In phase three, the categories I generated were then assigned to one of the three areas of athlete-centred coaching. Once this stage of the analysis was completed, I developed a final draft of the manuscript with my interpretation and invited the coaches to provide additional commentary on any aspect of the narrative.

## Results

In the first part of this section, I present results relative to team culture. In a second section, I present results from how the coaches used TGfU before presenting results regarding how the coaches used questioning. Finally, I present findings with respect to barriers the coaches noted with athlete-centred coaching.

## Team culture

The first step both coaches recognised as important was developing a philosophy associated with athlete-centred coaching. For example, both coaches noted the importance of them being a "facilitator", which Craig outlined as making himself "redundant" due to the creation of "an environment where the athletes . . . become experienced in solving problems, making decisions, steering direction". Chris agreed that it was important that he created "the conditions to learning . . . encouraging people to attain a better performance than they currently express evolving from a . . . responsibility environment". One caveat that Chris highlighted, however, was that he needed to "model" what he "expected of the athlete" in terms of "standards of feedback", "how to interact with each other" and "deliver to the group".

Craig had the opportunity to lead a centralised program where all the players lived close to the training facility and trained there on most days. Chris did not, and only saw a handful of his players on a regular basis, especially for team training. Consequently, Craig was able to gain the support of a contracted Director of Performance Science, team manager, as well as a sport psychologist. The latter role assisted Craig in his development of player leadership within the program, especially in delegating this responsibility to this individual, a trait he had learned in his earlier roles as Head Coach in the U21 Scottish and English programs. Delegating responsibility to the sport psychologist, Craig's team "started to develop leadership groups and . . . develop leaderful people" where "everybody's responsibility in the team was to think like a leader" via opportunities for "the whole group at different periods to be in leadership roles", although he admitted "some of course were not that into it". The *touchstone* that was created from these meeting was for the team to be UN1TED, where the '1' represented an "aspirational" desire for the players to be number 1 at everything they did.

Chris's role was more traditional and 'hands-on'; he drew on experience from his days as an associate head coach, where colleagues delegated to him responsibility for leading the development of "a lot of the team chemistry, team dynamics, elements within that side of the programs or teams". In the men's program, he therefore worked to "gradually gave the reins or the leadership to the athletes by . . . receiving feedback", which progressed to the athletes "planning [sessions] and developing [their own] a leadership group".

However, for both coaches, the importance of accountability and expectations was paramount to the development of "leaderful people" (Craig). For the women's program, Craig noted that "little interventions like the 'accountability wall' in the dressing room" provided a space where the players "would write some of their accountability goals . . . so . . . we as coaches knew what their accountability goals were", and through "buddy systems" players could provide each other with "peer to peer feedback". Chris also noted that delivering a set of "roles and responsibilities and expectations . . . between the coach and the athlete" was important "because . . . if they're not established and clear from both parties" it is not clear "how . . . that affect[s] the whole team and then therefore obviously, their acceptance."

Consequently, one critical element both coaches noted within team culture that was more 'open' was the notion of peer-to-peer feedback, which linked to accountability and expectations. Chris noted how he liked to "empower the athletes . . . to the point where, the . . . athletes . . . [are] . . . providing feedback to other athletes that I would have given five years ago . . . they are now . . . able to do it . . . themselves". Similarly, Craig highlighted how his sport psychologist was surprised "the amount of control as a Head Coach that I would concede to the staff and the players and, in his [the sport psychologist's] words not me, he didn't see as prevalent in coaching as it was with our program". Craig acknowledged how this was linked to his whole philosophy, which had "changed considerably over the years . . . from that transactional to transformational . . . approach to player development" to one where "the knowledge whenever I stood in a room . . . is generally looking back at me". Part of "conceding" power to his players was also dealing with failure. Craig noted that he was content that:

> if we are in a situation where there is a moment where we can get some great learning through having a failure then I was happy or comfortable to let it go to that point and just experience this for what it is, and then review it and we will take some great learning from it.

### Teaching Games for Understanding

With respect to the second element of athlete-centred coaching, TGfU, both coaches recognised the value of teaching through games, albeit they had both had different experiences up until becoming USA Head Coaches. One aspect which was vital to both coaches was game design. Good game design fulfilled many of the pedagogical principles of TGfU, which included representation, exaggeration, sampling and tactical complexity. For example, Craig noted that he felt:

> We had to be representative in training on what we were doing in games. We needed to bring it to life and we need to be representative of game[s] we are playing. So, the tempo, the condition of the 3-second restarts, all the different conditions and tempos situations we can bring to life in a game they absolutely reflected the way we played. And that was so important to us . . . and so things like exaggeration for example . . . we would set up pitch sizes and shapes and conditions, where we were constantly in these situations in a game and we are having to make decisions relevant to the pitch, specific to the area, appropriate numbers, mad moments of chaos. The pressure was our friend and chaos was our friend and we were desensitising ourselves to what could be considered normally typical pressured situations.

Similarly, Chris recognised the value in simplification of games through using adaptations to games to allow player learning of concepts.

> Sometimes the stick wasn't in the hand. It was just the ball or it was just a Frisbee . . . because it can be really frustrating at times and we just don't get it, so finding other ways to get to that endpoint by playing at different games with a basketball or soccer ball.

This ability for the coaches to design games to enable transfer to match play conditions was, therefore, critical.

Craig also responded to the challenge of integrating technical skills into coaching sessions that are led by games. He noted that he and his staff were aligned to notions expressed by the original designers of TGfU where they suggested that technical skills be developed when teachers/coaches saw them "break down" in the game form being practiced. When this occured, Craig and his staff tried to "recreate the types of situations in a more closed practice environment but there may be pressure from the coach with a tackle bag" before putting them back into the game so that they can then develop notions of "'Ah, this is how this works'". Craig stated that "trying to get that sort of contrast . . . from game into practice back into game that was something that was important for us".

Moreover, Craig noted how they also used games in the women's national team due to their holistic nature. As "every session of it was monitored" through GPS tracking devices, Craig felt using games "gave us our physical component. It gave us our tactical literacy when it comes to making decisions around, 'Where is our space? What options have I got? What's the next pass look like?'" Craig and Chris further articulated how the use of games was holistic because they also integrated a sense of "fun" into training. Chris acknowledged that "it's a high stress environment, but we also need them to be able to have fun at the same time". This point was further developed by Craig, who noted that "fun and enjoyment was a huge part of how we tried to set things up", since "having fun and an enjoyable time" made the players "want to come back tomorrow . . . because it [training] becomes an onerous challenge".

## Questioning

Both coaches explained how questions were an integral part of their coaching. They acknowledged the importance of using questioning as it helped align to their coaching philosophy, educational philosophy about how players learn, and their expectation for the team culture they had created. Craig noted this link:

> when you start to layer in . . . the start of the accountability and the standards and the behaviours you can then start to fall back onto and then the players, the power, as I said comes from the players then challenging each other in a way that is respectful. But at that point now my role is just to watch to see

how this plays out because it's now the players demanding of each other and that's where I think you get great growth.

Similarly, Chris initially used questioning to develop his team culture and get "their [his players] involvement in meetings . . . Then that sort of evolved to them either suggesting ideas for training, or suggesting, or coming, being given tasks or assignments to report back".

A critical piece to this development of questioning was its use on the field. Craig stated that he began using questioning from the first day of working with his players. He used a "whole gambit" of techniques with his players, from "'just with the person next to you, just give it some thought, what do you think about that last exercise? How would do better?'" to "think pair share". After using these more 'open' questioning techniques, he explained how it became easier for his players and even encouraged "some of the younger, often, quieter players [who] are the ones that don't typically want to contribute and gradually just bring it out of people". Chris further expressed the need to be "very open to begin with" and so it was "easy for them [the players] to respond". Once this was in place, "and as the athletes got more comfortable with that environment", Chris highlighted a need to "create more probing types of questioning . . . to get the athletes to think deeper about the game". Consequently, Chris acknowledged that his "knowledge was not needed so to speak" other than to "provide extra guidance" where needed.

### Barriers to athlete-centred coaching

While the coaches noted some barriers to using athlete-centred coaching, neither of the coaches felt these barriers were insurmountable. Both coaches expressed issues with their players, saying, "I don't want the responsibility of having to think about this" (Craig), and, "why we are having all these questions, why are we stopping now, why are we talking about this?" (Chris). Furthermore, when working with his athletes for the first time Craig was met with a "stony silence" and some athletes saying, "just tell me, just tell me what to do", but he was "comfortable with this silence, so patiently used wait time "to get a response to this question". Related to this notion of player frustration was time. Chris noted that using athlete-centred coaching and questioning "takes time and sometimes you don't have time", especially when he did not see his players in the men's program every day or consistently for longer periods of time Craig also highlighted time being an issue, stating that he and his staff and players "could have got to places quicker, if we had just jumped in and said right do this", but this would have gone against the team culture that he and his staff were trying to create.

### Discussion

In the discussion that follows, I will highlight how the athlete-centred coaching approach of the two Head Coaches linked to Positive Pedagogy, in particular

Antonovsky's three salutogenic elements of: a) comprehensibility, b) manageability and c) meaningfulness.

With respect to *comprehensibility*, the coaches' focus on using TGfU created a learning environment that was holistic and afforded opportunities for the players to see the links between the technical, tactical, physical and social aspects of being an elite-level games player. Depth of learning and inquiry was developed by coaches asking questions, revisiting concepts, having players provide each other with peer feedback and players in general holding a sense of curiosity, creativity, engagement and individuality in their learning journey as a member of the team, particularly evident in the women's team as depicted in Figure 7.1. The coaches supplemented game-based learning with technical skill development sessions. Players were given feedback (from coaches and peers) relative to their technical, tactical and physiological development. Indeed, both coaches presented specific examples about how they developed this complementarity between technical and tactical skill development with their players.

Participating in these practice sessions further encouraged *manageability*. Craig, for example, described how TGfU-based training was developed to enable his players to manage pressure, chaos and anxiety. Chris also designed games to facilitate his players learning around tactical problems, sometimes using the principle of simplification of practice so his players could develop initial understanding of concepts, before he gradually scaffolded their learning by him and his players adding additional layers of complexity. Coaches therefore encouraged manageability through the utilisation of strongly guided instruction. For example, the purpose of the games was shared with players, along with the specific skills they were to develop during these games. Moreover, the coaches explicitly made links to how the skills being developed matched those required by the players during competition match play. This process is supported by research by Mayer (2004), who argues that the constructivist view of learning is best supported by methods of instruction that involve cognitive as opposed to behavioural activity, instructional guidance rather than the implicit learning of pure discovery and curricular focus rather than unstructured exploration. In addition

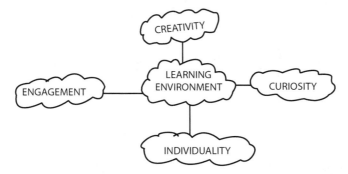

**FIGURE 7.1**  Main components of the athlete-centred coaching learning environment developed by the United States Women's National Team and staff.

to strongly guided and explicit instruction, manageability in the athlete-centred coaching environment was developed through players in the women's team meeting regularly with a contracted licensed sport psychologist to discuss their team identity. These meetings also occurred in the men's team, but were led by the Head Coach himself.

Both coaches also developed a culture within which they taught their players how to give and receive feedback. The development of the touchstone feature of UN1TED in the women's program was a further signature element of the positive development of manageability. Craig also described managing his staff appropriately so that they were continually able to meet the challenges of their roles. These features of manageability were part of the cumulative experience of both coaches in various socio-cultural contexts, where these experiences, and their reflection on them, had a profound impact on the coaches' learning, their beliefs about learning and 'how' to coach and ultimately their own coaching habitus (Light, 2017). This development of their coaching habitus meant the coaches saw themselves as co-participants or facilitators in learning, and could see learning in its holistic sense, further impacting how they designed the learning environment for their players both on and off the field.

*Meaningfulness* was developed by the coaches in specific ways. Both coaches expressed the need for training to be fun and enjoyable for their players to connect affectively and socially as well physically and intellectually. Coaches developed

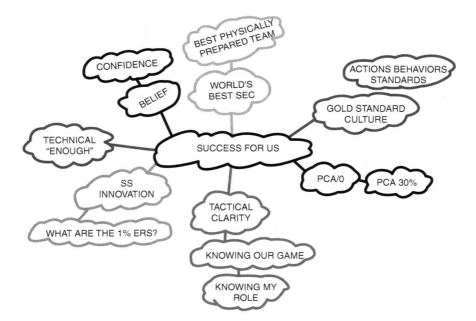

**FIGURE 7.2** Explicit features of Positive Pedagogy inherent in the United States Women's National Team developed by players and staff.

games that were explicitly linked to the team's style of play, a style which was explicitly referred to by the coaching staff after development *with* the players (see Figure 7.2). Questioning was utilised so that alignment between the culture being developed by the coaches linked to how the coaches managed their co-participant and facilitator behaviours in both practice and competition settings (Light et al., 2014). It further focused the players on seeing problems as obstacles to be overcome, and educating them in knowing the resources on which they could draw in different circumstances to gain a successful outcome, even if this was the realisation that the players needed more time or additional practice or challenges in a specific area (Light & Harvey, 2017). In addition, the coaches and support staff created a feedback loop mechanism where leadership groups could bring issues to the attention of the Head Coaches in a professional manner, so that the team was continually growing, developing and moving forward. Moreover, all activities in training, physical conditioning and psychologist sessions were conducted with a purpose, so that the initial goals of the team (e.g., UN1TED for the USWNT) were explicit and continually scaffolded during the team's development.

## Conclusions

Ascertaining a compelling narrative of how these two Head Coaches of a high performance coaching system have integrated athlete-centred coaching into their philosophy and practice enables the provision of transferable suggestions to other coaching cultures and organisations for how to cultivate an athlete-centred coaching system. Adopting an athlete-centred coaching approach to high performance field hockey coaching has enabled these coaches to develop a learning environment aligned to Positive Pedagogy. In this environment, players are consistently focusing on what they *can* do and the resources they can draw on to meet the new challenges they are faced with, in what could be a highly stressful environment (Light & Harvey, 2017).

## References

Antonovsky, A. (1979). *Health, stress, and coping* (1st ed.). San Francisco, CA: Jossey-Bass.
Antonovsky, A. (1987). *Unraveling the mystery of health* (1st ed.). San Francisco, CA: Jossey-Bass.
Glaser, B. G., & Strauss, A. L. (1967). *The discovery of grounded theory: Strategies for qualitative research*. Hawthorne, NY: Aldine de Gruyter.
Janesick, V. (1998). *"Stretching" exercises for qualitative researchers*. Thousand Oaks, CA: Sage.
Kidman, L. (2005). *Athlete centered coaching: Developing inspired and inspiring people*. Christchurch, NZ: Innovative Print Communications.
Light, R. (2017). *Positive pedagogy for sport coaching*. New York: Routledge.
Light, R., & Harvey, S. (2017). Positive pedagogy for sport coaching. *Sport, Education and Society, 22*(2), 271–287.
Light, R., Harvey, S., & Mouchet, A. (2014). Improving 'at-action' decision-making in team sports through a holistic coaching approach. *Sport, Education and Society, 19*(3), 258–275.
Lincoln, Y., & Guba, E. (1985). *Naturalistic inquiry* (1st ed.). Newbury Park, CA: Sage.
Mayer, R. (2004). Should there be a three-strikes rule against pure discovery learning? The case for guided methods of instruction. *American Psychologist, 59*(1), 14–19.

Partington, M., Cushion, C., Cope, E., & Harvey, S. (2015). The impact of video feedback on professional youth football coaches' reflection and practice behaviour: A longitudinal investigation of behaviour change. *Reflective Practice, 16,* 700–716.

Potrac, P., Jones, R., & Armour, K. (2002). 'It's all about getting respect': The coaching behaviours of an expert English soccer coach. *Sport, Education and Society, 7*(2), 183–202.

Purdy, L., & Potrac, P. (2016). Am I just not good enough? The creation, development and questioning of a high performance coaching identity. *Sport, Education and Society, 21*(5), 778–795.

Stake, R. (2000). Case studies. In N. Denzin & Y. Lincoln (Eds.), *Strategies of qualitative inquiry* (2nd ed., pp. 435–454). Thousand Oaks, CA: Sage.

# 8

# DEVELOPING THINKING PLAYERS

## A coach's experience with Game Sense coaching

*Shane Pill*

The coach worked with the author for two years developing a Game Sense coaching approach. The data explored in this paper comes from a semi-structured interview between the author and the coach after the first year of the collaboration. The shifts in pedagogical understanding by the coach, resultant experience of a changed relationship with the players, and positive change in 'ladder position' following the shift in coaching style are explored. Examples of practice forms that were included in the coach's practice as part of his shift to a Game Sense coaching approach are illustrated.

## The Game Sense coaching approach

The Game Sense coaching approach and, more broadly, the development of players' 'game sense' has long been associated with athlete-centred coaching (Kidman, 2001, 2005; Kidman & Lombardo, 2010; Light & Evans, 2010) and a 'player-centred' approach (Light, 2013). The approach emerged in Australia in the mid-1990s from the Australian Sports Commission (ASC) (ASC, 1996). The approach is based on the Teaching Games for Understanding (TGfU) model (Bunker & Thorpe, 1982, 1983) that 'flipped' skill teaching from a mechanistic technical-to-tactical linearity calling for conformity to stylised notions of play requiring replication of 'textbook techniques' before game play, to a tactical before technical direction with more emphasis on motor learning and cognition – 'teaching for understanding' (Pigott, 1982). The Game Sense approach contained a similar pedagogical 'toolkit' to TGfU, emphasising game play, game categorisation based on common principles of play, the modification and adaptation of games for specific teaching intentions, coaches guiding the development of player thinking through the use of questions in preference to 'telling', and greater player responsibility during play and discussions (ASC, 1996). However, the Game Sense approach is considered more flexible, nuanced, non-linear, and less structured than TGfU (Harvey & Jarrett, 2016; Light, 2013; Stolz & Pill, 2012; Zuccolo, Spittle, & Pill, 2014), and a refinement of TGfU for sport teaching (Stolz & Pill, 2014; Thorpe, 2005).

The Game Sense approach is not undirected or unguided game play. The approach has a specific educational intent and focus on intelligent performance by developing 'thinking players' (ASC, 1996; den Duyn, 1997) through the empowerment of players (ASC, 1996). The idea of intelligent performance, or the game intelligence sometimes referred to as a player's 'game sense', characterises whether the player is acting skillfully with intent and not by accident or good fortune. Consequently, developing 'thinking players' is a deliberate coaching focus on the cognition of players and player development of knowledge in the form of 'principles of play' (ASC, 1996). Determining player 'understanding' occurs by observation of the player's knowledge 'in action' in the form of principles of play reflected in the action competency within the context of a game (Stolz & Pill, 2012).

Action specific perception theory (ASPT) can explain what it means to be a 'thinking player'. According to ASPT, a player's action ability influences perception. Body size and shape, demands of the task, motivation, a player's 'energetic potential' (fitness) are some of the factors that influence a player's perception of the game environment. Action abilities are therefore dynamic as players 'see' the game in terms of their abilities and intentions (Witt, 2011). There is therefore a coupling between perception, decision-making, and action (Fajen, Riley, & Turvey, 2008). Affordances theory captures this mutual relationship between the environment and the player, and that perception of the environment leads to action. Affordances are the properties in the environment that indicate possibilities for action to the player (Turvey, 1992). The property will expose itself in certain conditions. This means that in some circumstances certain properties will be apparent. The implication is that the properties of an environment can only be an affordance if the player abilities pair with information from which the player can make meaning. The affordances are therefore relations between the athlete and game environment. The player disposition for action may be present, but its actualisation is only possible if the player has the functional ability to perceive and take action (Chemero, 2003).

Applied to sport coaching, at any given game moment a player is in an environment that provides some affordances and not others. Therefore, the appropriate way to describe the action context of the game is in terms of dynamics. Study of the game environment to figure out what it offers the athlete in order to then engage with the coaching prerogative to design a practice setting to prepare players to perform in the game, is studying the task dynamics. The task dynamic creates information. Therefore, game behaviour is shaped by how players perceive the game environment, and thus learning or preparing to play is a motor control–cognition energetic where the player learns to detect and use information to coordinate and control their game behaviour. Coaching for this outcome is then about creating practice contexts that enable the athletes to perceptually attune to the complex dynamics creating opportunities (dispositions) for action. Practice needs to be an environment that represents the same affordances and therefore the same information as 'the game', at task relevant complexity for the readiness of the players.

## Coaching at practice – intentionally designed spaces

A Game Sense approach attempts to develop the sport understanding of 'thinking players' through the promotion of player decision-making and problem solving abilities through empowerment of the player via a type of guided inquiry often labelled 'discovery' (Breed & Spittle, 2011; den Duyn, 1997; Light, 2014; Pill, 2016a). Mosston and Ashworth (2008) suggested that 'thinking' can be classified into three processes: memory, discovery, and creativity. *Memory* requires the reproduction of already known to the player knowledge or skills. *Discovery* requires the production of knowledge previously unknown to the player through a 'search' and cannot be done in one cognitive step. *Creativity* requires the production of something that is unique or original to the player. Creativity can be further broken down into convergent thinking associated with finding a single solution, and divergent thinking generating multiple ideas or solutions (Memmert, 2014; Mosston & Ashworth, 2008). It is a premise of Game Sense coaching that the coach will deliberately construct a game requiring players to focus on either a problem (a situation in the game) to solve using a principle of play (convergent thinking or tactical intelligence), or requiring players to create a solution (divergent thinking or tactical creativity) directly from the dynamics of the situation. In other words, the coach creates a context through which the player is taken across the 'discovery barrier' (Mosston & Ashworth, 2008) into an intentionally designed space to develop thinking players.

The Game Sense coaching approach is therefore 'deliberate coaching' (Memmert, 2011) that increases the range of skill configurations used by players at training through game forms as practice tasks. This contains the possibility of encouraging players to explore action possibilities and adaptability during play. The development of tactical awareness via player immersion in real game situations with similar game time and defence pressure constraints is cited as one of the benefits of Game Sense coaching (Smith, 2006; Pill, 2012). It is the balance struck between game-based learning and technique isolation, and the central role that questioning plays in moving instruction to that of guiding in Game Sense coaching, which makes it often unfamiliar to Australian coaches (Light, 2004, 2013; Light & Evans, 2010; Pill, 2015a).

## Coach development through appreciative inquiry research

This project was a collaborative process between the researcher in dialogue with the coach throughout an Australian football season. That dialogue culminated in an interview with the coach. Ethics approval occurred before the interview occurred and the coach provided informed considered consent to involvement in the interview and for the data to be used in publications stemming from the project. The interview brought together the narrative of the previous conversations between the coach and the researcher acting in the role of sports pedagogue into a coherent story providing the data for interpretative analysis. The analysis provided a portrait of learning situated in the practical experience of coaching, where ongoing interactions in the applied context of coaching combine with the personal interpretation of those experiences as a form of coach education (Harvey, Cushion, & Massa-Gonzalez, 2010). It is a portrait of a coach involved in continuous reflection, interpretation, and reinterpretation of the experience of coaching. The coach's pedagogical-content knowledge grows from the "distilled wisdom of practice" (Cushion, Armour, & Jones, 2003, p. 221) over the course of the season. This type of reflective activity in coaching settings creates a space for thinking and exploring one's coaching practice by learning through the practice of coaching (Gilbert & Trudel, 2005).

## A coach experience of using the Game Sense approach for the first time

Although the coach's philosophy was underpinned by a belief in facilitating and 'teaching' rather than directing players, his coaching at this club in the four years prior to this project had been directive and command-like. Unlike the coaching described in other Game Sense coaching research (Evans, 2006; Light, 2004; Smith, 2006), the coach embraced the idea of a more non-linear and dynamic coaching space when using questions and game play to scaffold player technical and tactical development. At the end of the previous season, the coach had reflected that things 'had to change' as the club had not played in finals during the tenure of his coaching to this point. Coaches contend with expectations of success and tenure based on win–loss results (McLean & Mallett, 2012).

The coach acknowledged the difficulty changing their habitus and structuring of coaching behaviour. Previous experience of coaching and of being coached profoundly shape a coaching behaviour (Light & Evans, 2013), and in Australia it is acknowledged that a directive 'coach-centred' practice is still a common coaching expression (Light, 2013; Pill, 2016b).

> The hardest transition I've found is putting the whistle away and allowing players to play out scenarios at training, and look for the teachable moment. Previously there would have been a lot of witches' hats and open-ended drills. I think a lot of a coaches still use these drills with little thought to the transfer to the game.

Evidence of a change from directing practice to noticing what was happening for the players and, in an educative sense, looking for opportunities to teach. Specifically, teachable moments using stops in practice to talk through the action of the moment and what can be learnt was a new addition to the coach's practice (Launder, 2001; Pill, 2016b). Teachable moments where players are 'frozen' in the moment of action can be used to directly link perception of the moment with action possibilities.

> In a Game Sense approach you look for the teachable moments in these game scenarios and emphasise aspects of the scenario, in particular, conceptual aspects such as "how to create space?" and spacing awareness of other players that individual players need to have.

The educational relationship between player and coach has tended to be coach-centred and thus autocratic and prescriptive (Potrac & Cassidy, 2006) or directive (Light, 2013) in nature. The potential issue with prescriptive directive coaching is that the player comes to feel undervalued and stops 'thinking' and just does what they are told to do. Potrac and Cassidy (2006) suggest one way to change this relationship is to position the sport coach as a 'more capable other' though a pedagogical expression that recognises player learning as both active and social process. They propose that this active and social process is possible by incorporating guided discovery of player understanding and problem solving, typical of coaching using a Game Sense approach. The shift of coach relationship to an educational stance by the coach becoming more a facilitator is evident in these reflections by the coach.

> I now use more discovery learning and guided discovery to promote effective learning through questioning the players. I find the most effective learning comes through questioning the player, "what did you do there?" "why did you move there? What was your thought and reasoning?"
>
> Bring the groups together, find out what each group was talking about so players can learn from each other. Each group may have come up with different solutions, ideas. Or, two teams, same activity but their group discussions have addressed slightly different things. We all grow by hearing what different players and different groups are thinking. I still use other methods, like direct instruction, but I think more about when it is best to use them as I am trying to create a space where learning occurs. I see myself as a facilitator of a session rather than leading. I now design for facilitation to occur. Players have more equal membership of the group, and I am more of an equal member.

The second of the two previous reflections is another example of the empowerment of the players for their thinking and action found in the coach adoption of 'tactical timeouts'. Typically, this coach allocated a member of the player leadership group to each team during game play match simulations and small-sided games. Play was called to a halt after about 8–10 minutes, and each team in the match/game play retreated to their defensive end for a team tactical discussion. These discussions were observed by one of the assistant coaches; however, the conversation between players was managed by the member of the player leadership group allocated to team leader for the practice. Players being able to take ownership of learning via input into the briefing, debriefing, and analysis of action at training encourages players becoming self-aware and therefore a better on-field decision-maker (Kidman & Lombardo, 2010; Kidman & Davis, 2006).

In addition to the redesign of the coaching environment at practice sessions by adoption of game-specific practice tasks using game forms at training and asking questions in preference to telling, there was evidence of shared leadership between the coach and senior players. This empowerment is one of the justifications used by Kidman (2001) for an athlete-centred approach. Whatever the coaching expression, the practice of coaching exists in an interplay between the coach brokerage of power and the players' entitlement for influence in their preparation, planning, and performance (Jones & Standage, 2006). In this instance, the change in coaching practice to the Game Sense approach had a positive effect on the coach.

> It has enthused me the most to see the players really enjoying themselves and expressing themselves really a lot more than waiting in a line waiting for the next turn. Seeing them thinking. You can hear it in my voice now, I am excited about that. They are actually playing football. There has been a lot more job satisfaction through the enjoyment of players.

The coach in this study identified the ability to better develop the individual player through feedback, taking the form of meaningful questions. Feedback is distinguished from encouragement by feedback containing information on actual performance relative to achieving an intended goal or performance. At its core, feedback is an exchange of information. The act of information exchange by asking questions rather than telling allows the player to reflect and frame a response: in other words, time to think and then verbalise those thoughts. A clear message about athlete-centred coaching is to ask meaningful questions of players (Kidman & Lombardo, 2010).

> This way of training has enabled me to much better develop the individual player. You develop the team, you develop the individual. Again, it's reinforcement. Internal satisfaction of the individual, he knows he is becoming a better player, improves, they have more input into a game. They get more satisfaction. Individual effort increases and the player is rewarded with more success. Individual development leads to team development and the results come. More success leads to more motivation; players want to be part of that.

While this project did not collect data on the players' perception of the changed coaching practice, it has been found that players who perceive their coaches as exhibiting a controlling or autocratic leadership style tend to experience positive outcomes to a lesser extent and are less satisfied with the coach–athlete relationship (Mageau & Vallerand, 2003). Central is the coach's ability to influence players to act.

> We are developing the individual to be an independent decision maker ... We have learnt to collaborate on ideas, take leadership when it is time, when it is

the players turn to show leadership. You don't get that following a line witch's hat to witch's hat . . . I think the players have found it enjoyable.

Another shift for the coach was to the practice of designer games. Designer games are game forms to use at training that package technical, tactical, and conditioning intentions into one task (Charlesworth, 1994; Pill, 2015b).

Designing training this way has made me think, I can show you all the game diagrams I have in my training book. Designing scenarios had been really stimulating.

The coach put a lot of time into designing game forms to teach offensive and defensive concepts. For example, it was identified that the previous season players were not good defensively at pressing into the space of the ball player, and compressing space around the player with the ball with defensive positioning that creates both player density and coverage around the ball. Players were inclined defensively to wait for the offensive player with the ball to come to them before defensively engaging the player. Opposition players could too easily take ground towards their goal. To begin teaching the concept, a variation of End Ball was used (Figure 8.1). In this game, passing was constrained to disposal by handball initially in a 6v6 game played in a 40m × 30m grid. Teams scored by passing the ball to a target player past the end line at the team's scoring end. To focus player attention on the learning intention of pressing to keep the ball in the teams attacking third, the constraint on the play was that a score could only occur if every member of the

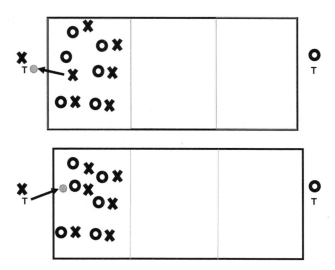

**FIGURE 8.1** Top: offensive team score with every team member in the attacking third can score. Bottom: the ball comes back into play after a score to the other team, and the team that scored is now in defence and already in a press.

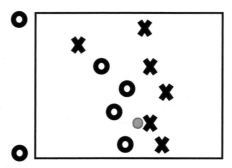

**FIGURE 8.2** 6v4 End Ball with target players. The player with the ball is closely guarded, as are the offensive support players in likely receiving positions. The defending player on the far side moves off the sideline or wing into a more midfield position, compressing space around the ball. If the ball is passed across the field to the far wing, the defence has time to slide across the field to cover space and contain ground.

team was in the attacking third of the field. When the ball turns over after a score, and returned into play from the scoring end by the other team, or the ball turns over by a lost ball pass, the previously attacking team is already in a high press.

After exploring a number of strategies associated with this team press, the game form expanded into a 9v9 small-sided football game. At this time, the handball game was modified to introduce a new defensive emphasis, to delay the opposition defensively when outnumbered using a sliding defensive. The sliding defence involved the defensive player closest to the ball pressing up into the space of the ball player, the next nearest defenders defending the likely pass and then further off the ball defending space to prevent a forward penetrating pass. To create the offensive overload, a 6v4 was created by two players from the team in defensive phase retiring to the end of the field, becoming the offensive team 'target player' (Figure 8.2). After a score, or upon a turnover from a lost ball, the two target players come into play and two players from the now defensive team retire to the end of the field. The concepts of pressing, sliding defence, closest defender going at the ball player, and compressing space moved from small-sided handball games to 9v9, 12v12, 15v15, and then 18v18 football games.

## Conclusion

Using the lens of appreciative inquiry (Pill, 2015a), the value proposition of a shift to athlete-centred coaching by using the Game Sense approach can be constructed from the experience of this coach. In an appreciative inquiry, value propositions are a series of statements that examine the situation from the position of strengths rather than the more common research in sport paradigm beginning with problems and then a testing of a solution/s. Because they are strength-based statements, value propositions therefore establish the advantage and the imagining of new possibilities (Ludema, Whitney, Mohr, & Griffin, 2003).

Proposition 1. Players practice to play so it makes sense to play for practice.

Proposition 2. It is important to train with replication of the affordances evident in the game at training to develop 'thinking' players.

Proposition 3. Using a guided rather than directive coaching style is promoted by questioning in preference to 'telling' players.

Proposition 4. The hardest transition to athlete-centred coaching is 'putting the whistle away' and observing practice for the teachable moment.

In this project, collaboration appeared to provide a useful direction for coach education and the grounding of sport pedagogy research in the 'natural' setting of coaching. If coaches are to learn the 'tricks of the trade' that come with understanding the pedagogical practice of athlete-centred coaching, then collaborative partnerships between sports pedagogues acting in the role of a 'more knowledgeable other' mentoring coaches should be considered by institutional sporting organisations.

## References

Australian Sports Commission. (2016). *Game sense: Perceptions and actions research report*. Belconnen, ACT: Australian Sports Commission.

Australian Sports Commission. (1996). *Game Sense: Perceptions and actions research report*. Belconnen, ACT: Australian Sports Commission.

Breed, R., & Spittle, M. (2011). *Developing game sense through tactical learning: A resource for teachers and coaches*. Melbourne: Cambridge University Press.

Bunker, D., & Thorpe, R. (Eds.) (1982). Reflecting on the teaching of games. *Bulletin of Physical Education*, *18*(1), Special Edition.

Bunker, D., & Thorpe, R. (Eds.) (1983). Games teaching revisited. *Bulletin of Physical Education*, *19*(1), Special Edition.

Charlesworth, R. (1994). Designer games. *Sports Coach*, *17*(4), 30–33.

Chemero, A. (2003). An outline of a theory of affordances. *Ecological Psychology*, *15*(2), 181–195.

Cushion, C., Armour, K., & Jones, R. (2003). Coach education and continuing professional development: Experience and learning to coach. *Quest*, *55*(3), 215–230.

den Duyn, N. (1997). *Game sense: Developing thinking players*. Belconnen, ACT: Australian Sports Commission.

Evans, J. (2006). *Developing a sense of the game: Skill, specificity and game sense in rugby coaching*. Proceedings of the Asia Pacific Conference on Teaching Sport and Physical Education for Understanding, University of Sydney. Retrieved from http://sydney.edu.au/education_social_work/professional_learning/resources/papers/Proceedings_TGfU_06_AsiaPacificSport.pdf

Fajen, B. R., Riley, M. A., & Turvey, M. T. (2008). Information, affordances and the control of action in sport. *International Journal of Sport Psychology*, *40*, 79–107.

Gilbert, W., & Trudel, P. (2005). Learning to coach through experience: Conditions that influence reflection. *The Physical Educator*, *62*(1), 32–45.

Harvey, S., Cushion, C., & Massa-Gonzalez, A. (2010). Learning a new method: Teaching Games for Understanding in the coaches' eyes. *Physical Education and Sport Pedagogy*, *15*(4), 361–382.

Harvey, S., & Jarrett, K. (2016). Similar, but not the same: Comparing the game based approaches of Teaching Games for Understanding (TGfU) and game sense. *eJRIEPS, 38*, 92–113.

Jones, R. L., & Standage, M. (2006). First among equals: Shared leadership in the coaching context. In R. L. Jones (Ed.), *The sports coach as educator* (pp. 65–77). New York: Routledge.

Kidman, L. (2001). *Developing decision makers: An empowerment approach to coaching.* Christchurch, NZ: Innovative Print Communications.

Kidman, L. (2005). *Athlete-centred coaching: Developing inspired and inspiring people.* Christchurch, NZ: Innovative Print Communications.

Kidman, L., & Davis, W. (2006). Empowerment in coaching. In W. Davis & G. Broadhead (Eds.), *Ecological task analysis perspectives on movement* (pp. 121–140). Champaign, IL: Human Kinetics.

Kidman, L., & Lombardo, B. J. (2010). *Athlete-centred coaching: Developing decision makers.* Christchurch, NZ: Innovative Print Communications.

Launder, A. (2001). *Play practice: The games approach to teaching and coaching sports.* Champaign, IL: Human Kinetics.

Light, R. (2004). Coaches' experiences of game sense: Opportunities and challenges. *Physical Education and Sport Pedagogy, 9*(2), 115–131.

Light, R. (2013). *Game sense: Pedagogy for performance, participation and enjoyment.* New York: Routledge.

Light, R. (2014). Quality teaching beyond games through game sense pedagogy. *University of Sydney Papers in Human Movement, Health and Coach Education, Special Game Sense Edition*, 1–13.

Light, R. L., & Evans, J. R. (2010). The impact of game sense pedagogy on Australian rugby coaches' practice: A question of pedagogy. *Physical Education and Sport Pedagogy, 15*(2), 103–115.

Light, R., & Evans, J. R. (2013). Dispositions of elite Australian rugby coaches towards game sense: Characteristics of their coaching habitus. *Sport, Education and Society, 18*(3), 407–423.

Ludema, J. D., Whitney, D., Mohr, B. J., & Griffin, T. J. (2003). *The appreciative inquiry summit.* San Francisco, CA: Berrett-Koehler.

Mageau, G., & Vallerand, R. (2003). The coach-athlete relationship: A motivational model. *Journal of Sport Sciences, 21*, 883–904.

McLean, K., & Mallett, C. (2012). What motivates the motivators? An examination of sport coaches. *Physical Education and Sport Pedagogy, 17*(1), 21–35.

Memmert, D. (2011). Sports and creativity. In M. A. Runco & S. R. Pritzker (Eds.), *Encyclopedia of creativity, second edition* (pp. 373–378). San Diego, CA: Academic Press.

Memmert, D. (2014). Tactical creativity in team sports. *Research in Physical Education, Sport and Health, 3*(1), 13–18

Mosston, M., & Ashworth, S. (2008). *Teaching physical education, first online edition*: Spectrum Institute for Teaching and Learning. Retrieved from http://www.spectrumofteaching-styles.org/pdfs/ebook/Teaching_Physical_Edu_1st_Online_old.pdf

Pigott, B. (1982). A psychological basis for new trends in games teaching. *Bulletin of Physical Education, 18*(1), 17–23.

Pill, S. (2012). *Play with purpose: Developing game sense in AFL footballers.* Hindmarsh, SA: ACHPER Publications.

Pill, S. (2015a). Using appreciative inquiry to explore Australian football coaches' experience with game sense coaching. *Sport, Education and Society, 20*(6), 799–818.

Pill, S. (2015b). *Play with purpose: The game sense coaching approach for football (soccer).* Hindmarsh, SA: ACHPER Publications.

Pill, S. (2016a). Game sense coaching: Developing thinking players. In M. Drummond & S. Pill (Eds.), *Advances in Australian football: A sociological and applied science exploration of the game* (pp. 42–49). Hindmarsh, SA: ACHPER Publications.

Pill, S. (2016b). Implementing game sense coaching in Australian football through action research. *Ágora Para La EfY El Deporte/Agora for PE and Sport, 18*(1), 1–19.

Potrac, P., & Cassidy, T. (2006). The coach as a 'more capable other'. In R. L. Jones (Ed.), *The sports coach as educator* (pp. 39–50). New York: Routledge.

Smith, W. (2006). Athlete-centred approach for elite players. In L. Kidman (Ed.), *Athlete-centred coaching: Developing inspired and inspiring people* (pp. 187–208). Christchurch, NZ: Innovative Print Communications.

Stolz, S., & Pill, S. (2012). Making sense of game sense. *Active and Healthy Magazine, 19*(1), 5–8.

Stolz, S., & Pill, S. (2014). Teaching games and sport for understanding: Exploring and reconsidering its relevance in physical education. *European Physical Education Review, 20*(1), 36–71.

Thorpe, R. (2005). Rod Thorpe on Teaching Games for Understanding. In L. Kidman (Ed.), *Athlete-centred coaching: Developing and inspiring people* (pp. 229–244). Christchurch, NZ: Innovative Print Communications.

Turvey, M. T. (1992). Affordances and prospective control: An outline of the ontology. *Ecological Psychology, 4,* 173–187.

Witt, J. K. (2011). Action's effect on perception. *Current Directions in Psychological Science, 20*(3), 201–206.

Zuccolo, A., Spittle, M., & Pill, S. (2014). Game sense research in coaching: Findings and reflections. *University of Sydney Papers in Human Movement, Health and Coach Education, Special Game Sense Edition,* 15–31.

# 9

# SUPPORTING WELLBEING

## Athlete transitions through elite to sub-elite sport

*Deborah Agnew and Andrew Marks*

Athlete-centred coaching and humanistic coaching are terms which can be used interchangeably and are related to the development of athletes' self-awareness, and holistic growth and development (Kidman, 2006; Lombardo, 2001). While athlete-centred coaching does not specifically focus on the development of wellbeing, positive wellbeing can be the by-product of positive coaching pedagogy (Light, 2017). Furthermore, Miller and Kerr (2002) stipulate that the improvement of holistic health and wellbeing comes through the pursuit of excellence in sport. The effect the coach has on the athlete's wellbeing, therefore, is dependent on the meaning athletes give to the coach's behaviours (Kidman, 2005). Well-planned training programs, continual monitoring of athletes' health and needs, the utilisation of support staff and the protection of the athletes' rights are key avenues through which positive athlete wellbeing can be achieved (Miller & Kerr, 2002) through athlete-centred coaching.

## Wellbeing

The World Health Organization (2004) identified that wellbeing is a key determinant in people's ability to cope with daily stressors. Athlete wellbeing includes all aspects of the athlete's life, including those that are not sport related (Dunn, 2014). Positive wellbeing, according to Light (2017), can be described as "an individual's or groups' state of being comfortable, happy and healthy" and includes their social, economic, medical, psychological and spiritual states (p. 40). Sport participation can be an avenue for the development of positive wellbeing through autonomy, competence and relatedness (Reinboth & Duda, 2006). However, sport participation alone does not guarantee wellbeing, and the adverse effects of elite sports participation have been documented in several studies (Bartholomew, Ntoumanis, Ryan, & Thøgersen-Ntoumani, 2011; Gould & Carson, 2008; Hellison & Cutforth, 1997).

## Sources of athlete stress

Noblet and Gifford (2002) determined that there are six broad sources of stress for Australian footballers: "(a) negative aspects of organisational systems and culture, (b) worries about performance, expectations and standards, (c) career development concerns, (d) negative aspects of interpersonal relationships, (e) demanding nature of the work, and (f) problems associated with the work/non-work interface" (p. 7). Stressors were identified at all levels of the sports experience and extended beyond sport-related commitments (Noblet & Gifford, 2002). Therefore, it is necessary to consider all sources of stress when developing wellbeing management strategies. Given that coaches have an influential role in the lives of athletes, positive pedagogies which focus on the development of the whole person and include avenues for achieving life balance between sporting and non-sporting pursuits have the potential to lead to happier and more well-rounded individuals (Price, Morrison, & Arnold, 2010). This is especially important as athletes transition from a playing role to another career.

## Career transitions and stress

One of the major sources of distress for athletes is the career transition out of sport (Stambulova, Alfermann, Statler, & Côté, 2009; Alfermann, 2000). Career transitions in sport are inevitable (Stambulova, Stephan, & Jäphag, 2007). Transitions can be expected (normative) such as the transition from junior to senior sport, or unexpected (non-normative), such as being abruptly deselected from the team or sustaining a career ending injury. Normative transitions, because they are relatively predictable, do not cause an overwhelming amount of stress for athletes. Non-normative transitions, however, can be extremely difficult for athletes as they are not expected (Stambulova et al., 2009).

The end of an athlete's career is often not a single moment, but rather the result of a longer process (Stambulova et al., 2009; Kelly & Hickey, 2008). How an athlete reacts to the termination of their athletic career depends on the circumstances surrounding their retirement and how the athlete feels about the decision as voluntary or involuntary (Fortunato & Gilbert, 2003; Stambulova et al., 2009). Those who are able to determine the timing of their retirement and have allowed time to prepare for life after sport enable a smoother transition than those who are forced into retirement through deselection or injury (Fortunato & Gilbert, 2003; Kelly & Hickey, 2008; Agnew, 2011). Alfermann (2000) and Professional Footballers Australia (2015) found that approximately 20% of retiring athletes experience very difficult transitions and may require professional assistance.

Research by Wylleman, Alfermann, and Lavallee (2004) stated that because they have little control over the timing of their retirement, deselected athletes often face the most difficulty during the transition process. Athletes who experience a non-normative transition through deselection from an elite sports team can be forced into retirement if they are unable to succeed in being selected for a rival team

(Fortunato & Gilbert, 2003). In a study by Fortunato and Gilbert (2003), deselected footballers suggested that remaining involved in football was imperative because the sport had been a major part of their lives and they still wanted to be involved. Therefore, it is plausible that these athletes may consider moving down a grade to sub-elite competitions or lower to continue playing even if they are no longer able to play professionally. Regardless of the circumstances surrounding retirement from elite sport, many athletes feel a sense of loss (Fortunato & Gilbert, 2003). The career transition process therefore can be associated with stress and uncertainty about whether the change will be positive or negative and usually comes with a specific set of demands relating to post-career adjustment (Stambulova et al., 2009; Alfermann & Stambulova, 2007).

Career transition research generally focusses on the transition out of elite sport rather than on transitions within an athlete's sports career (Pummell, Harwood, & Lavallee, 2008; Stambulova et al., 2009; Nesti, Littlewood, O'Halloran, Eubank, & Richardson, 2012). The end of a sports career is an important transition faced by athletes; however, it is not the only transition they face within their careers (Alfermann & Stambulova, 2007). Other important transitions within athletic careers include being sold to another team, facing a significant injury or illness and being permanently deselected from a team (Nesti & Littlewood, 2011). Kelly and Hickey (2008) argue that the transition out of elite sport must be seen as a process rather than a single moment. Given athletes can also move up, down or horizontally across the sport system (Lavallee, Wylleman, & Sinclair, 2000), they may choose to move down a competition level rather than discontinue sport participation all together, and yet little is known about these experiences.

## Significance of the research

There is currently no literature on Australian footballers who transition out of the elite AFL competition through sub-elite competitions such as the South Australian National Football League (SANFL), the Victorian Football League (VFL) and the West Australian Football League (WAFL). This research therefore aims to understand the experiences of footballers transitioning out of the elite AFL competition through state-based football clubs. Understanding the process of retirement through sub-elite competitions may provide important information not only for the sub-elite football clubs on how to best support the footballers, but also for the AFL Players' Association to assist in the development of programs to support the transition out of elite AFL football.

## Methodology

This research utilised a phenomenological design to investigate the lived experience of retirement transitions out of elite sport. Phenomenology is best suited for research in which the shared experience of individuals is sought (Creswell, 2013), and therefore is an appropriate method of inquiry for this study.

## Participants

Ten footballers who had retired from the AFL and were currently playing with an SANFL football club took part in this study. At the time of data collection, participants were currently playing for three SANFL football clubs in the senior teams. Nine of the footballers were forced into retirement from the national AFL competition through being deselected from the AFL team and one chose to return to the SANFL after contract negotiations with their AFL team did not conclude satisfactorily.

Participants were recruited purposefully through the football managers in the SANFL clubs, who invited the footballers who had previously played in the national AFL competition to take part in the study and provided the contact details of the researchers to those who were interested. The football managers were provided with an information letter detailing the study, which was forwarded to the footballers.

## Interviews

In this study, a life world interview was used to develop an understanding of the lived everyday experience from the perspective of the participants (Kvale & Brinkmann, 2009). Interviewing is one of the most common data collection techniques in phenomenological research (Creswell, 2013). Participants are selected who are central to the phenomenon being investigated. The interview length depends on the "amount of self-reflection the participant feels comfortable with and the topic of study" (Polkinghorne, 1989, p. 48). Interviews need to allow enough time for the phenomena under investigation to be explored in depth and can involve either single or multiple interviews with participants (Creswell, 2013; Polkinghorne, 1989). Participants took part in a semi-structured interview which lasted between 28 minutes and one hour.

Van Manen (2017) argues that a common misconception in phenomenological research is that "phenomenological questions will emerge in the conduct of unstructured interviews" (p. 776). He warns that this is a dangerous assumption, as not having a clear direction for the research may not lead to the collection of appropriate data. Therefore in this research a semi-structured interview guide was utilised to ensure similar questions were asked of participants; however, this also allowed for the interview to be directed by participants, depending upon their responses (Patton, 1990). Each interview explored topics including experiences in the national AFL competition, the difficulties faced by footballers during the transition process back to the SANFL competition, the support needed by footballers during this period and the responsibility for player wellbeing. Moustakas (1994) suggests participants in phenomenological research are asked two broad questions:

What have you experienced in terms of the phenomenon? and What contexts or situations have typically influenced or affected your experience of the phenomenon? In this study, participants were asked:

- "What was your retirement transition experience?" and
- "What were the circumstances surrounding your retirement transition?"

These two key questions enabled a textual and structural description of the experience to be gained, which provided an understanding of the common retirement transition experiences of the participants (Creswell, 2013). All interviews were audio-recorded with the permission of the participant and transcribed verbatim by a professional transcription service.

## Analysis

Phenomenological data analysis involves several steps, including horizonalisation, developing clusters of meaning and describing the essence of the experience (Creswell, 2013). Horizonalisation, as outlined by Moustakas (1994), involves going through the data to highlight statements of significance that can lead to an understanding of the participants' experience of the phenomenon. In order to highlight the statements of significance, this study utilised a detailed line by line approach in which each sentence was examined and coded (Van Manen, 2016; Creswell, 2013; Thomas & Harden, 2008). Following the line by line examination of the data, the codes that were developed in the horizonalisation stage were then grouped together into larger themes to form the clusters of meaning (Moustakas, 1994; Creswell, 2013).

*Trustworthiness.* Creswell and Miller (2000) discuss eight strategies for establishing validity in qualitative research: prolonged engagement and persistent observation; triangulation; peer review or debriefing; negative case analysis; clarifying researcher bias; member checking; rich, thick description; and external audits. Creswell (2013) recommends that at least two of these strategies should be used to enhance the validity of the research. The current study utilised member checking and peer review or debriefing in addition to an audit trail.

Lincoln and Guba (1985) argue the most important criterion in establishing credibility in qualitative studies is member checking. Through this process the participants have a key role in determining the accuracy and credibility of the research (Creswell, 2013). In this research participants were sent a copy of their interview transcript and given two weeks to contact the researcher with any changes they would like made. Provision for the use of their interview transcript was included in the consent form. No participants requested changes to the transcripts, all deeming them to be an accurate account of the conversation.

Throughout this study, the primary researcher kept in regular contact with an expert in player welfare to discuss the process and proposed findings to gauge their accuracy. Written accounts of the meetings were kept as part of the audit trail. This also enabled peer review of the analysis. Peer review or debrief is the process of externally checking the research process (Lincoln & Guba, 1985). The purpose of the peer reviewer is to ask the difficult questions about methods, meanings and interpretations, and allows an avenue through which the researcher can discuss their feelings to a sympathetic listener (Creswell, 2013; Lincoln & Guba, 1985).

Ary, Jacobs, and Sorensen (2010) suggest that another area through which trust-worthiness or dependability can be achieved is through documentation of the research process. An audit trail was established through which the raw data gathered in interviews, records of the primary researcher's decisions about who, what and why to interview, the hypothesis developed from the raw data and subsequent refinement and the coding process were kept in a well-organised and retrievable form.

## Results and discussion

Two themes emerged from the data relating to supporting wellbeing through an athlete-centred approach: 1. Taking responsibility; and 2. Support beyond football. These themes will be discussed in detail below.

### *Taking responsibility*

Athlete-centred coaching is about putting the focus on the athlete (Kidman, 2010). The footballers in this study who have transitioned or are transitioning from an elite level to sub-elite levels state that the major issues they are facing include financial difficulties, unfinished or no qualifications in an alternative vocation and an increase in leisure time. Light (2017) states that athletes who worry about being humiliated are unlikely to want to be empowered, and may want to just do as they are told. Australian footballers who have been deselected unexpectedly can often feel worthless and that they are no longer useful (Agnew, 2011). Participants in this study highlighted that the period immediately following deselection from a football club is the most critical in terms of wellbeing. Being deselected can lead to feelings of failure and not being good enough, and therefore wellbeing can be negatively affected. Participants recognised that all footballers go through this period and that it can be a dangerous period with regard to feelings of self-worth and wellbeing. For example, one player noted:

> No different to anyone else, I don't want to sit here and say mine was too much different to anyone else. Everyone has gone through it, I think – I do think it's a dangerous period for players. I think a lot of players mentally – "Am I good enough? Was I good enough? Will that be the only – will this be the thing that defines me as a person?" I think we sort of search for acceptance a bit, because it's – AFL is pumped up so much nowadays through the supporters, and it's just such a big game that if we feel that we didn't make

it and have the ten year career you feel like you may have let yourself down, or failed a little bit.

Given the footballers may be searching for acceptance, returning to a state-based league can provide an avenue for acceptance in a new team. Being involved in a team environment has a significant influence on footballers' identities; therefore, gaining a sense of belonging and acceptance through returning to state-based football has important implications for how well the transition is made (Agnew & Drummond, 2011).

Athlete-centred coaching is the process of enabling athletes to have ownership and responsibility for their sporting environment (Kidman, 2010). The role of the coach is then to assist athletes to learn and perform better. However, the athlete also needs to do a significant amount of professional development in order to learn and perform better (Kidman, 2010). This is particularly so for footballers who return to state-based competitions from the elite AFL competition, with the professional development particularly related to off-field behaviours and tasks. The footballers in this study recognised the need to take responsibility and have an active role in their own professional development; however, they also highlighted that support and guidance through this period is required. This is exemplified in this comment:

> Yeah, it's definitely harder. And I guess they – and they – that's AFL clubs, they probably try and prepare you as best they can to exit comfortably or whatever out of the system. But there's going to [be] things that you need to learn for yourself, and do for yourself, and they're going to be a little bit hard to pick up at first. But hopefully with a bit of guidance, and a bit of help, you'll find your way.

When reflecting on their transition out of AFL football, participants indicated they at least in the initial stages found the increase in leisure time difficult. As a result, some of the men engaged in behaviours which were not health promoting. Once they realised their behaviours were not assisting the transition period, there was a need to take responsibility for their actions and make some changes that were more positive, as outlined by this participant:

> Yeah, I probably left myself with a bit too much time on my hands here and there. I did work a couple of different jobs at times, so – yeah it was a bit of both. Sort of left myself a bit of time to still work but then – yeah sort of coming to the end of that I guess I probably was spending a bit too much time [participating in] nightlife and that sort of stuff. And I think that was a big point for me in terms of wanting to change things up a little bit. And had a big part in me coming to Adelaide for something a bit different so.

### Support beyond football

At the AFL level, from the interviews with these players it appears as though the focus is away from some of the key tenets of athlete-centred coaching. The footballers indicated they operate within a heavily structured environment where they have little autonomy. The footballers in this study stated they are used to the AFL football clubs "doing everything" for them. Therefore, integrating into a more athlete-centred coaching environment during the transition out of AFL into the SANFL can be challenging. It was apparent that initially, there was is an underlying expectation that the SANFL club would provide a similarly heavily structured environment.

From the footballers' perspective, at the sub-elite level athlete-centred coaching includes broader assistance than just sport-related matters from coaches and other staff members. The majority of footballers in this study believed the staff at the SANFL clubs should be assisting them with finding subsequent employment, as at the sub-elite level game payments cannot provide a player with a living. Football clubs are perceived as being well connected and, therefore, having the ability to assist beyond football. It was also evident that players considered that adopting an athlete-centred approach extended beyond the coaching staff to the football development managers. It was perceived by the footballers that part of the football development manager's role is to assist with many off-field related needs. This included helping the footballers find employment and supporting their transition out of the AFL system.

> Well [football operation manager] really he was really good; I guess it came with the job a little bit but just speaking to him about moving out of footy and yeah it sort of went hand in hand with the job I suppose but he's been really good in sort of thinking about what I'm doing and the future and yeah preparing me for what's next type thing.

Humanistic coaching is often used interchangeably with athlete-centred coaching. The idea of humanistic coaching is that it promotes athletes as thinking, feeling humans with a life outside of sport, which can then influence how they practice and perform in competition (Light, 2017; Kidman, 2006). In addition, the humanistic coaching perspective recognises the coach can have an influence on athletes' lives outside and beyond sport (Light, 2017). Sub-elite Australian football is not considered full-time employment; therefore, one way coaches can demonstrate an athlete-centred approach is to be supportive of a balanced lifestyle, and be approachable for the footballers to speak to. The footballers in this study highlighted the relationships they currently had at the SANFL club since transitioning out of the AFL as being positive, and an avenue through which their wellbeing can be supported. As highlighted by this participant, having a coach who is approachable about any problem, not just football related issues, is appreciated by the team:

> Anything footy related – I think the good thing about this club is [coach] has a great rapport with every single player on the list, so I think it doesn't matter whether it's a football problem; a personal problem; a financial problem – a whatever problem – I reckon every single person would go and talk to

[coach]. Where at other clubs I don't think it would be like that. I think the coach would be up here and the players would be down here and wouldn't feel comfortable talking to [coach] or their senior coach about off-field problems but I think here you would either go and talk to him or [Football Operations Manager] I reckon.

Tricker (2010) argues that a key point in athlete-centred coaching is that the coach needs to be able to identify the athlete's ability to cope with taking ownership, especially if they have not previously been exposed to an athlete-centred approach. During the initial months of transition from an elite AFL club to a sub-elite SANFL club, there is a need to provide an empathetic, supportive environment to support wellbeing and promote self-awareness, responsibility, learning and ownership (Light, 2017). In this way, a gradual move towards the footballers taking control of the decision making can be encouraged (Tricker, 2010). The footballers in this research highlighted the first few months as being a critical period where a higher level of support and direction is required. As stated by this footballer, without defined boundaries in the initial months of the transition, footballers may be susceptible to behaviours which do not promote wellbeing:

> That's the dangerous period where blokes need guidance more than ever through that period, and the dangers are instead of finding positive ways of letting out that – those emotions and that through golf, whatever, reading a book, doing those things. Blokes can easily fall into the drinking, the drugs, gambling, they're probably your big three when players don't have the borders around themselves, and the people telling them what to do, that they can definitely fall into those traps. And I would probably say that there probably needs to be more – I don't know someone touching base more often or something like that, and at a closer level for sure yep.

Athlete-centred coaching is about developing athletes who are self-aware and who have gained control over the decision-making process (Kidman, 2006). It is arguable that despite footballers wanting SANFL clubs to provide a structured environment in which everything is done for them, such an approach would not be beneficial long-term as it does not empower the athletes to assume self-responsibility in key areas of their lives.

Footballers transitioning from elite AFL to SANFL football appear to require clear direction and boundaries to assist them through this difficult time. The behaviours of the coach during this period can have a significant effect on the wellbeing of footballers both within and beyond the sport. Therefore, having a clear focus on the needs of the athlete, being able to identify the ability of the footballer to take ownership of the situation or not and adoption of positive coaching pedagogies which are focussed on the development of the whole person are avenues through which the state-based club can use athlete-centred coaching to support footballers. This would also allow players the possibility to gain ownership and control of the situation (Light, 2017; Tricker, 2010; Kidman, 2010).

# Conclusion

Much of the literature on athlete-centred coaching focusses on player preparation for competition. In this chapter, we have suggested that an athlete-centred coaching perspective and the use of positive coaching pedagogies are important strategies to support footballers transitioning out of the elite competition through sub-elite or state-based competitions. Retirement from sport, while inevitable, is a difficult time for athletes. Forced retirement through delisting is particularly challenging as the timing is unexpected and therefore can exacerbate the difficulties faced by athletes. Footballers who have been forced into retirement through permanent deselection from the team may choose to move down a competition grade to state-based leagues in order to continue their participation in sport. The decision to continue participation in state-based leagues is one avenue through which footballers can take some ownership of the unexpected or non-normative transition they are facing.

From the interviews with these players, it appears that the elite Australian Football competition (AFL) appears to operate within a coach- or club-centred approach to player wellbeing, with little autonomy for footballers. In the initial stages of transitioning out of the elite competition to state-based competitions, footballers require additional support structures, guidance and boundaries to minimise their engagement in non-health promoting behaviours such as drinking, drugs and gambling. During the first few months, footballers may need more of a directed approach. However, this approach is not sustainable long-term, and players need to be empowered through no longer having everything 'done for them'. Therefore, a gradual shift towards the players taking responsibility and control of the decision-making processes in football and non-football related matters is required. It is evident that an athlete-centred approach needs to be adopted by the whole football club and not just the coaches.

Coaches who are amenable to being available for footballers to talk to regarding both on-field and off-field matters are more likely to be providing the support mechanisms necessary to promote wellbeing; however, other key personnel, such as the Football Operation Manager, also have a significant influence on the footballers' lives. Therefore, in order to support wellbeing, athlete-centred concepts need adopting as a 'whole club' approach.

The research focussed on supporting athlete wellbeing through an athlete-centred approach during their transition out of elite sport through sub-elite competitions, from an athlete's perspective. Future research could investigate athlete-centred coaching from the perspective of the coaching and support staff within the sub-elite sporting context. The research reported in this chapter was also contextualised within Australian football; therefore, further research within other sports where the transition out of elite sport can be a process through sub-elite competitions is warranted.

# References

Agnew, D. (2011). *Life after football: The construction of masculinity following a career in elite Australian Rules football*. doctoral dissertation. Retrieved from Flinders University Digital Thesis Collection. Retrieved from https://theses.flinders.edu.au/view/ce0ce638-fac6-4129-b75e-4f558c8f35a9/1

Agnew, D. R., & Drummond, M. J. (2011). A sense of belonging: Sport, masculinity and the team environment. In G. Dodd (Ed.), *Moving, learning and achieving: Edited proceedings of the 27th ACHPER international conference* (pp. 267–273). Adelaide, SA: ACHPER Publications.

Alfermann, D. (2000). Causes and consequences of sport career termination. In D. Lavallee & P. Wylleman (Eds.), *Career transitions in sport: International perspectives* (pp. 44–58). Morgantown, WV: Fitness Information Technology.

Alfermann, D., & Stambulova, N. (2007). Career transitions and career termination. In G. Tenenbaum & R. Eklund (Eds.), *Handbook of sport psychology* (3rd ed., pp. 712–733). Hoboken, NJ: John Wiley & Sons Inc.

Ary, D., Jacobs, L., & Sorensen, C. (2010). *Introduction to research in education* (8th ed.). Belmont: Wadsworth.

Bartholomew, K., Ntoumanis, N., Ryan, R. M., & Thøgersen-Ntoumani, C. (2011). Psychological need thwarting in the sport context: Assessing the darker side of athletic experience. *Journal of Sport and Exercise Psychology, 33*(1), 75–102.

Creswell, J. W. (2013). *Qualitative inquiry and research design: Choosing among five approaches.* Thousand Oaks, CA: Sage.

Creswell, J. W., & Miller, D. L. (2000). Determining validity in qualitative inquiry. *Theory into Practice, 39*(3), 124–130.

Dunn, M. (2014). Understanding athlete wellbeing. *Sport Health, 32*(2), 46.

Fortunato, V., & Gilbert, K. (2003). *Reconstructing lives: The problem of retirement from elite sport.* Altona, VIC, Australia: Common Ground Publishing.

Gould, D., & Carson, S. (2008). Life skills development through sport: Current status and future directions. *International Review of Sport and Exercise Psychology, 1*(1), 58–78.

Hellison, D. R., & Cutforth, N. J. (1997). Extended day programs for urban children and youth: From theory to practice. *Issues in Children's and Families Lives, 7*, 223–252.

Kelly, P., & Hickey, C. (2008). *The struggle for the body, mind and soul of AFL footballers.* North Melbourne, VIC, Australia: Australian Scholarly Publishing.

Kidman, L. (2005). *Athlete-centred coaching: Developing inspired and inspiring people.* Christchurch, NZ: Innovative Print Communications Ltd.

Kidman, L. (2006). *Humanistic coaching – Teaching Games for Understanding.* Conference paper at Asia Pacific Conference on Teaching Sport and Physical Education for Understanding, The University of Sydney. Retrieved from http://sydney.edu.au/education_social_work/professional_learning/resources/papers/Proceedings_TGfU_06_AsiaPacificSport.pdf#page=59

Kidman, L. (2010). *Athlete centred coaching: Developing decision makers.* Worchester: IPC Print Resources.

Kvale, S., & Brinkmann, S. (2009). *Interviews: Learning the craft of qualitative research.* Thousand Oaks, CA: Sage.

Lavallee, D., Wylleman, P., & Sinclair, D. (2000). Career transitions in sport: An annotated bibliography. In D. Lavallee & P. Wylleman (Eds.), *Career transitions in sport: International perspectives* (pp. 29–44). Morgantown, WV: Fitness Information Technology.

Light, R. (2017). *Positive pedagogy for sport coaching: Athlete-centred coaching for individual sports.* Abingdon, Oxon: Routledge.

Lincoln, Y., & Guba, E. (1985). *Naturalistic inquiry.* Thousand Oaks, CA: Sage.

Lombardo, B. J. (2001). Coaching in the 21st Century: The education models. In B. J. Lombardo, T. J. Caravella-Nadeau, K. S. Castagono, & V. H. Mancini (Eds.), *Sport in the twenty-first century: Alternatives for the new millennium* (pp. 3–10). Boston, MA: Pearson.

Miller, P. S., & Kerr, G. A. (2002). Conceptualizing excellence: Past, present, and future. *Journal of Applied Sport Psychology, 14*(3), 140–153.

Moustakas, C. (1994). *Phenomenological research methods.* Thousand Oaks, CA: Sage.

Nesti, M., & Littlewood, M. (2011). Making your way in the game: Boundary situations in England's professional football world. In D. Gilbourne & M. B. Andersen (Eds.), *Critical essays in applied sport psychology.* Champaign, IL: Human Kinetics.

Nesti, M., Littlewood, M., O'Halloran, L., Eubank, M., & Richardson, D. (2012). Critical moments in elite premiership football: Who do you think you are? *Physical Culture and Sport: Studies and Research, 56*(1), 23–32.

Noblet, A. J., & Gifford, S. M. (2002). The sources of stress experienced by professional Australian footballers. *Journal of Applied Sport Psychology, 14*(1), 1–13.

Patton, M. Q. (1990). *Qualitative evaluation and research methods.* Thousand Oaks, CA: Sage.

Polkinghorne, D. E. (1989). Phenomenological research methods. In R. Valle & S. Halling (Eds.), *Existential-phenomenological perspectives in psychology* (pp. 41–60). New York: Springer.

Price, N., Morrison, N., & Arnold, S. (2010). Life out of the limelight: Understanding the non-sporting pursuits of elite athletes. *The International Journal of Sport and Society, 1*(3), 69–79.

Professional Footballers Australia. (2015). *Retired and transitioned players report 2015.* Melbourne, VIC, Australia: Professional Footballers Australia.

Pummell, B., Harwood, C., & Lavallee, D. (2008). Jumping to the next level: A qualitative examination of within-career decision in adolescent event riders. *Psychology of Sport and Exercise, 9*(4), 427–447.

Reinboth, M., & Duda, J. L. (2006). Perceived motivational climate, need satisfaction and indices of well-being in team sports: A longitudinal perspective. *Psychology of Sport and Exercise, 7*(3), 269–286.

Stambulova, N., Alfermann, D., Statler, T., & Côté, J. (2009). ISSP position stand: Career development and transitions of athletes. *International Journal of Sport and Exercise Psychology, 7*(4), 395–412.

Stambulova, N., Stephan, Y., & Jäphag, U. (2007). Athletic retirement: A cross-national comparison of elite French and Swedish athletes. *Psychology of Sport and Exercise, 8*(1), 101–118.

Thomas, J., & Harden, A. (2008). Methods for the thematic synthesis of qualitative research in systematic reviews. *BMC Medical Research Methodology, 8*(1), 45–55.

Tricker, D. (2010). New Zealand black sox (men's softball) former coach. In L. Kidman (Ed.), *Athlete centred coaching: Developing decision makers* (pp. 229–255). Worchester: IPC Print Resources.

Van Manen, M. (2016). *Researching lived experience: Human science for an action sensitive pedagogy.* Abingdon, Oxon: Routledge.

Van Manen, M. (2017). But is it phenomenology? *Qualitative Health Research, 27*(6), 775–779.

World Health Organization. (2004). *Promoting mental health: Concepts, emerging evidence, practice: Summary report.* Retrieved from www.who.int/mental_health/evidence/en/promoting_mhh.pdf

Wylleman, P., Alfermann, D., & Lavallee, D. (2004). Career transitions in sport: European perspectives. *Psychology of Sport and Exercise, 5*, 7–20.

# 10

# BODY IN MOVEMENT

## Better measurements for better coaching

*Carlos Gonçalves, Humberto Moreira Carvalho
and Luís Catarino*

It may be argued that sport training is best represented by bodies in movement, and the individual body is the point of intersection of diversities. This fundamental characteristic supports the idea that organising, planning and executing a practice session is a sequence of drills aiming to reach the best physiological and technical adaptations. Literature and coaching tradition therefore encourage planning based on the bio-scientific principles of athlete performance. However, Denison (2010) argues that coach planning is much more complex than manipulating physiological variables, and thus, it remains over-simplified and under-problematised in coach education curricula. Coach education curricula tend to prioritise biological disciplines as fundamental tools to build scientific-based session plans. However, the tension between biological and behavioural areas is evident in recent literature (Grecic & Collins, 2013; Jacobs, Claringbould, & Knoppers, 2016), and this situation does not help researchers and coaches to develop a clear understanding of the athletes' needs.

For athletes and coaches, sport is more than a corporeal phenomenon or an embodied experience. The word embodiment is vague, and can quickly become an explanation of motivation and what produces action. In this limited way, the practice/embodied approach is a phenomenological account of post hoc explanations that may be given by those concerned. Our argument is that sport is a living laboratory where diversity is the rule. Athletes are biological beings and the adaptations to the training environment mean corporeal experiences. If satisfaction in practice does not flow throughout the body, the adoption of sport will hardly be deemed justifiable and worthwhile.

Adolescent and specialised athletes are often seen as relatively homogeneous in functional capacity and sport-specific skills. Interestingly, this homogeneity is often apparent with relatively different patterns of training experience. Consequently, we describe some of the sources of biological diversity and offer practical resources for coaches to deal with the problem. We also present our critique of contemporary solutions to optimise athletes' preparation.

For the purposes of the chapter, we must define what we mean by athlete. The question is relevant because contemporary sport organisations offer organised practices and competitions starting at 6 years of age, with highly variable levels of engagement, going from a sporadic contact with sport to strict programs with qualified coaches. The discussion about early specialisation is beyond the scope of this chapter, and thus when we write 'athlete' we mean an individual in the path to sport specialisation that, arbitrarily, starts around 12 years of age. We also consider that a weekly training volume of four hours is the lowest limit to produce significant physiological adaptations, occurring in three sessions per week, in an organised, supervised environment.

The athletes' biological diversity in the training process must be seen through three lenses and levels of analysis:

(a) Before practice; individuals arrive at sport carrying their own singularity and keep it during their entire career. Participants are very different at any stage of their sporting life, but especially during the specialisation years, when every person experiences the process of growth and maturation at very uneven paces;

(b) During the training years; the effects of the training load are experienced by participants in an absolute individualised way. Coaches cannot expect that the same drill or the same environment stressor have the same physiological or biomechanical effect with all the athletes; and

(c) After practice; the accumulated effects of training make the athletes even more different – those with bigger volumes of work exceling compared to the others, as excellent performance in sport has a strong positive relationship with the accumulated number of hours of practice (Gonçalves et al., 2009; Helsen et al., 2000).

The role of physical growth and functional performance in sports tends to be underestimated, when late maturing individuals may be systematically excluded in favour of average and early maturing individuals as chronological age and sport specialisation increase. On many occasions, these analytic decisions may fail to account for influence of aggregation or clusters of individuals within a specific context. Although exposed to organised training programs, often at early ages, adolescent athletes are going through an interactive process of growth, maturation and development (Sherar, Cumming, Eisenmann, Baxter-Jones, & Malina, 2010). This implies changes in body size, physique, proportions and composition, maturation of the different body systems. Furthermore, adolescents vary substantially in the timing and tempo of biological maturation, which has a significant influence on body dimensions, physiological functions (Armstrong, Welsman, & Chia, 2001; Armstrong, Welsman, Williams, & Kirby, 2000; Beunen et al., 2002; Beunen et al., 1988; Thomis, Rogers, Beunen, Woynarowska, & Malina, 2000; Van Praagh & Dore, 2002) and likely on behavioural characteristics. The impact of individual differences in the timing of maturation may afford to the early maturing potential athletic advantages (greater size, strength, speed, power and endurance), although likely transient, particularly between the ages of 11 to 14 years, when maturity associated variation in size and function is more evident (Cumming, Lloyd, Oliver, Eisenmann, & Malina, 2017).

Chronological age has been traditionally used as reference in youth sports to group teams both in training and competitive settings, and to inform decisions about the promotion of young players through the sport or exercise prescription (Lloyd, Oliver, Faigenbaum, Myer, & De Ste Croix, 2014). Thus, a mismatch between chronological age and biological age may lead to the exacerbation of the relative age effects (i.e., an overrepresentation of players born within, at or just after the age cut-off points), likely as consequence of an overrepresentation of players in specific maturity stages within sports where role of physical growth and functional performance is determinant. For example, early maturing players in football (Malina et al., 2000) and basketball (Carvalho et al., 2011) or late maturing gymnasts (Thomis et al., 2005).

## The study

Using the data from an ongoing research project, we illustrate the analysis and interpretation of adolescent athletes' performance, considering a multidimensional approach with an examination of the variation in body size, and functional capacities of female and male adolescent basketball players associated with differences in biological maturity status, chronological age and years of training experience. One hundred and eight adolescent basketball players (female players, n=50; male players, n=58) aged 9.6 to 15.8 years were considered. Variables included chronological age, estimated age at peak height velocity (Mirwald, Baxter-Jones, Bailey, & Beunen, 2002), stature and body mass by anthropometry. As functional capacities indicators for basketball we used the Line Drill test (Carvalho, Gonçalves, Grosgeorge, & Paes, 2017; Semenick, 1990) and Yo-Yo Intermittent Recovery level 1 (Yo-Yo IR1) (Bangsbo, 2004; Castagna, Impellizzeri, Rampinini, D'Ottavio, & Manzi, 2008).

The data were modelled using varying intercepts models, within a Bayesian multilevel framework. We generally used weakly regularising prior distributions for population-level, normal priors (0, 10), and for group-level effects, Cauchy priors (0, 2). Vaguer regularising prior distributions (uniform distribution) for group-level effects were considered and noted when used. Posterior estimates were based on a chain with 20,000 iterations with a warm-up length of 5,000 iterations, implemented via Markov Chain Monte Carlo (MCMC) simulation and using Hamiltonian Monte Carlo and its extension, the No-U-Turn Sampler using Stan (Stan Development Team, 2015), obtained using "brms" package (Burkner, in press), available as a package in the R statistical language (R-Core-Team, 2014).

A detailed description of the statistical analysis was chosen because the significant variability inter-athletes at baseline is an issue, particularly relevant in longitudinal studies. At the same time, distribution in sport populations tends to be skewed. These two factors should advise researchers to be careful and sophisticated with the statistical methods and techniques used to make inferences or to predict success or failure.

The data showed that maturation is the main factor that can explain changes in body size (Figure 10.1) and aerobic and anaerobic performance in both boys and girls (Figures 10.2 and 10.3). If maturation depends on individual genetics, years of experience may represent an effect of the coach decision, based on observation and competitive results. It is important to stress that body size, and aerobic and anaerobic performance, are the most relevant parameters valued by the coach to support his/her decisions. We will return to this subject later in the chapter.

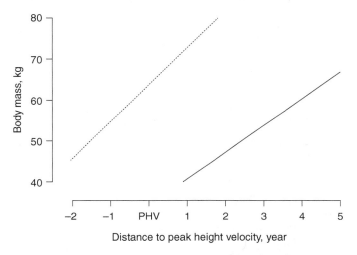

**FIGURE 10.1**    Body size aligned for estimated age at peak height velocity of female (n = 50) and male (n = 58) adolescent basketball players (full line: girls; dotted line: boys).

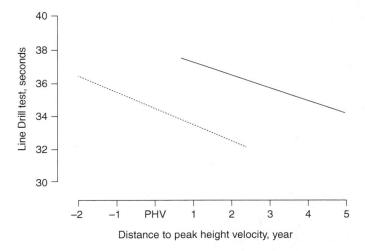

**FIGURE 10.2**    Functional performance (Line Drill test) aligned for estimated age at peak height velocity of female (n = 50) and male (n = 58) adolescent basketball players (full line: girls; dotted line: boys).

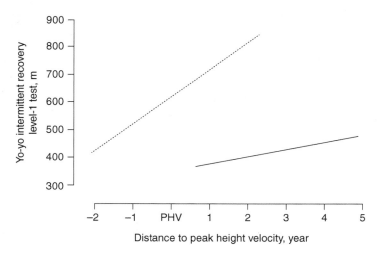

**FIGURE 10.3** Functional performance (Yo-Yo Intermittent Recovery test level 1) aligned for estimated age at peak height velocity of female (n = 50) and male (n = 58) adolescent basketball players (full line: girls; dotted line: boys).

The process of growth and maturation is inescapable and raises important peda-gogical and organizational problems for coaches to solve. It is a matter of planning, long-term vision, patience and flexibility. Coaches must profoundly know their athletes. As coach John Wooden put it once: "they don't care how much you know, before they know how much you care". From an athlete-centred coaching perspec-tive, good coaches know and care, and that is the best path to deal with diversity.

## Bio-banding

To minimise the possibilities of errors, models of athlete development have been elaborated, based on an age-linked choice of priorities (Côté & Vierimaa, 2014). However, the problem with all models is that they envision the long-term out-comes, whether continuity in participation or talent identification, and most young athletes live the fun of the moment and the enjoyment of their actual sporting life. Some solutions have been posed recently. Although not new, the application of bio-banding in youth sports' competitions, talent identification and strength and conditioning have been re-emphasised (Cumming et al., 2017). The concept involves grouping and/or evaluating athletes on the basis of size and/or maturity status rather than chronological age (Cumming et al., 2017). In applied contexts, the application of bio-banding has been explored mostly in professional clubs or academies, in the search of the young 'elite' athletes.

Even considering accounting for age- and maturity-associated variation on physiological performance in young athletes, important individual differences remain accounted to training exposure (Carvalho et al., 2013; Carvalho et al., 2011;

Carvalho et al., 2012) and likely other environmental factors (e.g., competition exposure and level, or coaching). Furthermore, misclassification of players by maturity group is a potential concern, as a growing body of information has highlighted the limitations of predictive equations to estimate maturity status, particularly with young athletes (Malina et al., 2006; Malina & Koziel, 2014; Moore et al., 2015). As Cumming and colleagues recognise, despite grouping athletes on the basis of physical characteristics, it does not preclude the consideration of psychological and/or technical skills (Cumming et al., 2017). This implies a major drawback in applied youth sports contexts where sport participation in school contexts, local clubs and other forms of youth sports promotion, which involves most of youth sports participation, is constrained by social and cultural contexts than need to be considered. Although the concept of bio-banding appears valid, and in many cases applicable, such as weight groups in wrestling, it may be more useful as one more resource for coaches to improve their interventions within their teams and clubs, whether grouping players within training exercises, or promoting occasional competitions by size or 'biological age'.

The critical use of development models is useful to set points of reference to guide the coaches' interventions during the specialisation years, but it does not establish rules or define the practical decisions of coaches. The study of good coaches may represent a viable way to reveal the mechanisms that underpin the excellence in coaching that is undoubtedly athlete-centred. Good coaches present remarkable flexibility to adapt their plans, training loads, instructions and feedback to individual athletes, according to their capabilities and competitive level (Turnnidge, Côté, Hollenstein, & Deakin, 2014).

## The athlete

Athletes perceive and experience training loads and task difficulty in individualised ways. The same drill can have diverse impacts on athletes' physiological responses. For instance, the magnitude of the effects of altitude training varies from athlete to athlete. Fatigue and recovery from fatigue after the same training load appear sooner, or later, depending of the individual. Coaches must know their athletes' reactions and how to deal with them.

There are several tools that allow coaches to monitor their athletes and prescribe an individualised training load. In professional sport, the task of the coach is easier, as there is a high-qualified staff that manages effort and recovery according to the actual capacities of the athletes. In youth sport or in a less structured environment, where coaches are frequently alone, portable technology devices, such as cardiofrequencimeters, and/or scales of Perceived Exertion – Foster scale, REST-Q or POMS are the most common – and represent valuable and necessary resources which can be used on a daily, weekly or monthly basis (Kelly & Coutts, 2007).

There is anecdotal evidence that professional athletes have their own personal trainer to maximise the gains of a customised training. In other settings and with scarce resources, good coaches observe each athlete, register their reactions to effort and recovery and re-plan sessions and drills accordingly. In this particular area of intervention, the quantification of the training load and the measurement of athletes' performances are mandatory. The 'eye' of the coach is not enough.

Another issue for an effective athlete-centred coach is the risk of injuries, because they are another individualised effect of training. Athletes with certain morphological or functional characteristics (e.g., body size or particular muscular fragilities) are more prone to injuries. Coaches must prescribe or avoid specific drills for specific athletes in order to prevent negative outcomes or to facilitate a complete recovery from previous problems. This part of the role framing of the coach is especially important during the specialisation years or in sports with tough physical contact (rugby, combat sports), when the prevalence of injuries is very high.

## The performer

Participation in sport increases the inter-athletes' diversity; it does not make them more homogeneous. Forsman et al. (2016) showed that the differences at the baseline among athletes in technical and functional skills increase or remain the same after a competitive season. A third chronosystem, time of practice, is in play, interacting with chronological age and biological age, influencing athletes' development. Training age, or formal years of training experience, which refers to the number of years an athlete has been participating in formal training (Lloyd et al., 2014; Myer, Lloyd, Brent, & Faigenbaum, 2013), has been noted to influence variation in young athletes' physiological performance (Berry, Abernethy, & Cote, 2008; Gonçalves, Rama, & Figueiredo, 2012; Gonçalves, Silva, Carvalho, & Gonçalves, 2011).

As noted above, the incidence of injuries is correlated in the amount of hours of training and with the level and intensity of competition (Steinberg, Aujla, Zeev, & Redding, 2014). Furthermore, athletes recover from injuries at different paces, associated with their previous amount of practice and type of preparation (Gilson, Heller, & Stults-Kolehmainen, 2013).

We are in a field where to look for general causes or causal mechanisms seems impossible because the interaction of multiple factors is unique for each athlete. Coaches cannot control the previous the outcomes of their training process, but they can control their decisions about the athletes' careers – such as selection vs. deselection, talent development, playing time or the evaluation of success and failure.

## Coaches' interpretations and decision-making: what coaches need to know?

Coaches interpret reality and make decisions based on several observable parameters, mediated by their knowledge of sport, and by their own philosophies. These biological observable parameters are measurable and evaluated through reference values, either cut-off values for a given population or for the individual athlete. Therefore, the coach must know how to locate and rank the athlete among his/

her peers and must track the personal development trajectory of the athletes he/she coaches. The specific, ecological knowledge of the coach operates in two levels: (a) planning, organising and evaluating practice sessions, prescribe the training load and the recovery periods, prevent injuries, managing competitions; and (b) following the athletes' evolution in response to training, growth and maturation, identifying and developing talent, preparing for higher competitive demands.

To deal with the first level of knowledge, coaches have at their disposal simple and easy-to-use tools that can offer enough information to assess the athletes' performances and to individualise the training loads. Coach education programs provide expertise about non-invasive or mild-invasive resources that coaches can use to monitor and prescribe the balance between effort and recovery. Heart rate, blood lactate and perceived exertion scales are familiar to coaches and, even without the precision of more sophisticated and expensive methods, are viable ways to uncover the unique responses of athletes to physical stressors. However, in most cases coaches use these resources only to store information and do not build their practices on an authentic athlete-centred approach. The consequences, especially with inexperienced athletes, can result in injuries, burnout, overtraining syndrome or dropout. The motto for coaches must be: 'what is technically and tactically desirable for each athlete must be physically possible'.

Regarding the second level of knowledge, the risk is that coaches tend to overlook athletes late in biological maturity that may be at a slower growth rate than those advanced in biological maturity status that are taller, heavier, stronger and faster. This belief has powerful pedagogical consequences.

Early adolescent players are frequently exposed to specialisation in sport programs, where athletes are oriented towards competitive success, being submitted to standards of training intensities and volume required by excellence performance. Thus, the interpretation of physiological signs among adolescent players should consider growth and maturation-related influences on behavioural changes with pubertal development.

Coaches have at their disposal reliable tools to assess the athletes' maturation status. The use of X-rays is the most precise measurement, but it requires exposure to radiation and a trained expert to interpret the images. The use of less precise but easier to use measurements, such as the maturity offset or the calculation of the predicted mature stature, provides sufficient and accurate information. We exclude the systematic observation of secondary sexual characteristics due the potential legal problems. The key point is that coaches must map the athlete's path and pace of development and act accordingly. It is not only the talent identification issue or the quest for victories, but also and mainly a healthy and enjoyable participation in sport. Interpretation of the interactions between body dimensions, functional capacities and psychological and social characteristics needs to consider appropriate analytical approaches. Multilevel regression models allow examining variance components and determining if mean body dimensions, functional capacities and pedagogical environment vary notably by maturity status.

## Conclusions

The chapter focused on the biological side of training. Planning practice sessions and quantifying the training loads are normally well known by coaches, and extensively delivered in formal coaching education. The issues linked to growth and maturation of adolescent athletes are beginning to occupy a central place among coaches' interests, and are important in an athlete-centred context.

There are sufficient material and scientific resources to help coaches to measure, quantify and evaluate the idiosyncrasies of every athlete. It remains the pedagogical problem of how to adapt effort and recovery for each individual without compromising team building and team cohesion. Coaches must also be aware of the level, beliefs and expectations of the people who they work with, in order to weight the possible solutions and choose the most adequate to their specific environment. However, researchers and practitioners must never forget that biology per se does not explain everything and that the individual is unique not only in his or her body, but as a complex, sensitive, autonomous human being. It seems evident that any advance in this understanding process needs to adopt a multi-factorial approach.

## References

Armstrong, N., Welsman, J. R., & Chia, M.Y. (2001). Short term power output in relation to growth and maturation. *British Journal of Sports Medicine, 35*(2), 118–124.

Armstrong, N., Welsman, J. R., Williams, C. A., & Kirby, B. J. (2000). Longitudinal changes in young people's short-term power output. *Medicine & Science in Sports & Exercise, 32*(6), 1140–1145.

Bangsbo, J. (2004). *Fitness training in soccer: A scientific approach.* Spring City, PA: Reedswain.

Berry, J., Abernethy, B., & Cote, J. (2008). The contribution of structured activity and deliberate play to the development of expert perceptual and decision-making skill. *Journal of Sport and Exercise Psychology, 30*(6), 685–708.

Beunen, G., Baxter-Jones, A. D., Mirwald, R. L., Thomis, M., Lefevre, J., Malina, R. M., & Bailey, D. A. (2002). Intraindividual allometric development of aerobic power in 8- to 16-year-old boys. *Medicine & Science in Sports & Exercise, 34*(3), 503–510.

Beunen, G., Malina, R. M., Lefevre, J., Claessens, A. L., Renson, R., & Simons, J. (1988). *Adolescent growth and motor performance: A longitudinal study of Belgian boys.* Champaign, IL: Human Kinetics Books.

Burkner, P-C. (2017). Brms: An R package for Bayesian multilevel models using stan. *Journal of Statistical Software, 80*(1), 1–28.

Carvalho, H. M., Gonçalves, C. E., Grosgeorge, B., & Paes, R. R. (2017). Usefulness and validity of the line drill test for adolescent basketball players: A Bayesian multilevel analysis. *Research in Sports Medicine, 25*(3), 333–344.

Carvalho, H. M., Silva, M., Eisenmann, J. C., & Malina, R. M. (2013). Aerobic fitness, maturation, and training experience in youth basketball. *International Journal of Sports Physiology & Performance, 8*(4), 428–434.

Carvalho, H. M., Silva, M., Figueiredo, A. J., Gonçalves, C. E., Philippaerts, R. M., Castagna, C., & Malina, R. M. (2011). Predictors of maximal short-term power outputs in basketball players 14–16 years. *European Journal of Applied Physiology, 111*(5), 789–796.

Carvalho, H. M., Silva, M., Santos, J., Gonçalves, R. S., Philippaerts, R., & Malina, R. (2012). Scaling lower-limb isokinetic strength for biological maturation and body size in adolescent basketball players. *European Journal of Applied Physiology, 112*(8), 2881–2889.

Castagna, C., Impellizzeri, F. M., Rampinini, E., D'Ottavio, S., & Manzi, V. (2008). The Yo-Yo intermittent recovery test in basketball players. *Journal of Sports Science and Medicine, 11*(2), 202–208.

Côté, J., & Vierimaa, M. (2014). The developmental model of sport participation: 15 years after its first conceptualization. *Science and Sports, 29*, S63–S69.

Cumming, S. P., Lloyd, R. S., Oliver, J. L., Eisenmann, J. C., & Malina, R. M. (2017). Bio-banding in Sport: Applications to competition, talent identification, and strength and conditioning of youth athletes. *Strength & Conditioning Journal, 39*(2), 34–47.

Denison, J. (2010). Planning, practice and performance: The discursive formation of coaches' knowledge. *Sport, Education and Society, 15*(4), 461–478.

Forsman, H., Gråstén, A., Blomqvist, M., Davids, K., Liukkonen, J., & Konttinen, N. (2016). Development of perceived competence, tactical skills, motivation, technical skills, and speed and agility in young soccer players. *Journal of Sports Sciences, 34*(14), 1311–1318.

Gilson, T. A., Heller, E. A., & Stults-Kolehmainen, M. A. (2013). The relationship between an effort goal and self-regulatory efficacy beliefs for division i football players. *The Journal of Strength & Conditioning Research, 27*(10), 2806–2815.

Gonçalves, C. E., Figueiredo, A., & Coelho e Silva, M. (2009). Multidimensional analysis of dropout in youth basketball: 2-year follow-up among Portuguese initiates. In T. Jurimae, N. Armstrong, & J. Jurimae (Eds.), *Children an exercise XXIV* (pp. 190–195). London: Routledge.

Gonçalves, C. E., Rama, L. M., & Figueiredo, A. J. (2012). Talent identification and specialization in sport: An overview of some unanswered questions. *International Journal of Sports Physiology & Performance, 7*(4), 390–393.

Gonçalves, C. E., Silva, M., Carvalho, H. M., & Gonçalves, A. (2011). Why do they engage in such hard programs? The search for excellence in youth basketball. *Journal of Sports Science and Medicine, 10*(3), 458–464.

Grecic, D., & Collins, D. (2013). The epistemological chain: Practical applications in sports. *Quest, 65*(2), 151–168.

Helsen, W. F., Hodges, N. J., Van Winckel, J., & Starkes, J. L. (2000). The roles of talent, physical precocity and practice in the development of soccer expertise. *Journal of Sport Sciences, 18*, 727–736.

Jacobs, F., Claringbould, I., & Knoppers, A. (2016). Becoming a "good coach". *Sport, Education and Society, 21*(3), 411–430.

Kelly, V. G., & Coutts, A. J. (2007). Planning and monitoring training loads during the competition phase in team sports. *Strength & Conditioning Journal, 29*(4), 32–37.

Lloyd, R. S., Oliver, J. L., Faigenbaum, A. D., Myer, G. D., & De Ste Croix, M. B. (2014). Chronological age vs. biological maturation: Implications for exercise programming in youth. *The Journal of Strength & Conditioning Research, 28*(5), 1454–1464.

Malina, R. M., Claessens, A. L., Van Aken, K., Thomis, M., Lefevre, J., Philippaerts, R., & Beunen, G. P. (2006). Maturity offset in gymnasts: Application of a prediction equation. *Medicine & Science in Sports & Exercise, 38*(7), 1342–1347.

Malina, R. M., & Koziel, S. M. (2014). Validation of maturity offset in a longitudinal sample of Polish boys. *Journal of Sports Sciences, 32*(5), 424–437.

Malina, R. M., Pena Reyes, M. E., Eisenmann, J. C., Horta, L., Rodrigues, J., & Miller, R. (2000). Height, mass and skeletal maturity of elite Portuguese soccer players aged 11–16 years. *Journal of Sports ScienceS, 18*(9), 685–693.

Mirwald, R. L., Baxter-Jones, A. D., Bailey, D. A., & Beunen, G. P. (2002). An assessment of maturity from anthropometric measurements. *Medicine & Science in Sports & Exercise, 34*(4), 689–694.

Moore, S. A., McKay, H. A., Macdonald, H., Nettlefold, L., Baxter-Jones, A. D., Cameron, N., & Brasher, P. M. (2015). Enhancing a somatic maturity prediction model. *Medicine & Science in Sports & Exercise, 47*(8), 1755–1764.

Myer, G. D., Lloyd, R. S., Brent, J. L., & Faigenbaum, A. D. (2013). How young is "too young" to start training? *ACSMs Health & Fitness Journal, 17*(5), 14–23.

R-Core-Team. (2014). *R: A language and environment for statistical computing.* Vienna, Austria: R Foundation for Statistical Computing. Retrieved from www.R-project.org/

Semenick, D. (1990). Tests and measurements: The line drill test. *Strength & Conditioning Journal, 12*(2), 47–49.

Sherar, L. B., Cumming, S. P., Eisenmann, J. C., Baxter-Jones, A. D., & Malina, R. M. (2010). Adolescent biological maturity and physical activity: Biology meets behavior. *Pediatric Exercise Science, 22*(3), 332–349.

Stan Development Team. (2015). *Stan: A C++ library for probability and sampling.* Retrieved from http://mc-stan.org/

Steinberg, N., Aujla, I., Zeev, A., & Redding, E. (2014). Injuries among talented young dancers: Findings from the UK Centres for Advanced Training. *International Journal of Sports Medicine, 35*, 238–244.

Thomis, M., Claessens, A. L., Lefevre, J., Philippaerts, R., Beunen, G. P., & Malina, R. M. (2005). Adolescent growth spurts in female gymnasts. *Journal of Pediatrics, 146*(2), 239–244.

Thomis, M., Rogers, D. M., Beunen, G. P., Woynarowska, B., & Malina, R. M. (2000). Allometric relationship between body size and peak VO2 relative to age at menarche. *Annals of Human Biology, 27*(6), 623–633.

Turnnidge, J., Côté, J., Hollenstein, T., & Deakin, J. (2014). A direct observation of the dynamic content and structure of coach-athlete interactions in a model sport program. *Journal of Applied Sport Psychology, 26*(2), 225–240.

Van Praagh, E., & Dore, E. (2002). Short-term muscle power during growth and maturation. *Sports Medicine, 32*(11), 701–728.

# 11

## ATHLETE-CENTRED COACHING AND TEACHING GAMES FOR UNDERSTANDING

## Not quite the perfect match

*Adrian P. Turner*

For the past decade, I have been involved with coaching competitive travel soccer (8–14-year-olds) at the grass roots level in the American Midwest – initially as the coaching facilitator at a community soccer club. In this capacity, I received the following email from a concerned, and highly informed, soccer parent.

Adrian,

I was talking with my son Jason (pseudonym) yesterday afternoon about school, life, etc. I asked him what he enjoyed most about school. "Recess," was his answer. He elaborated. I then asked him what he enjoyed most about soccer. "Playing the games." Predictable. And then after a brief pause his tone of voice got sad and he reported in the simple language of a six year old, "When I pop the ball up the coach takes me out." He paused. "Then I sit on the bench and I have to wait until after the game to play soccer with you guys." I asked him what he meant by "popping the ball up." He wasn't very articulate (he's six years old), but he mumbled something about his coach not liking it when he juggles the ball.

You might recall me telling you about what happened a month ago in practice when Jason, at full speed, received a ball, flicked it up, bounce-juggled it four times in the air before volleying it into the back of the net. Instead of celebrating a bit of creative soccer genius, his coach responded by yelling "No, no, no" and then lectured Jason on how you don't juggle in soccer games and told him that he didn't want to see that anymore. As I told you following the incident, I didn't say anything to his coach (Andrei, pseudonym) or my son. I didn't think it was my place.

But after my conversation with Jason yesterday, I feel like I need to say something.

I appreciate Andrei's work and enthusiasm with the kids. He clearly cares. And I respect his soccer credentials, his playing and coaching experience. Still, we can all learn. While I don't have a soccer playing background, I played a lot of sports growing up and I know how to do research. I've spent a great deal of time reading, watching, and most importantly, observing and talking with people who know a lot about soccer over the last decade. I've watched and played a lot of street and organized soccer in Argentina, Italy, Mexico, and Spain over the years. I could go on. I won't. In short, I may not have played semi-professional soccer, but I'm not an imbecile.

With that I'll cut to the chase. Andrei's style of over-coaching will in the short-run win games. He has plans to work with our boys all winter long to prepare them for spring ball. Very laudable. Based on my observations, he will teach our kids to become great passers and classic finishers. They will become ruthlessly effective. With their innate talent they will win many games. The vast majority of parents will be tremendously pleased. But in the process, he will snuff out the sparks of genius that our kids possess. He will tell my son to pass, pass, pass. He will tell my son not to flick the ball up, as he naturally wants to do. He will discourage risk taking.

How do I know? Because I've watched the evolution of this team over the last few games. Our boys look so much more organised and so much more effective. But the dribbling runs have disappeared. My son's little flick dribble has disappeared. When he gets a run going instead of looking to juke his opponent, I see him looking around for someone to pass to.

Effective? Yes.

Moronic? If we're talking about the long-term development of a six year old, no doubt about it.

In two years of close observation, I have never once heard Paul Smith (pseudonym) – by far the most talented coach we have out there – tell Jeff Jones (pseudonym) to pass the ball. In fact, he really doesn't tell any of his players to pass the ball. And I've certainly never heard him discipline a player for taking a risk. Certainly, he teaches them the value of passing in practice. But he doesn't work on tactics. He teaches them skills and then lets them go out and govern themselves. Let Jeff use his genius to figure stuff out on his own. Let the others try as well. And that's been with 10, 11, and 12 year olds.

So what are we doing over-coaching 6 and 7 year olds?

To conclude, I don't think I'm just an angry parent. I can be objective. I can see that my eldest son would rather be playing chess and doing magic tricks. My daughter just wants to have fun. But Jason LOVES soccer. And he has a bit of genius in him. Some of the stuff he comes up with is crazy. To be sure, a lot of it is pointless. But it's the craziness that makes for the greatest players. Maradona, Garrincha, Pele, Ronaldinho, Zidane, Messi . . . They did/do crazy, fundamentally unsound stuff. The greatest tennis players in history – they changed the game because they WERE fundamentally unsound. The greatest basketball players. They're street ballers.

We're fools if we snuff the street ball out of our kids. We're fools if we let Andrei do that.

I've given a big chunk of the last five years of my life to this club. But I'll take Jason elsewhere if he's going to spend the winter having the spark snuffed out of his game.

I'd like to discuss this with you and I'd be fine if you shared this with Andrei although that's your call. But I've been worried about this for six months and have been biting my tongue. With the talent and passion Andrei has, this could be a very easy fix. Just get the kids together, teach them correct principles, but then let them govern themselves! Easy fix. But it needs to be fixed.

Thanks.

## Athlete-centred coaching

In his email, the parent makes several cogent points pertaining to a request for a more athlete-centred approach to coaching. In the coach-centred scenario that the parent witnessed, the focus appeared to be on facilitating short-term outcomes (i.e., winning) rather than long-term player development advocated by athlete-centred coaching proponents (Kidman & Lombardo, 2010). The impetus from the email also concurs with Cooper's (2010) positions on an athlete-centred approach to coaching regarding the importance of street soccer and playing games in young players' talent development. The parent implies that the coach viewed his son's actions as those of a maverick and a potential threat to conformity and coaching control. In the United States the stereotypical coaching culture has frequently identified the coach as both the controller and director whose authority is above question by athletes (Humm, 2010). The parent also recognises the importance of opportunities for creativity as essential to his son's soccer development. The juggling and shooting example illustrates the premise presented in athlete-centred coaching missives of acquiring unique solutions to movement problems via discovery learning and exploration (Holyoak, 2005; Renshaw & Chappell, 2010).

## Teaching Games for Understanding

About a month prior to receipt of the parent's email, the coach, Andrei, participated in a workshop on games-based approaches (see Turner, 2014a). He was one of three coaches purposefully sampled from among the workshop attendees to participate in a yearlong study examining novice coaches' experiences in learning to negotiate Teaching Games for Understanding (TGfU). The juggling example that the parent witnessed was recorded on videotape. In addition to Andrei, the Under 8-year-old (U8) boys' team coach, two other coaches also participated in the project: Ken, the U10 boys' team coach, and Sally, the U11 girls' team coach. Ken was a church minister and had been a goalkeeper in high school; although Sally had not played competitive soccer, she was the only one of the three with a coaching qualification at the time of the research project – a "D" license obtained from the

United States Soccer Federation. The study (see Turner, 2014a) utilised Windschitl's (2002) four-dimensional model to analyse the conceptual, cultural, pedagogical and political dilemmas confronting these three travel soccer coaches when attempting to use TGfU. In this chapter, I will draw directly from selected excerpts from the coaches' transcripts reported in that study to illustrate the challenges that the coaches experienced in relation to an athlete-centred approach to coaching, which, while broader than TGfU, incorporates several of its key elements. I will begin with the conceptual challenge experienced by coach Andrei.

## Conceptual challenges

Andrei experienced a challenge in employing an athlete-centred approach focusing on games-based learning rather than a coach-centred approach where techniques were learned in drills prior to games. As Andrei elaborated:

> before you start making them think creativity on the field you have to fix your basics . . . It's like Chess OK, before they start to think on the board they have to know how to use the figures on the desk right. Because if they don't know about (can execute) passing and how to stop the ball, what kind of creativity can you expect from them?
>
> *(Turner, 2014a, p. 73)*

Andrei's point represents a concern expressed by some leading scholars in physical education and sport in criticism of games-based/athlete-centred approaches that an initial level of control of a ball is necessary before tactics can be employed in most elementary game settings (Rink, 2010). The game may be modified to avert the skill, but ultimately in returning to the initial/actual game the tactics will typically be restricted by an inability to execute technique (Rink, 2010). In contrast, the other two coaches were more accepting of a need for learners to acquire games concepts in dynamic tactical situations (Turner & Martinek, 1995). As Ken suggested:

> Well it's like passing if you did a skill in a non-game drill, but then you get to the game and there's so many emotional variables and adrenaline that are going on that what they learned by passing one with one in a warm-up (practice) that's fine but if you're trying to coach passing, it's nothing like the game. The ball's not bouncing, their adrenaline is not going, they're not moving the same way quickly into space it's completely different.
>
> *(Turner, 2014a, p. 75)*

Ken's statement illustrates how TGfU coaching is anchored in a humanistic athlete-centred approach, as it potentially increases athletes' motivation and intensity because of the meaningful nature of the tasks that create situations more representative of the pressure in games competition (Kidman & Lombardo, 2010). He is also cognisant of the importance of learning to play in context to facilitate a better understanding of the game (Thorpe, 2001). The learning tasks make more sense to the athletes when they relate to the core concepts of the sport. In soccer, an invasion game, those elements include time and space (Light, 2017), as Ken acknowledged in his statement. In learning to play games effectively, tactics, decision-making and skill execution are all connected as knowledge-in-action (Light, 2017).

## Cultural challenges

In an attempt to re-orientate coach and player roles to a more 'hands-off' approach to coaching, all three coaches designed modified games using task constraints to 're-culture' the learning environment during team practices (Kidman & Lombardo, 2010; Renshaw & Chappell, 2010). They manipulated game objectives, game progression and possession rules, space, equipment and team numbers during modified games (see Turner, 2014a).

In order to create more player involvement in the learning process, the coaches utilised questioning to promote an interactive athlete-centred culture. Ken's questioning ability evolved over the duration of the study. Initially he asked lower order convergent questions and sought athlete responses that confirmed his anticipated answer – the use of an initiate–response–evaluation scenario (Forrest, 2014). Ken indicated:

> I think they know some answers I want so I have to figure out a different way to ask questions, cause it's like, 'passing, passing, passing'. Kind of like a Sunday school answer 'Jesus, Jesus, Jesus' so I need to work out a different way to question.
>
> *(Turner, 2014a, p. 78)*

Over time Ken's approach to questioning progressed to more divergent inquiry and he was able to pose questions within game problems that he set for the athletes.

> I'm allowing them to self-direct one another, asking the question and seeing during the game period them correct one another. OK, what is wrong, and then self-coaching one another. They get it, you know, maybe they're not in an effective position but another player understands and explains what they are doing.
>
> *(Turner, 2014a, p. 78)*

The use of higher order questions provided opportunities for athletes to interpret questions and evaluate responses independently. Furthermore, in a team game setting he provided a venue for athletes to debate different solutions, empowering the players to make decisions on the field of play during his coaching (Kidman & Lombardo, 2010). Lyn Gunson (international netball coach) has indicated that in order to be effective questions must be open-ended and create ownership for the athletes (Kidman &

Lombardo, 2010). By learning independently of the coach, mistakes will be made that athletes can examine as part of social learning in an athlete-centred approach (Light, 2017). Some games-based scholars have also suggested that by verbalising their understanding, it is brought to all athletes' consciousness as they become explicitly aware of the construct, and have the opportunity to experiment with the concept in their subsequent movement performances (Harvey, Cushion, & Massa-Gonzalez, 2010).

Martens (2012) suggests that "team culture is the way things are done on a team – it's the social architecture that nurtures the team psyche" (p. 34). The team culture created by athletes and coaches was based on shared values and provided direction and focus. Examples of concepts impacting team culture on these TGfU coached teams included presentation of a multi-coloured rubber band at the end of every match to an opponent who demonstrated good sportsmanship – voted on by the athletes. Before, during and after every game the coaches encouraged athletes to provide their perspectives on various issues. For example, before a game, players provided input on perceived strengths and weaknesses of opponents. In most instances players had knowledge of opponents from previous league play. At halftime players were encouraged to provide their perspectives on what their team had done well and what they needed to work on during the second half. At the conclusion of the game, players were requested to convey to the team what they had learned from the match. As part of team tradition before the game, at halftime and after the match the players recited a team cheer that they created. After each game, all players shook hands with every opponent and the referees – always thanking the referee regardless of game outcome. Before leaving the playing field all rubbish was collected by team players. The team area and touchline was always left clean. Whenever the team lost a game the coach identified positive elements in the team's play and informed the team of these elements before they left the playing field.

## Pedagogical challenges

One of Rod Thorpe's (2001) primary tenets underpinning TGfU is the creation of games experiences that enable young athletes to achieve tactical understanding for themselves. The three coaches recognised the importance, but also had difficulty in addressing this premise. As Ken noted, "we could look like idiots sometimes if the modified games don't work but unless we try we're never going to be stretched and the players won't improve" (Turner, 2014a, p. 80).

In the first week of the project, Ken created a learning activity in a 20-by-10-metre area where three offensive players (beginning at one end of the area) had to make four passes and circumvent an advancing defender from the opposite end in order to cross the goal line to score. In an initial trial, the attacking players positioned very close together made four very short passes and then one of them dribbled by the defender. The players' creativity was impressive, but Ken was frustrated and criticised them for undermining his learning task – which he had designed to facilitate passing and moving to space. In the subsequent trial the attacking players started the same way and the defender rushed out to close the attackers down, only this time on the third pass an attacker chipped the ball long into space behind the advancing defender for his teammate to run on to and make a sideways pass to his teammate over the goal line. The 'short-short-long' passing tactic they created worked well, as the athletes were focused on the objective of the game task and how it could be achieved. The problem was solved by working within the rules of the activity to create a solution learned by the players that could then provide a viable tactical alternative in future games.

When to intervene as a coach and when to allow athletes to work through situations is a difficult choice for a coach and may depend on the context (Kidman & Lombardo, 2010). Over time, Ken's preference was to wait and see if the problem and solution emerged from the modified game rather than implementing conditions to address the issue too quickly. It has been posited that this lengthier observation process enables athletes to make decisions for themselves in an athlete-centred approach (Humm, 2010).

There were also instances when modified games required assistance or intervention to facilitate the development of play. In one example, Sally was coaching a four versus four game on a 30-by-25-metre field with four goals. Each team was attacking two small goals offset towards each touchline of the field on their opponent's goal line. One team was creating multiple scoring opportunities on both opponents' goals. After several minutes Sally stopped the game and asked the teams to reflect on their level of success in creating scoring opportunities. After a brief discussion, the less successful team suggested that they were not creating many goal-scoring opportunities because they were keeping two players back as pseudo goalkeepers when they were on offense. As a consequence, they were typically outnumbered all over the field. She then asked the team how they could amend this predicament by formulating a different strategy. After further discussion, the team suggested using one player (the last defender) to cover both goals when they were attacking. This player would position only far enough forward when her team was on offense that she could run to cover either goal in the event of a turnover. The team subsequently used one of their players as a 'sweeper-keeper' to facilitate their game performance. The evolution of the 'sweeper-keeper' solution devised by one of the teams is an example of a mistake being made into a positive learning experience, with time provided by the coach for reflection and analysis by the athletes to create a strategy to amend the game problem (Light, 2017). The ability of the coach to develop a game to maintain an appropriate level of challenge by analysing player performance is critical to athlete-centred coaching approaches (Turner, 2014b).

## Political challenges

The parent's email presented at the beginning of this chapter requested a more athlete-centred focus to coaching, but research on sport teaching and coaching practices has suggested that practitioners often modify their athlete-centred pedagogy to mediate parent and administrator expectations for more formal technique instruction (Curry & Light, 2014). Scholars in youth sports have indicated many parents hold unrealistic performance expectations for their children (Hyman, 2009) and focus on fast changes in observable performance rather than learning (Thorpe, 2001). The parent comments from the touchline at one of Ken's games were critical of the 9-year-old players' abilities to play defence, due to an apparent lack of coaching and their inability to take throw-ins legally. At another game Ken actually stopped coaching his team, walked around the edge of the soccer field and requested parents to refrain from coaching their children. This was frustrating, as he had recently reported the development of a more athlete-centred approach during matches. As Ken indicated, "I'm having to talk less as a coach which is my goal in the games and so they were doing things; the defense was telling each-other to support, they switched fields without being told" (Turner, 2014a, p. 83).

The youth soccer league rules were only partially conducive to athlete-centred coaching at the time of the study. Teams were permitted six players on the field for U8–U10 age level competition and eight players for U11–U12 games; but the goals were 2.13 metres high and 6.40 metres wide. Goalkeepers had little chance with high shots and some club coaches encouraged their teams to play on this opposition weakness. Although the fields were appropriately sized for fewer players, younger age goalkeepers often had difficultly clearing their own penalty areas on goal (place) kicks. Opposing players would stand at the edge of the penalty area waiting to pounce as the ball slowly exited the penalty box. Goalkeeper punts were a much more effective weapon though, as goalkeepers would frequently punt the ball a long way on the miniature field to be chased after by a fast attacker who was frequently through on goal for a scoring opportunity at the other end of the field with no offside law enforced.

While the goals still remain too big for young players, the youth soccer league finally amended its playing rules in autumn 2016 to preclude goalkeepers from punting or drop-kicking the ball at the U10 or younger age level. When the goalkeeper possesses the ball, the opposing team must now retreat behind a 'build-out' line adjacent to the top of the penalty area (and marked four metres beyond it) until the goalkeeper has thrown, rolled or kicked the ball into play. The intent of this constraint is to enable players to build play from the defensive third of the field with the ball being passed into play from the goalkeeper position under reduced defensive pressure. It appears to be a valid attempt by the youth soccer league administration to "get the modified game right" (Thorpe & Bunker, 2008) by making it developmentally appropriate for young players. In 2016, due to concerns pertaining to young athletes sustaining concussions, the United States Soccer Federation introduced legislation to preclude all athletes aged 10 and younger from heading the ball during games or practice settings. There are clear implications for young players learning tactics and skills to play games in accordance with this new safety constraint.

## Summary

Scholars have indicated that coaches who utilise a TGfU approach are well advanced on the continuum towards athlete-centred coaching (Kidman & Lombardo, 2010). TGFU is grounded in a humanistic, athlete-centred approach where players learn to solve their own game-related problems. Conceptually it presents a challenge to some coaches, but when learning is situated in modified games that simulate the actual game it provides meaning to the learning activities not addressed in isolated technique practice. By engaging athletes in active dialogue via questioning, the coaches can re-negotiate the pedagogical environment to one where they listen to and respect players' perspectives in order to create an interactive athlete-centred learning culture. The creation of modified games experiences that test athletes and enable them to develop tactical understanding is a primary pedagogical challenge for sports teachers and coaches. Mistakes are part of the instructional process and provide opportunities for athlete-centred learning. By amending the game context players are challenged to create new ways to solve tactical problems they encounter as additional problems arise during their games. While some parents still favour a short-term emphasis on winning and formal coaching instruction, the email at the beginning of this chapter suggests a change in that perspective towards athlete-centred coaching that may continue to grow with ongoing initiatives in parent coaching education. The changes in the youth soccer league laws also suggest a trend towards long-term athlete development as well as an increased concern for players' safety as part of an athlete-centred focus.

## References

Cooper, P. (2010). Play and children. In L. Kidman & B. J. Lombardo (Eds.), *Athlete-centred coaching: Developing decision makers* (2nd ed., pp. 137–150). Worcester: IPC Print Resources.

Curry, C., & Light, R. L. (2014). The influence of school context on the implementation of TGfU across a secondary school physical education department. In R. L. Light, J. Quay, S. Harvey, & A. Mooney (Eds.), *Contemporary developments in games teaching* (pp. 118–132). New York: Routledge.

Forrest, G. (2014). Questions and answers: Understanding the connection between questioning and knowledge in game-centred approaches. In R. L. Light, J. Quay, S. Harvey, & A. Mooney (Eds.), *Contemporary developments in games teaching* (pp. 167–177). New York: Routledge.

Harvey, S., Cushion, C. J., & Massa-Gonzalez, A. N. (2010). Learning a new method: Teaching Games for Understanding in the coaches' eyes. *Physical Education and Sport Pedagogy*, *15*(4), 361–382.

Holyoak, D. (2005). Practice, instruction and skill acquisition. *Journal of Sport Sciences, 23*(6), 637–650.

Humm, R. (2010). How's your coaching. In L. Kidman & B. J. Lombardo (Eds.), *Athlete-centred coaching: Developing decision makers* (2nd ed., pp. 256–275). Worcester: IPC Print Resources.

Hyman, M. (2009). *Until it hurts: America's obsession with youth sports and how it harms our kids*. Boston, MA: Beacon.

Kidman, L., & Lombardo, B. J. (2010). *Athlete-centred coaching: Developing decision makers* (2nd ed.). Worcester: IPC Print Resources.

Light, R. (2017). *Positive pedagogy for sport coaching: Athlete-centred coaching for individual sports*. New York: Routledge.

Martens, R. (2012). *Successful coaching* (4th ed.). Champaign, IL: Human Kinetics.

Renshaw, I., & Chappell, G. (2010). A constraints-led approach to talent development in cricket. In L. Kidman & B. J. Lombardo (Eds.), *Athlete-centred coaching: Developing decision makers* (2nd ed., pp. 151–172). Worcester: IPC Print Resources.

Rink, J. (2010). TGfU: Celebrations and cautions. In J. Butler & L. L. Griffin (Eds.), *More Teaching Games for Understanding: Move globally* (pp. 33–47). Champaign, IL: Human Kinetics.

Thorpe, R. (2001). Rod Thorpe on Teaching Games for Understanding. In L. Kidman (Ed.), *Developing decision makers: An empowerment approach to coaching* (pp. 22–36). Worcester: IPC Print Resources.

Thorpe, R. D., & Bunker, D. (2008, May). *Teaching Games for Understanding: Do current developments reflect original intentions?* Paper presented at the Fourth International Conference: Teaching Games for Understanding, Vancouver, British Columbia, Canada.

Turner, A. P. (2014a). Novice coaches negotiating Teaching Games for Understanding. *University of Sydney Papers in Human Movement, Health and Coach Education, 3*, 67–89.

Turner, A. P. (2014b). Learning games concepts by design. In R. L. Light, J. Quay, S. Harvey, & A. Mooney (Eds.), *Contemporary developments in games teaching* (pp. 193–206). New York: Routledge.

Turner, A. P., & Martinek, T. J. (1995). Teaching for understanding: A model for improving decision-making during game play. *Quest, 47*, 44–63.

United States Soccer Federation. (2016). *U.S. Soccer concussion initiative.* Retrieved from www.recognizetorecover.org/head-and-brain/#head-brain-conditions.

Windschitl, M. (2002). Framing constructivism in practice as the negotiation of dilemmas: An analysis of the conceptual, pedagogical, cultural and political challenges facing teachers. *Review of Educational Research, 72*(2), 131–175.

# PART III

# Researcher-practitioner perspectives on athlete-centred coaching

# 12

# ATHLETE-CENTRED COACHING FOR INDIVIDUAL SPORTS

*Richard Light*

Over the past two decades game-based approaches to coaching and teaching such as Teaching Games for Understanding (TGfU) and the Game Sense approach have attracted increasing interest from researchers and practitioners across the globe. Given their focus on the athlete as an active learner, athlete empowerment and consideration of athletes from a more humanistic perspective as thinking, feeling human beings with a life outside their sport, game-based approach (GBA) are athlete-centred. In particular, they offer considerable opportunity for advancing coaching in team sports and have influenced coaching at all levels, from children's sport to elite level, professional sport across a wide range of team sports (see Light, Evans, Harvey, & Hassanin, 2015). Indeed, the complexity and social nature of team sports make them highly suitable for the implementation of athlete-centred coaching, which I suggest is why this is where its development has been focused.

The continuing development of athlete-centred coaching in team sports offers great promise across a range of cultural and institutional settings, from children's first exposure to sport to elite levels of sport (see Chen, & Light, 2006; Chappell & Light, 2015; Jones, 2015; Wang & Ha, 2009). However, thinking about athlete-centred coaching has not moved far beyond team sports, with individual sports largely overlooked. This is likely due to a number of reasons, among which are assumptions that technique and skill can only be coached through direct instruction in skill-intensive sports and the significantly reduced importance of tactical knowledge and 'at action' decision-making (Light, Harvey, & Mouchet, 2014) in individual sports.

There have been suggestions made for adopting a constructivist-informed, learner-centred approach to teaching individual activities such as dance (see Chen, 2001) and primary school physical education (Chen & Rovegno, 2000) using pedagogy that is similar to athlete-centred coaching. More recently, I have worked with a range of international colleagues on adapting the principles of athlete-centred coaching to coaching individual sports such as swimming and athletics (Light &

Wallian, 2008; Light & Kentel, 2015). This work, further research and reflection on my own practice informed the development of a framework for adapting the features of Game Sense to coaching individual sport and making learning positive that I have since labelled Positive Pedagogy (PPed) for individual sports (Light & Harvey, 2017; Light, 2017). This approach modifies the Game Sense pedagogical framework (Light, 2013) to suit individual sport while drawing on Antonovsky's (1979, 1987) Sense of Coherence (SoC) model and Positive Psychology to augment the inherently positive learning experiences provided by athlete-centred coaching approaches for team sports. This chapter outlines PPed, then provides an example of coaching using this approach.

## The Positive Pedagogy framework

The PPed framework for coaching has three core features that guide the coach but are not intended to be prescriptive. It is not a model but instead is intended to provide a framework for thinking and modifying practice that guides the coach but allows him/her to adapt the ideas and features of PPed to suit the coach's disposition and the particulars of the situation. In adopting a PPed approach for individual sport, the coach would:

(1) Design and manage physical learning experience that engages the athlete;
(2) Emphasises asking questions to stimulate thinking and interaction in *preference* to telling athletes what to do; and
(3) Adopts an inquiry-based approach to coaching and athlete learning.

### *Designing and managing the learning environment/ experience*

The holistic and humanistic focus in PPed for individual sports is on the whole person, rather than on the whole game as in the Game Sense approach. It involves all the senses and other dimensions of experience, often with an emphasis on 'feel'. It typically requires designing learning experiences aimed at achieving specific outcomes of the session by placing physical constraints on the athlete to create a problem for him or her to solve. In PPed the aim of imposing a restraint is not to produce a predetermined movement or movement pattern, as it is in Constraints Led Theory (see Renshaw, Chow, Davids, & Hammond, 2010). Its aim is to create problems to be solved by the athlete through the interaction between processes of non-conscious thinking/learning (adaptation) and conscious thinking/learning promoted through questioning and interaction. Owing to the skill-intensive nature of most individual sports, this usually (but not always) involves using a discovery learning approach (Bruner, 1961) or, more narrowly, Mosston and Ashworth's (1986) guided discovery teaching style. Here the coach guides the athlete's discovery of the most efficient way for them to perform a skill or technique, which tends to involve more of a convergent thinking than divergent. It is important here to recognise that, despite the detail involved in teaching technique, every athlete interprets and adapts technique differently (Light & Wallian, 2008). When using PPed for coaching individual sports, constraints are commonly used to create awareness of a movement or create a problem that is to be solved through interaction and active learning (see Light, 2017). This would normally involve the inquiry learning approach first proposed by Dewey (see Barrow, 2006) a century ago that involves identifying and clarifying the problem, formulating a solution, testing and evaluating it and then applying it.

### Ask questions to generate dialogue and thinking

Designing and managing practice games for learning and questioning for learning seem to be the most challenging aspects of adopting these athlete-centred approaches (Harvey & Light, 2015). Questioning is one of the central mechanisms employed for promoting learning in PPed and GBA but typically presents challenges for coaches (Harvey & Light, 2015; Roberts, 2011). In PPed, questions are asked to promote thinking, reflection and dialogue and/or to assist in the discovery of effective technique, but it takes time for coaches to become skilful enough with questioning to guide discovery and achieve these aims. In team sport, questions should stimulate a range of possible answers or solutions; this is possible in some individual sports, but more often they assist athletes in discovering pre-determined knowledge with a smaller range of response options than in team sports (Harvey & Light, 2015). However, each athlete interprets skill execution according to his/her previous experiences, dispositions and physical attributes, with subtle individual variations (Light & Wallian, 2008).

Although questions asked in PPed tend to be designed to help athletes discover pre-determined knowledge, it requires a coaching disposition toward promoting a sense of curiosity and positive disposition toward inquiry where possible. When a solution does not work, the coach should ask the athlete to reflect upon why it did not work and how it could be modified to make it work, or decide it cannot work and seek a different solution. This could be in pairs, small groups or in one-on-one situations between coach and athlete. It is 'solution-focused', which allows it to provide a positive experience by focusing athlete attention on the goals of the activity and what they can do to achieve these goals, instead of on their weaknesses and eliminating mistakes (Grant, 2011). It can also be seen as a strength-based approach (see McCuaig, Quennerstedt, & Macdonald, 2013). The athlete solves problems by drawing on the resources (including social) available, with discussion focused on solutions to keep the athlete(s) engaged in the task (Grant, 2011).

### Adopt an inquiry-based approach to athlete learning

PPed adopts an inquiry-based approach that helps athletes improve while developing as independent learners and remaining motivated to participate in the activity for the longer term (Renshaw, Oldham, & Bawden, 2012). The social interaction involved in this process should also lead to athletes understanding each other in humanistic ways and can encourage empathy, compassion, meaningful relationships and a sense of connection. In PPed, coaches develop an environment in which athletes feel secure to not only seek to discover but also experiment and take chances, and in which they understand that mistakes provide positive opportunities for learning (Light, 2013; Renshaw et al., 2012). When working with children and young people in particular, the emphasis is on the process of learning through inquiry more than on the product. They provide positive learning experiences with the provision of opportunities for adequate reflection and analysis.

## Enhancing positive experience and learning

The three core features of Positive Pedagogy encourage positive learning experiences, but this is enhanced by drawing on Antonovsky's Sense of Coherence (SoC) model (1979, 1987) and Positive Psychology, with a focus on the PERMA model (Seligman, 2012).

### Sense of Coherence model

Antonovsky's SoC model (1979, 1987) focuses on the socially constructed resources that facilitate attaining and maintaining health and wellbeing. He proposes that specific personal dispositions made individuals more able to cope with the stresses of life and thus remain healthy by providing them with a 'sense of coherence'. His focus on experience offers a way of working with an holistic focus on the affective and social dimensions of sport that are emphasised in athlete-centred approaches (Kidman & Lombardo, 2010; Light, 2013) instead of taking a purely cognitive approach to creating positive experiences of practice. In PPed, I appropriate the three features of Antonovsky's SoC model to help make athlete learning positive by making practice *comprehensible, manageable* and *meaningful*. These concepts are used in PPed to create conditions that promote positive experiences of learning I briefly describe below.

*Comprehensibility* is developed through experience and refers to the extent to which things make sense for the individual by being ordered and consistent. For learning to be comprehensible in sport, it should help athletes to know, not only *how* to do something, but also *when, where* and *why*. It should also foster deep understanding of the concepts or 'big ideas' (Fosnot, 1996) that underpin learning and performance in sport (Light, 2017). Comprehensive understanding in sport involves not only rational, conscious and articulated knowing, but also a practical understanding or 'sense' of the game or activity (Bourdieu, 1986) developed through experience and engagement in the unfolding of knowledge.

In PPed, *manageability* refers to the resources available from interaction between athletes and between an athlete and the coach in dialogue. Here the athlete should feel that the challenges of learning are manageable and can be met by drawing on individual resources such as skill, physical capacity, knowledge and/or social resources such as social interaction with teammates and the coach.

Activities that engage athletes affectively and socially as well as physically and intellectually are more likely to provide *meaningfulness* for them. For example, when a swim or athletics coach adopts PPed, s/he might ask his/her athlete to reflect upon the feel of his/her skill execution and discuss it with a training partner who provides an external, objective perspective that can be drawn on along with the athlete's subjective perspective and focus on feel. In this case, learning emerges from interaction between the two athletes and the sharing of two different perspectives. This should involve them linking its technical detail to one of the core concepts of reducing resistance or increasing propulsion. As is emphasised in TGfU in relation to team sport, understanding *why* they are doing activities and how they relate to the aims of the session and even the season are central to learning. This not only promotes physical, affective, intellectual and physical engagement in learning but also gives meaning to practice through deep understanding of *why* a technique is performed as it is. It empowers the athlete to work through problems and challenges as they arise (Light, 2014) by providing manageability.

## Positive psychology and the PERMA model

Positive Psychology sets out to redress a preoccupation in psychology with pathologies and repairing the 'worst aspects' of life by discovering and promoting life's positive qualities (Seligman & Csikszentmihalyi, 2000). It focuses on what is good about life and what the individual can do to make life better by promoting satisfaction in the past, happiness and the experience of *flow* in the present and hope and optimism in the future (Jackson & Csikszentmihalyi, 1999). Positive Psychology aligns with the aims of Positive Pedagogy, but it is the PERMA model (Seligman, 2012) that best frames the intent of PPed to promote positive experiences, dispositions and learning (Light, in press).

PPed fosters positive learning that can contribute toward wellbeing and aligns well with all five elements of Seligman's (2012) PERMA (positive emotions, engagement, relations, meaning and achievement) model. It encourages positive emotions and engagement (emotional, intellectual and physical) that contribute to the meaningfulness of practice. Setting the challenges the athlete must meet through the design of activities, and being able to adjust them through observation and humanistic understanding of athlete learning, can provide positive experiences of achievement. These aspects and the emphasis on building trusting relationships between athletes and between athletes and the coach all meet what the PERMA model suggests are needed to be happy and enjoy wellbeing.

In the second half of this chapter, I ground my explanation of Positive Pedagogy in practice by reflecting upon my own experiences of coaching swimming, as based on a chapter from my book, *Positive Pedagogy for Sports Coaching* (Light, 2017).

## PPed in action: developing feel for the water in breaststroke

Here I draw on a reflective account of taking a Positive Pedagogy approach to coaching from *Positive Pedagogy for Sport Coaching* (Light, 2017) but add to it some recent experience of teaching athlete-centred coaching at a Japanese University for six weeks. It focuses on helping swimmers develop *feel* for the water as an important aspect of learning to swim breaststroke well. The concept of feel is important in a number of sports but is vague and difficult to pin down or measure. Although important in other sports, such as equestrian sports and surfing (Dashper, 2012; Light, 2016), it has been overlooked in the coaching literature because coaching for feel "moves beyond technique into the realm of the phenomenon of the swimmer's connections with the water" (Light, 2008, p. 142). It involves the swimmer's adaptation to moving through, and connecting with, a literally fluid environment that does not lend itself to the precise focus placed on stroke technique and correction.

Swim coaches typically teach feel by providing particular experiences, referred to as drills, through which the swimmer learns by doing and adapting to the constraint. Activities used by coaches to enhance feel for the water in breaststroke impose constraints that encourage the swimmer to find ways of compensating for them and which intensify the experience and awareness of contact with the water.

Coaches use these 'drills' because they work, but rarely do they consider how their swimmers learn or how to enhance this learning. Nor do they talk about how or why they work with their swimmers or ask them to describe or reflect upon how they felt as in Positive Pedagogy. Learning to improve feel through performing these 'drills' occurs at a non-conscious level through performance of them over time, during which the swimmer adapts to the demands of the task. To develop feel for the water in the hands, fingers and forearms in breaststroke, coaches typically have their swimmers perform two types of 'sculling' as the two halves of the breaststroke pull. These are the front, or outward, scull, in which the swimmer propels him/herself by using only the first part of the stroke from the 'catch' (out-sweep), whereby the swimmer first catches the water, and the inward scull (in-sweep) as the second part of the stroke. Sometimes the swimmer is allowed to use a small flutter kick, but more often no kick at all is allowed to place more emphasis on the stroke. In the session that I most recently ran I made all the swimmers use 'pull buoys' (leg float), which is a flotation device they clamp between their legs to keep their body level in the water and stop them kicking.

Sculling helps develop a sensitivity to contact between the forearms and hand/fingers and the water and improve efficiency in getting hold of the water from the beginning of the pull. In this activity, the swimmer solves the problem of moving through the water by exploring the most efficient ways to perform in response to the constraints imposed, leading to improving feel for catching and using the water. The swimmer has to solve the problem of moving forward by only using half the normal stroke and no kick, which involves adapting to the constraint through reflection *in* action that can promote a state of mindfulness (Varela, Thompson, & Rosch, 1991), and which occurs at a non-conscious level using a standard coaching approach. Mindfulness refers to a state of awareness of the individual's being and doing (Cohen, 2010) in Buddhist traditions but has been appropriated as a coping mechanism in psychology and to circumvent some of the limitations of Western dualism (see for example, Varela et al., 1991; Seligman & Csikszentmihalyi, 2000).

For most swim coaches using sculling to develop their swimmers' feel, their pedagogy does not go beyond setting the task and having the swimmer perform the drill but may include some direct instruction. When teaching this approach to Japanese postgraduate students recently, I asked them to scull beginning by asking them to do the out-sweep action. At the end of each 25 metre lap, I asked them questions such as "how does that feel?" and "how can you move through the water more efficiently with these constraints?" These students were not competitive swimmers and were of mixed ability, which meant that for the first few laps (25 metres) a couple really struggled to make any progress in the water. In trying to have them focus consciously on developing sensitivity to contact with the water, I asked if they could feel the water on their palms, fingers and forearms.

After five minutes or so when they had all begun to scull more efficiently I told them that they had to now close their fists and perform the same activity. I asked them to experiment with ways of catching as much water as possible with this intensified constraint, after which they determined that having thumbs down and palms out was the most efficient way. I then asked them to scull again but pay attention to where their elbows were when adopting this use of their fists (elbows up). After a quick discussion on this they then did another lap concentrating on keeping palms out and elbows up and were asked how that felt.

The next step for me was to begin removing the constraints for them to begin to apply learning in action by allowing them to extend two fingers on either hand to swim one lap. I then and asked them, "how did that feel?", "could you feel the water on your extended fingers?" and "did you feel yourself moving through the water better?" I then allowed them to open their hands and after a couple of questions, asked them to do full breaststroke and kick, with all saying that they felt they were swimming much better and had developed feel for the water. Finally, I asked them to try to glide for at least two seconds and was surprised at the improvement of a couple of students in particular, who were also elated at what they perceived as their improvement in swimming and the knowledge of breaststroke they felt they had developed in one hour.

Like many PPed sessions that I have conducted, this session started slowly as they struggled to adapt to both the constraints imposed on them and the coaching pedagogy I used. As I have often experienced when coaching this way, there was a point they seem to reach as a group where it all comes together as learning and positive emotions flow.

Learning from reflection *on* (after) action can be enhanced by verbally encouraging athletes to reflect *in* action. When asking them to scull with fists closed, this involved asking them to swim and think about, "how can you catch the most water with your fists closed?" I also asked, "when you scull I would like you to experiment with the angle of your fist to see how you can catch the most water" and "where can you feel the water?" Rotating the fists to a 'palm out' position 180 degrees for the catch and the outward movement will enable the swimmer to move forward most efficiently and requires having elbows up high in the water. In striving to catch water with their fists turned out, swimmers will invariably raise the elbows without being asked to. Instead of just telling them what to do, s/he could ask, "when you were sculling with your fist turned out where were your elbows?", "why do you think your elbows were up?" and "this time think about where your elbows are and why this might be?" This type of questioning helps comprehensibility and meaningfulness due to understanding why they need to have their elbows up.

This session design provides for learning feel at an embodied level while also offering opportunity for the coach to enhance this learning by bringing experience to consciousness for rational consideration and representation through dialogue. The constraints that the activities suggested in this chapter impose are aimed at having the swimmer explore and discover possibilities as *enabling constraints* (Davis, Sumara, & Luce-Kapler, 2000). The use of language, dialogue and questioning brings this learning experience to a conscious level for discussion, debate and the formulation of ideas, but there is a limit to which non-rational learning(s) can be rendered rational and consciously knowable.

## Discussion

The idea of adapting the principles or core features of the Game Sense approach to coaching individual sport is long overdue but not such a radical proposal. To some, it would appear to be common sense. It is also likely that many coaches already do something similar and perhaps without any detailed conscious consideration, but the specific demands of most individual sports mean that in practice it will in fact be quite different. For the coach, it may require deep thinking, critical reflection and adaptability. There are good reasons why there are so few suggestions for doing this in a systematic way and why applying athlete-centred coaching to team sports has long seemed unsuitable for individual sport.

The demands of a focus on skill and technique, such as in changing the baton in the 4 x 100 track relay event or throwing a javelin, require a more structured approach and narrow focus than team sport does. It requires a degree of compromise and adaptation, and being able to see what is possible. While coaching individual sports using PPed typically involves the discovery of knowledge, it maintains the humanistic and holistic approach of Game Sense (Light, 2013). Indeed, the ability to empathise with and fully understand the progression of learning and the nature of whole-person experience is more important with individual sport. PPed also builds productive relationships and emphasises reflection as well as promoting dialogue and the conversation between non-conscious learning (body) and conscious learning (mind).

The central importance of skill and technique in individual sports requires a narrow focus on what is learned, and the use of discovery learning where team sport coached using athlete-centred coaching often takes a problem-solving approach to encourage divergent thinking. This places PPed for individual sport between athlete-centred coaching for team sports, with its athlete-centred inquiry approach, and the technique-centred, direct instruction as the dominant coaching method used in coaching individual sport. PPed for individual sport can thus provide a bridge between traditional directive pedagogy and the open ended, problem solving Game Sense and similar game-based approaches. Given the variation across game-based approaches and in the emphasis on skill that coaches adopt, this allows for a view of a pedagogical spectrum from direct instruction to the problem-solving or problem-posing approach suggested by Friere (1970) that is evident in game-based approaches.

# References

Antonovsky, A. (1979). *Health, stress and coping.* San Francisco, CA: Jossey-Bass.

Antonovsky, A. (1987). *Unraveling the mystery of health: How people manage stress and stay well.* San Francisco, CA: Jossey-Bass.

Barrow, L. H. (2006). A brief history of inquiry: From Dewey to standards. *Journal of Science Teacher Education, 17,* 265–278.

Bourdieu, P. (1986). *Distinction.* London: Routledge & Kegan Paul.

Bruner, J. S. (1961). The art of discovery. *Harvard Education Review, 31,* 21–32.

Chappell, G., & Light, R. L. (2015). Back to the future: Developing batting talent through game sense. *Active +Healthy Magazine, 23*(2/3), 31–34.

Chen, Q., & Light, R. (2006). I thought I'd hate cricket but I love it!' Year six students' responses to game sense pedagogy. *Change: Transformations in Education, 9*(2), 7–15.

Chen, W. (2001). Description of an expert and novice teachers' constructivist-oriented teaching: Engaging students critical thinking in learning creative dance. *Research Quarterly for Exercise and Sport, 72*(4), 366–375.

Chen, W., & Rovegno, I. (2000). Examination of expert and novice teachers' constructivist-oriented teaching practices using a movement approach to elementary physical education. *Research Quarterly for Exercise and Sport, 71*(4), 357–372.

Cohen, E. (2010). From the Bodhi tree to the analyst's couch and then into the MRI scanner: The psychologisation of Buddhism. *Annual Review of Critical Psychology, 8,* 97–119.

Dashper, K. (2012). Together, yet still not equal? Sex integration in equestrian sport. *Asia-Pacific Journal of Health, Sport and Physical Education, 3*(3), 213–225.

Davis, B., Sumara, D., & Luce-Kapler, R. (2000). *Engaging minds: Learning in a complex world.* Mahwah, NJ: Lawrence Erlbaum Associates, Inc.

Fosnot, C. T. (Ed.) (1996). *Constructivism: Theory, perspectives and practice.* New York, London: Teachers College, Columbia University.

Friere, P. (1970). *Pedagogy of the oppressed.* New York: Continuum.

Grant, A. M. (2011). The solution-focused inventory: A tripartite taxonomy for teaching, measuring and conceptualising solution focused approaches to coaching. *The Coach Psychologist, 7*(2), 98–105.

Harvey, S. & Light, R. L. (2015). Questioning for learning in games-based approaches to teaching and coaching. *Asia Pacific Journal of Health, Sport and Physical Education, 6*(2), 175-190.

Jackson, S.A. and Czikszentmihalyi, M. (1999). *Flow in sports.* Champaign, IL: Human Kinetics.

Jones, E. (2015). Transferring skill from practice to the match in rugby through game sense. *Active and Healthy Magazine, 22*(2/3), 56–58.

Kidman, L. & Lomabardo, B. J. (Eds.) (2010). *Athlete-centred coaching: Developing decision-makers.* Worcester, UK: IPC Print Resources.

Light, R. (2008). *Sport in the lives of young Australians.* Sydney: Sydney University Press.

Light, R. L. (2013). *Game sense: Pedagogy for performance, participation and enjoyment.* London, New York: Routledge.

Light, R. L. (2014). Learner-centred pedagogy for swim coaching: A complex learning theory informed approach. *Asia-Pacific Journal of Health, Sport and Physical Education, 5*(2), 167–180.

Light, R. L. (2016). *Children, young people and sport: Studies on experience and meaning.* Newcastle, UK: Cambridge Scholars Press.

Light, R. L. (2017). *Positive pedagogy for sport coaching: Athlete-centred coaching for individual sports.* London, New York: Routledge.

Light, R. L. (2018). Positive Pedagogy for sport coaching: The influence of Positive Psychology. In A. Brady & B. Grenville-Cleave (Eds.), *Positive psychology in sport and physical activity: An introduction.* Oxford: Routledge.

Light, R. L., Evans, J. R., Harvey, S., & Hassanin, R. (2015). *Advances in rugby coaching: An holistic approach.* London, New York: Routledge.

Light, R. L., & Harvey, S. (2017). Positive pedagogy for sport coaching, *Sport, Education and Society, 22*(2), 271–287.

Light, R. L., Harvey, S., & Mouchet, A. (2014). Improving 'at-action' decision-making in team sports through a holistic coaching approach. *Sport, Education and Society, 19*(3), 258–275.

Light, R. L., & Kentel, J. A. (2015). *Mushin*: Learning in technique-intensive sport as uniting mind and body through complex learning theory. *Physical Education and Sport Pedagogy, 20*(4), 381–396.

Light, R., & Wallian, N. (2008). A constructivist approach to teaching swimming. *Quest, 60*(3), 387–404.

McCuaig, L., Quennerstedt, M., & Macdonald, D. (2013). A salutogenic strengths-based approach as a theory to guide HPE curriculum change. *Asia-Pacific Journal of Health, Sport and Physical Education, 4*(2), 109–125.

Mosston, M., & Ashworth, S. (1986). *Teaching physical education* (3rd ed.). Columbus: Merrill.

Renshaw, I., Chow, J. Y., Davids, K., & Hammond, J. (2010). A constraints-led perspective to understanding skill acquisition and game play: a basis for integration of motor learning theory and physical education praxis? *Physical Education and Sport Pedagogy, 15*(2), 117–137.

Renshaw, I., Oldham, A. R., & Bawden, M. (2012). Non-linear pedagogy underpins intrinsic motivation in sports coaching. *The Open Sports Sciences Journal, 5*, 1–12.

Roberts, S. J. (2011). Teaching Games for Understanding: The difficulties and challenges experienced by participation cricket coaches. *Physical Education and Sport Pedagogy, 16*(1), 33–48.

Seligman, M. E. P. (2012). *Flourish: A visionary new understanding of happiness and wellbeing.* Sydney, NSW: Random House.

Seligman, M. E. P., & Csikszentmihalyi, M. (2000). Positive psychology: An introduction. *American Psychologist, 55*(1), 5–14.

Varela, F. J., Thompson, E., & Rosch, E. (1991). *The embodied mind: Cognitive science and human experience*. Cambridge, MA: MIT Press.

Wang, C. L., & Ha, A. (2009). Pre-service teachers' perception of Teaching Games for Understanding: A Hong Kong perspective. *European Physical Education Review, 15*(3), 407–429.

# 13

# THE AUTOETHNOGRAPHIC JOURNEY OF ATHLETE-CENTRED EXPERIENCES, RESEARCH AND LEARNING

## Athlete to researcher, now coach, and beyond

*Karlene Headley-Cooper*

This chapter will share my autoethnographic journey of athlete-centred experiences, research and learning. My path spans over twelve years and continues to this day. My years as an international athlete motivated me to study athlete-centred coaching, which then encouraged me to implement my research findings as a high-performance level coach. As a qualitative research method, autoethnography uses narratives of self to tell stories (Dench, 2003). Andrew Sparkes' sporting autoethnographies draw on personal experiences to extend sociological understanding of sporting cultures (Holt, 2003; Sparkes, 2000). The connections made can be powerful, emotive, self-reflexive for the writer, and engaging for the reader (Holt, 2003). Autoethnography will be used to connect my lived experiences and perspectives to the social world of athlete-centred coaching (Cooper, Grenier, & Macaulay, 2017; Ellis, 2004; Holman Jones, 2005).

The goal is to share a perspective on how experiences can stimulate research, motivate the application of theory into practice, enhance knowledge and spark questions that enable learning to continue, all within the context of athlete-centred coaching.

## The athlete-centred journey begins – communication

My experiences of athlete-centred coaching started in 2005 when I began my career as an international athlete. After a last-minute flight from Toronto to London, a lot of rain, only two games played and a first pitch of the game home-run at the last pre-season open trial weekend, I was selected as a member of the 2005 Great Britain (GB) Women's National Softball Team. I had made the national side and I was going to spend my 21st birthday at the European Championships in Prague,

Czech Republic. As I landed at the Prague airport, I not only started my softball career on international soil, but I also began the experience of being an athlete in a world full of diverse coaching philosophies and behaviours. There was no athlete textbook to refer to for guidance, just as there was no coaches' manual for 'what to do or say' or, more importantly, 'what not to do or say'. What became evident very quickly was that communication matters. One of the most important and often extremely challenging key skills involved in the coaching process is communication (Kidman, 2005). This is where my autoethnographic journey started.

As we stepped off the plane (I remember this as if it were yesterday), I was walking alongside the GB Head Coach, my new coach. As we walked the long hallway in the airport terminal, he said, "Hi Karlene . . . you're here because several other players couldn't get a passport". My initial thought was, 'wow, that's quite a welcome . . . can I get back on that plane and go home?' Possibly of greater significance is what happened next – I kept walking. I kept going for that summer, and nine more summer seasons. At the time, this was an impactful moment, in which key aspects of athlete-centred coaching, such as the importance of communication, the significance of empowering athletes and recognition of the athlete as a holistic person, were not felt, but the determined athlete in me kept going.

## Combining my lived experiences and academic research

The combination of my lived experiences and academic research aims to resonate with readers whose individual path to coaching may also be varied, or to broaden the perspectives of those who are primarily driven by practice or theory. All my GB experiences, especially the moments I will share in this chapter, motivated me to pursue graduate research studying Canadian *Coaches' Perspectives on Athlete-Centred Coaching*, under the supervision of Dr Gretchen Kerr at the University of Toronto (Headley-Cooper, 2010).

Three athlete-centred principles will be featured in this unique story: communication, knowledge and empowerment. Communication is a fundamental skill needed for all coaching styles; however, previous athlete-centred research does not specifically feature effective communication as an explicit focal point (Headley-Cooper, 2010; Kidman, 2005; Kidman & Lombardo, 2010). All the Canadian national team coaches who participated in my academic research (Headley-Cooper, 2010) discussed communication involving their athletes. One of the most important roles of a coach is to facilitate two-way communication: coach to athlete and athlete to coach. However, despite this prominent research finding, unfortunately unidirectional messages from coach to athlete are still prevalent in many high-performance sport environments.

Returning to the interaction with my GB coach in the Prague airport and continuing throughout my years as a high-performance athlete representing GB, many interactions were hierarchical, assertive and firm in nature. On several occasions, my fellow athletes and I were told, in what I perceived to be a threatening tone, "I have emails and videos from other players, and if I watch their videos and they are better than you, they could come and take your spot". This message intimidated me. I regularly acted and played in fear of losing my position on the team. Receiving communication from Coach was often a daunting and emotional experience. I fully understood and appreciated that playing for a national team is a privilege to be earned. I also knew there were only three positions to play in the outfield of a softball team and that there were five people listed as outfielders on the roster. As such, this assertive style of communication was not getting the best out of me. I did not feel empowered in the pursuit of performance or personal excellence (Miller & Kerr, 2002). Coaches in my research commented that communication between coaches and athletes needs to be open, honest, fair and based on the needs of the athlete. While some people might refer to fairness and honesty with a negative tone as 'tough love' or constructive feedback, coaches who utilise an athlete-centred approach will find ways to facilitate ongoing communication that empowers their athletes.

My experiences of communication between my coach and I were in stark contrast to the comments made by the participants of my research. Those coaches identified the importance of giving athletes a voice, listening to athletes, allowing athletes to express their opinions and reaching a mutual agreement. Several coaches explained how they asked questions of their athletes, either to gather information and feedback, or to get to know their athletes better. In addition to these findings, one coach added an additional dimension of coaching whereby a coach is sensitive to the verbal and non-verbal cues they send and receive.

Communication is a skill that needs to be practiced. It is no longer sufficient to read coaching manuals, attend coaching conferences, have a polished coaching philosophy or detailed practice plan. Coaches need to reflect on their words, body language and tone with the same dedication that they analyse video and scout opponents. As a coach, it is essential to be aware of not only what you are saying, but also how you are saying it. Encouraging and empowering athletes to pursue performance and personal excellence requires attention to what happens in real-time day-to-day interactions, which support and enable athletes to be the best they can be, on and off the field.

## The journey continues: sport specific knowledge and empowerment

In addition to the coaches' abilities to speak appropriately with their athletes, there is the need for athlete-centred coaches to effectively communicate sport specific knowledge to their players. Coaches may come from one of two schools. Many are extremely encouraging, supportive and friendly but lack expert sport specific training, while other coaches have extensive physical skill and tactical knowledge but are unable to communicate in a way that supports their athletes' psychological, emotional and social development. My experiences with my former GB coach exemplified him as the latter. It was that realisation that led me to my graduate research area of study. My research findings led to the understanding that athlete-centred coaches seek to combine the best of both worlds as effective communicators of sport specific knowledge.

My former GB coach was an expert practice and game planner. Without a doubt, he was the most organised and knowledgeable softball coach that I have ever played or coached with. Practice drills, diagrams, time allocations, the division of players into groups or scrimmage teams, opposition scouting and game plans were always well prepared. In this regard, the business blueprints were 'on point'. His sport specific knowledge was well represented in his competitive strategies, disciplined approach and win-centred philosophy. These were Coach's strengths and methods. This was in contrast to an athlete-centred style in which specificity, competition and organisation are still valued, but within an environment that also recognises the importance of respectfully communicating with the athletes.

Every day in practice, Coach would set up pressured, game-like drills and situations. The drill was called 21 outs. The objective was to get 21 defensive outs without letting any runners score. We often played with non-starters or 'bench' players as the runners. As a result, early in my GB career, I ran a lot! As a runner, I was always trying to implement Coach's philosophy to compete and put teammates under pressure. This served two purposes: to try impress Coach but also to make my teammates work harder defensively than I was working running.

Later in 2006, my perseverance paid off. Coach's competitive nature was heavily grounded in the pursuit of performance excellence. Game wins were important. The reality of international sport is that results matter. The drive for skill execution and team-centred motivation can enhance the path to achieving greatness. I greatly benefitted from my actions and Coach's desire to strive for excellence during the 2006 World Championships in Beijing, China. Heading into the fifth day of competition, GB had a 1–3 record and off the field the team was beginning to suffer from some internal communication issues. Up to that point, I had not seen much playing time, which was to be expected as I was once again the last player named to the team roster. Fast forward from the selection process to the evening of August 31, 2006, when GB played DPR Korea.

Day by day, Coach's philosophy was being put to the test. GB needed a win against Korea, and it was clear that Coach wanted to continue to stay true to his competitive approach. The attitude he exuded was that if he was not satisfied with the performance of one player, they could be replaced, and a non-starter might start the next game. Coach's philosophy, combined with my patience, hard work and dedication to play, resulted in my first big game at Worlds. Enter GB #12 Karlene Headley-Cooper into the line-up! I batted last in the order and played defence in the outfield. With the score 0–0 in the bottom of the third inning, I stepped to the plate. A few pitches into the at-bat, I hit a shot to deep left field – homerun! It was the biggest swing of my softball career! GB battled the rest of the game and we won, 1–0! GB went on to finish a record placing high of 10th in the world. It was an amazing turn of events, from bench to starter, from feeling inadequate within the team and coaching environment around me to feeling useful and purposeful. In my mind, I had been upgraded from a replaceable piece to an active participant.

These changes were largely due to the team culture that Coach had created via the business-like processes and competitive style that he intentionally implemented every day. Performance excellence was clearly valued.

Qualities such as being tough, competitive, aggressive, strategic and strong are important characteristics that are often used to describe successful high-performance coaches. However, my experiences and research have taught me that being holistic, respectful, accountable, open, a leader, facilitator and fun are also necessary descriptors of talented athlete-centred coaches. Effective verbal and non-verbal communication skills are vital competencies that all coaches need to develop and implement.

Throughout my first three years with the GB program, Coach and I had a few challenging verbal conversations; however, the written review of the 2006 season had a significantly different tone. Below is an excerpt of encouragement that highlights the importance for coaches to find ways to regularly and genuinely communicate with their athletes in order to empower them to be their best within the established competitive team culture:

> World Championships: Finally, we asked you to join the team going to China. Once again you had to be patient, and initially you were still fighting for a starting place. But the main thing you accomplished in Beijing was to move from a non-starter to one of the starters, and for that you truly deserve to be commended. You never gave up or stopped believing in yourself. You hit consistently in this tournament against mostly tough pitching . . . You also aided the team by scoring four runs and I'm sure you'll remember that game-winning blast against North Korea for a lifetime!
>
> *(GB staff, personal communication, February 13, 2007)*

These positive comments would have been incredibly powerful if said to me in person some time during the 2006 season. The end-of-season report also provided me with detailed individualised sport specific analyses, comments for improvements and statistics. There was no doubt to me that Coach knew the game, had high standards, could organise physical routines, anticipate strategic plays and give tactically appropriate signals. However, above these sport specific applications, Coach was not equally proficient in his verbal communication skills. Comments such as the sample excerpt are best communicated to the athlete in a timely manner so that the psychological support and physical changes can be appreciated and made during the playing season. In that way, the sport specific knowledge that Coach had (better than many other opposition coaches) could be effectively utilised and implemented to empower the athlete and team to be their best. A lack of, or poor communication does not benefit the coach, athlete or team performance, culture or mind-set. Athlete-centred research has identified many athlete-centred coaching principles and practices that focus on enhancing athletes' holistic health and well-being through the pursuit of excellence in sport (Miller & Kerr, 2002). The first part of this principle was often lacking in my GB experiences. The goal of the

GB team was always excellence (e.g., to be the best team in Europe, qualify for the World Championships or qualify for the Olympics). However, athlete support and empowerment did not always accompany these targets. Upon reflection, it is likely that this was a contributing factor to our difficulties and unfulfilled goals – GB finished 4th and 5th at Europeans in 2005 and 2007, got a wildcard position to the 2006 Worlds and did not qualify for the 2008 Olympics. As with any other high-performance athlete or team, physical skills are often the most significant components of performance and subsequent results; however, within an athlete-centred approach, non-physical attributes should not be undervalued or ignored.

In addition to concepts of holism and empowerment, communication is of paramount importance as the means by which many other athlete-centred characteristics can be exhibited. Previous research has shared many ideas about athlete-centred coaching; however, communication has not been at the forefront of the literature (Headley-Cooper, 2010; Kidman, 2005; Kidman & Lombardo, 2010). My lived GB experiences highlight that coaches need to be effective communicators to best foster both holistic personal development and pursue performance excellence.

## The journey shifts from athlete and researcher to coach: putting lessons learned into action

Several of the athlete-centred characteristics that were shared by the Canadian national team coaches who participated in my master's thesis research echoed previous athlete-centred research findings. Interviewed coaches spoke about the importance of empowering athletes' holistic development, enhancing team cohesion, extending responsibility outside of sport, facilitating athletes' independence, fostering opportunities for leadership development and the value of respect (Clarke, Smith, & Thibault, 1994; Headley-Cooper, 2010; Kidman, 2005; Miller & Kerr, 2002). Results which are unique to my study included comments about recognising the athlete as part of a greater whole, enlisting a support team around the athletes, remembering to make sport fun and defining success as goals that are attainable (Headley-Cooper, 2010).

Upon completion of my master's, I had experienced these findings in a theoretical academic field rather than lived in-action on the field of play. This is when part three of my journey started, as I endeavoured to apply my learning and implement an athlete-centred approach into my next coaching opportunity: as Assistant Coach of the University of Toronto (U of T) Women's Squash Team from 2012 to 2014.

My academic research provided evidence-informed learning that I continue to draw from to create my own version of an athlete-centred coaching style. I had gained valuable insight into athlete-centred coaching behaviours and attitudes, and my goal was to include and implement many of my research findings into my coaching philosophy and daily coaching practices. There were many athlete-centred characteristics that my research confirmed and revealed; however, six were notably significant to me. I wanted to bring to life the following athlete-centred coaching practices: enabling effective two-way communication that aimed to provide sport specific knowledge as well as empower the athletes, engaging in multiple roles within the support team, recognising the athlete as part of a greater whole, enhancing team cohesion, defining success as achieving attainable set goals, and showing respect to everyone within the sporting environment (Headley-Cooper, 2010).

Many people within the U of T squash and GB softball communities did not know my background in both sports. Softball was my number one sport, and I began playing squash as my winter sport to keep fit when I could not be outside playing ball (which is October–March in Canada!). Coaching the U of T Varsity Blues Squash team was a fantastic next step for me. The Head Coach of the team considered himself to be an athlete-centred coach. He also encouraged me to put into practice the information that my research had confirmed and revealed about coaching. We made a great pair! As a young coach, I was eager to implement an athlete-centred coaching philosophy into my daily coaching behaviours. From 2000 to 2015, the Varsity Blues Squash Team was one of the strongest women's university programs in Canada. I was fortunate to be a member of the team for eight seasons (2002–2009) while I was a student at U of T. My experiences as a player and then as Assistant Coach enabled me to quickly appreciate the importance of having a quality team culture (Kidman, 2005). One of my goals as Assistant Coach was to immerse myself in the process of putting athlete-centred research into practice to help build a unified team culture and collaborate with the athletes to foster a meaningful experience.

Some days it was easy to use an athlete-centred approach, whereas other days I found it more challenging. That is the reality of coaching. In the world of academia, many research findings are significant in theory, but can be difficult to implement in the real world. In addition to this, the expectations and pressures to win and perform can be overwhelming in high-performance sport. I spoke with my athletes regularly. I asked them about school, work and life. I recognised that life as a university student–athlete existed outside of the two domains of school and squash. I could tell that many athletes appreciated that communication. Previous athlete-centred coaching literature and coaches in my master's research referred to this as extended responsibility (Headley-Cooper, 2010). It takes a purposefully planned and executed process to help people develop on and off the court. I sought out opportunities to attend to and better my athletes' emotional, psychological and social well-being. Once again, the learning I had gained from studying Miller and Kerr (2002) solidified my desire to help my athletes pursue personal and performance excellence throughout their experiences within an athlete-centred environment.

On and off the court, I continued to communicate with the athletes. This communication integrated multiple forms: verbal, non-verbal (i.e., demonstrations), one-on-one, in small groups and as a whole team. We spoke about and practiced technical skills and tactical strategies, played drills and conditioned games, acknowledged successes and provided encouragement after mistakes. Almost every day, I found myself playing multiple roles as Assistant Coach. I was sometimes the team sport psychologist working with the athletes on their positive self-talk or

S.M.A.R.T. goal setting. At least once a week I was the strength and conditioning trainer who planned and ran the team fitness sessions. I also did my best impersonation of a cheerleader when the playing environment needed a boost of enthusiasm, energy or music. On a several occasions, I was the social convenor of team bonding events such as playing cards or watching movies while on the road. My role as nutritionist included reminding athletes to stay hydrated and preparing their snacks. To comply with school policy, I was frequently one of the team chauffeurs driving the student-athletes to their matches. And, last but certainly not least, I was proud to be a role model of a successful squash alumna who had the utmost respect for the program. Attending to the holistic needs of my athletes was important. Upon reflection, all the roles I played were grounded in my belief and knowledge in the power an athlete-centred approach to coaching.

Despite countless positives, the U of T Squash experience was not all happiness and rainbows. The reality of many high-performance coaching positions is that they are political and bureaucratic in nature. However, on and around the squash courts I tried to create an environment where the larger administrative challenges did not matter. In my approach, the athletes truly were at the centre of the program. I take away many positives and learning moments from this experience, none bigger than the appreciation that successfully implementing athlete-centred coaching behaviours is a multi-faceted, life-long process.

It is important to recognise that not all coaching endeavours are smooth sailing. The GB Softball Head Coach from 2009 to 2014 used the phrase "row the GB boat" to represent the need for all athletes, coaches and staff to be rowing in the same boat, going in the same direction and rowing together as one unit. This saying and analogy has stayed with me. Sir Clive Woodward, Coach of the 2003 Rugby World Cup Champions, used a similar phrase to galvanise his England Rugby Team. Woodward borrowed from Sir John Harvey-Jones, saying "to create success, everyone's noses must be pointing in the same direction" when he spoke about the need to change the mind-set of English Rugby prior to the 2003 World Cup (Woodward, 2004, p. 186).

My most recent coaching opportunity lead me back to the GB Softball Team boat, but unfortunately, we went through some rougher waters with our noses misaligned in 2015 and 2016. By then, my international playing career with the GB Women's Team had finished. Between 2005 and 2014, I was fortunate to have over 100 caps for GB while competing in four World Championships (2006, 2010, 2012, 2014), five European Championships (2005, 2007, 2009, 2011, 2013), two World Cups (2006, 2011) and a Euro–Africa Olympic Qualifier (in 2007 for 2008). A few weeks after my last game as an athlete, I exchanged my playing uniform for a GB coaching shirt. I was extremely honoured to join the GB under-19 Junior Girls Softball Team coaching staff as an assistant in 2014, remain with them in 2015 and as a group move up to coach the GB Women's Team at the 2016 World Championships in Surrey, Canada. These recent experiences provided my next opportunity to implement athlete-centred coaching attitudes and behaviours. Interestingly, this time my approach elicited mixed results.

As a GB Assistant Coach in 2015 and 2016, I once again had many different roles. I assisted with organising team bonding events. It was a yearly GB Softball occurrence to have the players, coaches and staff together for the first time approximately a week prior to the first game of the tournament. This meant that we had limited time to bond, get to know each other, practice together and play as a team before the first national anthem was sung and the umpire said 'play ball'. As a coaching staff, we spoke about the importance of helping the team gel as a cohesive unit and begin to form a team culture, but despite my knowledge that this was a key aspect of being athlete-centred, there never seemed to be enough time dedicated to fully engage in team bonding activities. This was problematic. My research and experiences support Miller and Kerr's (2002) finding that athletes can only achieve performance excellence (i.e., results) when it is coupled with the pursuit of personal excellence (i.e., holistic development). Understanding this athlete-centred philosophy acknowledges that supporting athletes' social and emotional development will help build a foundation that can strengthen their physical performances on the field.

A lack of team unity can significantly contribute to individuals not knowing their roles within the team. My experiences in 2015 and 2016 also highlighted that coaches play a huge role in creating a positive team environment. Coaches in my research spoke about their need to be facilitators of leadership opportunities (Headley-Cooper, 2010). Many coaches discussed the importance of athletes being leaders. Athletes play an important role in contributing to their own growth and performance as well as the development and success of the whole team. Coaches commented that being a leader involves taking responsibility for yourself and the larger team unit.

In addition, this experience confirmed that one of the most important skills needed to foster these athlete-centred attitudes is effective interpersonal communication. Moreover, in a team setting, all relationships that exist within a high-performance team (i.e., coach–athlete, athlete–athlete, coach–coach) need to be supported. From my perspective, these leadership and communication skills were not present within the GB Women's team in 2016. Throughout my experience, I felt uncomfortable in my position on the coaching staff. That feeling discouraged me from voicing my concerns and undoubtedly negatively influenced my ability to put my athlete-centred knowledge and experience into action. I continue to reflect and grow with confidence, knowing that challenging situations in combination with positive learning opportunities and evidence-based research findings all help me build a stronger self and coaching outlook.

## Conclusion

A common thread throughout my lived experiences and research has been the need for effective communication skills. Possibly the greatest challenge I experienced in 2015 and 2016 was working with coaches who were clearly from the opposite school than my former GB Coach. In contrast, these coaches were extremely encouraging, supportive and friendly but were weaker in their sport specific knowledge. These sociable coaches may have great communication skills, but their comments are often more general and positive in nature rather than specific and constructive. Fostering development and achievement at a high-performance level requires support and detail. This learning epitomises the common adage that coaching is both an art and a science.

My lived athletic experiences seemed to have uncovered two coaches who sit at opposite ends of a communication and skills continuum: one at the critical, knowledgeable, sport specific end and the other on the friendly, uplifting, indecisive end. As a result, it is my ambition to learn from my research, U of T opportunities and GB experiences. I aspire to be a coach who develops, utilises and promotes skills in three areas: communication, sport specificity and empowerment. Within my athlete-centred approach, I understand that proficiency in those domains can empower my athletes' pursuits of personal and performance excellence.

My attempt to weave my lived experiences and research findings into this autoethnographic journey has allowed me to also continue the process of self-reflection. I have come to better appreciate the need to take time to reflect on past lessons and events. It is my hope that this autoethnographic approach of combining lived experiences with academic research has sparked you to reflect on your own coaching philosophy, behaviours and journey. I encourage you, the reader, to take a few moments to think about your own path, your own lived experiences and lessons learned from your own setting (i.e., on the field or in research). To help you connect some of this story and make it matter to you, in conclusion, I ask you to consider the following questions and how they relate to you:

1   "How does an athlete-centred coach communicate with their athletes?"
2   "How does a coach using athlete-centred coaching effectively communicate sport specific knowledge to their athletes?"
3   "How does an athlete-centred coach empower their athletes to be the best that they can be?"
4   "How do you communicate, share sport specific knowledge and empower your athletes?"

## References

Clarke, H., Smith, D., & Thibault, G. (1994). *Athlete-centred sport: A discussion paper*. Federal/Provincial/Territorial Sport Police Steering Committee.

Cooper, J. N., Grenier, R. S., Macaulay, C. (2017). Autoethnography as a critical approach in sport management: Current applications and directions for future research. *Sport Management Review, 20*(1), 43–54.

Dench, L. N. (2003). Telling tales in sport and physical activity: A qualitative journey. *The Sport Psychologist, 17*(3), 372–374.

Ellis, C. (2004). *The ethnographic I: A methodological novel about teaching and doing autoethnography*. Walnut Creek: AltaMira.

Headley-Cooper, K. J. (2010). *Coaches' perspectives on athlete-centred coaching*. Master's Thesis, University of Toronto.

Holman Jones, S. (2005). Autoethnography: Making the personal political. In N. K. Denzin & Y. S. Lincoln (Eds.), *Handbook of qualitative research* (3rd ed., pp. 763–792). Thousand Oaks, CA: Sage.

Holt, N. L. (2003). Representation, legitimation, and autoethnography: An autoethnographic writing story. *International Journal of Qualitative Methods, 2*(1), 1–22.

Kidman, L. (2005). *Athlete-centred coaching: Developing inspired and inspiring people*. Christchurch, NZ: Innovative Communications.

Kidman, L., & Lombardo, B. (Eds.) (2010). *Athlete-centred coaching: Developing decision makers*. Worcester: IPC Print Resources.

Miller, P. S., & Kerr, G. A. (2002). Conceptualizing excellence: Past, present, and future. *Journal of Applied Sport Psychology, 14*, 140–153.

Sparkes, A. C. (2000). Autoethnography and narratives of self: Reflections on criteria in action. *Sociology of Sport Journal, 17*, 21–43.

Woodward, C. (2004). *Winning!* London: Hoder and Stoughton.

# 14

# ATHLETE-CENTRED COACHING IN SWIMMING

## An autoethnography

*Terry Magias*

This chapter blends an autoethnographic vignette of the author with coaching literature to examine hegemony within South Australian learn to swim settings. A narrative is provided around the application of athlete-centred coaching perspectives in swim teaching. Specifically, shifting power discourses related to movement performance away from the coach to place greater value in the embodied athlete experience. For the practitioner, this narrative may serve as a philosophical inspiration in empowering athletes to have active and purposeful decision-making over their own skill learning. Although this chapter focuses on skill learning considerations, the significance of the discussion hinges on the potential to place greater value in participation outcomes beyond performance.

## Background

### Swimming in Australia

Acknowledging that Australia is the most 'beach-bound' country in the world (Booth, 2001), the pervasiveness of swimming within its cultural identity is unsurprising (Winterton, 2010). Although it remains unclear if and how swimming was a part of Aboriginal Australia pre-colonisation, historians note its contribution to developing a certain brand of national identity since British occupation. International success in the sport since the early nineteenth century has solidified that branding (Cashman, 2002; Winterton, 2010).

Competitive origins for swimming can be traced back to Robinson's Baths in Sydney 1845, where the first Australian swimming event was historicised (Light & Rockwell, 2005). Ocean bath competitions grew in popularly, peaking from the early 1900s until 1949 ("Find a Pool", n.d). Today, competitive swimming continues to reinforce this sporting-cultural identity in Australia, with swimming being the country's most significant Olympic sport, 58 of its current 135 Olympic Gold medals achieved in swimming events ("Swimming Australia: Olympic History", n.d.). Successes in the Melbourne (1956), Rome (1960) and Tokyo (1964) Olympics drove support for more swimming pools to be built and positioned them as a standard local government community facility around the country ("Find a Pool", n.d).

Arguably, these competitive origins laid a philosophical foundation in aquatic learning largely focused on competitive stroke development. Although water safety and game play have penetrated private and public swimming curriculum in Australia, the dominance of stroke competency continues to pervade aquatic learn to swim for both youth and adult programs. In this chapter, I will critique pedagogical implications that this has had for Australian aquatic education at pedagogical and curriculum levels. Components of athlete-centred coaching are then considered as a conceptual basis toward an alternative philosophy of aquatic learning, challenging the current coach-centred hegemony. I discuss athlete empowerment for decision-making on two distinct but interrelated coaching dimensions. The first is concerned with enabling greater athlete decision-making around intra-individual functional movement performance. The second is providing learn to swim opportunities that transcend traditional competitive stroke development focuses, pervasive in public and private swim settings in Australia. This chapter references my experiences in aquatic learning in both active and observatory roles whilst drawing parallels with coaching literature.

## Swim coaching hegemony

A lack of consensus regarding the nature of coaching and, subsequently, a poorly defined conceptual base, I argue, has left many coaches practising without reference to any coaching model (Cushion, Armour, & Jones, 2006). Instead, coaches are largely grounding their practice in intuition, feelings and events (Cushion et al., 2006), with the principle source for both novice and more seasoned coaches coming from previous coaching experiences (Nelson & Cushion, 2006). As such, coaches' selection of pedagogical strategies may be influenced by methods they have experienced as a participant or by observation of other coaches (Cassidy, Jones, & Potrac, 2008). Sport coaching practice for many, particularly those involved with children and youth coaching, is likely to be formed by an apprenticeship of observation involving personal experience of having been coached and not a clear pedagogical philosophy for practice. For the author's experience in aquatic education, learn to swim programs are no exception here (Magias & Pill, 2013).

Traditionally, there has been a strong impetus for swim coaches to have significant control and direction over the coaching–learning exchange. This is grounded in a hierarchal power relationship where the coach is understood as knowledgeable on swimming mechanics and the athlete is the empty vessel to be programmed for movement (Cassidy et al., 2008; Jones, 2006). This experience is perhaps best articulated by Shogan, who states, "although what athletes do may be more important than what coaches do . . . what coaches say is much more important than what athletes say" (Shogan, 1999, p. 41). In this instance, the author would extend this statement further to "*what is planned for is much more important than anything unplanned for*". This extension of the quote reflects my experience of a resistance in learn to swim settings to actively diverge during learning time from planned curriculum and/or the expected pedagogy. In my six years working in the learn to swim context, coaches learnt to coach by observation and mimicry of an experienced coach. Learning is typically controlled by incremental progression, recognised as milestones that must be satisfied in order for swimmers to advance to further learnings for any given stroke mechanic, or to graduate to an entirely different class with a new stroke focus. For example, 'achieve five consecutive bent-elbow recoveries'. The specificity of the phrasing around progression milestones does not usually acknowledge the roll of movement variability in what is considered skill competency.

Within a set curriculum, an imperative is placed on the coach to ensure movement adherence rather than exploration. Such an approach, where all knowledge is espoused directly from the coach to athlete, is said to disempower athletes' involvement in the learning process (Kidman, 2010). Specifically, in this imperative an emphasis is placed on the learner memorising or mimicking demonstrated movement competencies rather than understanding or solving problems (Kidman, 2010) related to the organismic constraints of individuals moving through water. Multiple terms have been used to encapsulate such practices, including method coaching (Abraham & Collins, 1998), leadership style (Kidman, 2010), coach-centred (Kidman, 2010) and technique-centred (Hewitt, 2015). These terms collectively reflect a behaviourist understanding of learning which dominated the 1980s and 1990s (Light, 2008). From my experience of learn to swim programs, an almost exclusive focus on physical skill acquisition is a typical of behaviourism (Drewe, 2000), where the athlete's body is viewed as a biological 'machine' that can be improved by compliance through training (Cassidy et al., 2008). Movement through water is conceived entirely as a 'progressive-part' mechanical process. Competitive stroke development becomes a focus, with techniques compartmentalised into components, repeated for isolation from each other, before eventually the pull phase is reassembled with the recovery phase timing (Light, 2008; Stolz & Pill, 2012). Directive 'practice' and 'command' styles (Cross & Lyle, 1999) are almost exclusively the preference in this context to achieve performance compliance to predetermined stroke models.

Highly structured training sessions are used to sequentially progress through segmented stoke mechanics in order to internalise objective knowledge (Light, 2008). Sessions therefore typically consist of demonstrative cues to introduce and consolidate key stroke mechanics with static practice standing up in water or on the edge of pool – participants might stand, waist deep in water, and replicate what the coach demonstrated. Tinning called this demonstrate–explain–practice (Tinning, 2015). Short game play orientated around races or 'dive and seek' objectives are commonly used to conclude sessions. In summary, resting on the assumption of the fundamentals of biomechanically 'optimal' stoke techniques (Stolz & Pill, 2012), teacher-directed instruction is used to demonstrate, correct, praise, verbalise feedback and question athletes on their technical performances (Claxton, 1988; Lacy & Darst, 1985; Rupert & Buschner, 1989; Smith, Zane, Smoll, & Coppel, 1983; Williams & Hodges, 2005). An emphasis is placed on coaches' specialist knowledge of sport (swimming) related technique and the provision of sequenced technical instruction to deliver it. Demonstration has been a common pedagogical instrument synonymous with a focus on technique, providing learners with a visual template or criterion model for the intended movement pattern (Williams & Hodges, 2005).

Collectively, these pedagogical features are synonymous with what is referred to as a linear approach to skill learning. Here, proportional changes in demonstration/movement response, mono-stable movement outcomes, invariant movement patterns and internal rather than external influences on learning are expected (Chow, Renshaw, Button, Davids, & Keat, 2013). Traditional linear approaches have been criticised for focusing only on 'how' to execute a skill, omitting the 'when, where and why' of its application (Wein, 2007). This criticism has historically been in reference to game-based sports, with the argument being made that closed-skill drill practice conditions fail to acknowledge the contextual and cognitive nature of the game (Pill, 2012; Wein, 2007). Where closed learning is characterised by predictable performance environments devoid of dynamic variables, at face value it may appear attractive to a context such as aquatic learning. This may be understood from a perspective where the swimming pool environment is predictable and desired stroke mechanics are largely invariant. In athlete-centred literature, it is contended that such an understanding has failed to acknowledge social and cultural elements inherent to the athlete development process (Cushion et al., 2006).

Particularly where coaching involving games/tactical/team sports are concerned, a coach-centred perspective has arguably softened in since the introduction of 'game-based' approaches that advocate pedagogical tools that place greater emphasis on exploratory student-centred forms of learning (Light, 2013). The shift in the pedagogical landscape for games learning remains untrue for individual athletic performance-focused sports such as swimming.

Various efforts have been made to extend understandings of coaching beyond the pyscho-motor, to social, cultural and ethical domains (Cassidy et al., 2008; Crisfield, Cabral, & Carpenter, 2005; Drewe, 2000). Underpinning these efforts, arguments for coaching as an inherently social, problematised human process have been made (Potrac, Brewer, Jones, Armour, & Hoff, 2000). Within this discussion there have been calls for a more holistic coaching model, repositioning power discourses to value athletes' knowledge and experiences, facilitating more equitable contributions from the athlete toward their own development and performance (Cassidy et al., 2008). This coincides with a view of coaching as 'educating' as opposed to 'training', with strong parallels being drawn to PE (Drewe, 2000).

## Discussion

My first exposure to athlete-centred ideologies came as a pre-service Physical Education teacher. During this period, I worked part-time as a learn to swim instructor for both children and adults. My interest in sport pedagogy was spurned by my lived experience in learn to swim programs, where I encountered practices entrenched in hegemonic traditions akin to those aforementioned. As my studies progressed, my philosophy as a swimming instructor and an educator changed, and increasingly the swim coaching behaviour expected of me contrasted with educative philosophy of athlete-centred approaches.

This was probably the most confronting and personally challenging time I've experienced as a sport coach/educator. Increasingly, I questioned the specific applications of movement demonstrations, physical technique manipulation and verbal cues common across my aquatic instructing experiences. The answers to these questions became that much more significant under the time constraints swimming instructors typically work within. Often, I only had contact with my students once a week for 30 minutes. Moreover, parents/caregivers were sometimes limited in how many lessons they could enrol their children in, constrained by the considerable cost of swimming lessons. Parents would often ask me what was required to see their child progress to the next class level where new swimming competencies would be introduced. Sometimes children would remain in a single class level for half a year while younger peers would be assessed as competent in class outcomes by a supervisor and graduate to the next class much sooner. Collectively, these pressures to 'push students through' and achieve benchmarked learning objectives came into conflict with a coaching philosophy and pedagogical behaviours that were considered best practice in my teacher education coursework. I began to question if what I was doing as a swim coach was 'as good as it could be'.

I looked to my physical education lecturers and teacher education studies for guidance. At this time, there was a paucity of research or discussion around pedagogical practice in individual sports such as swimming. The little research that did exist seemed to be dwarfed by the popularity of game-based pedagogies like the Game Sense approach (den Duyn, 1997) and Teaching Games for Understanding (TGfU) (Bunker & Thorpe, 1982), heralded for their pedagogical and curriculum efficacy and a philosophical grounding aligned to the athlete-centred philosophy (Thorpe, 2005). This initially led me to consider if an athlete-centred focus might also be efficacious for skill acquisition within my practice as a swimming instructor. I distinctly recall feeling confident in my thinking, although I had trouble articulating what this might look like in practice. In an effort to conceptually flesh out my thinking, I pursued discussions with physical education peers and lecturers and attended sport and physical education conferences, networking with experienced professionals in the field. My ideas (discussed later) were met with enormous resistance and/or dismissal in some quarters, to the point where I felt incredibly frustrated and disheartened by the hegemonic conventions of swimming coaches, especially in learn to swim settings.

My frustrations were compounded in the pool. As my thinking around athlete-centeredness advanced, shortcomings in existing discourses on swim coaching become more evident in my eyes. With competitive stroke development being almost the sole focus in the particular learn to swim programs I had been involved within, I perceived shortcomings around the concept of generating propulsion in water, particularly with hand/arm movements. I was confident that while almost all of my students understood the demonstrated movement patterns, the process of using these movements to generate propulsion was far slower to develop, if it developed at all. As an example, when learning freestyle students would be shown the 'S-pull' through water, replicating the movement standing upright at one end of the lane. Using kickboards, students would then be required to start 'chain' laps and adhere to the S-pull movement representation in their freestyle stroke mechanics. As an instructor, I was required to position myself in the centre of the lane and physically manipulate arms into S-shaped pull trajectories. In the initial stages of learning this technique, students comprehended the S trajectory and were able to trace its path through water both standing and performing chain-lap swimming. However, typically the process of generating propulsion from the movement took the most significant amount of time for competency in freestyle stroke mechanics. Initially, I reasoned this to strength-related development. However, at closer examination I felt the true issue lay in what Light (2008) refers to as developing 'feel for the water'. This relates to the swimmer's perceptual connection to the kinaesthetic experience of purposefully feeling out water resistance (Light, 2016). The underlying problem I had observed was inefficiencies of aforementioned coach-centred practices in creating what Davids et al. (2008) refer to as perception–action coupling. That is, consciously feeling water resistance and embodying action that serves to increase resistance against the hands and arms throughout the S-pull trajectory, thus increasing propulsion.

## Perception-action coupling

How can perception of this feeling be coached for? Influenced by an athlete-centred coaching perspective, I believed the answer to this question lies in shifting my swim coaching practice away from the understanding that the coach is in the sole position of power to decide which movements satisfy task requirements. Inherent to this perspective was that because the coach possesses the biomechanical knowledge around optimal movement performance, the learning experience is tightly controlled whereby desired techniques are demonstrated, verbally reinforced and physically adjusted for. Returning to the freestyle example, I made a decision to preference the S-shaped trajectory rather than a straight arm movement in the pull phase. This was based on the biomechanical understanding that an S shape is longer than a straight arm pull, and therefore may generate greater propulsion. However, adopting an athlete-centred perspective, I also believed that there was room for flexibility for a certain type of movement exploration, valuing the embodied athlete experience. This was also in part informed by recognition of an ecological perspective (Davids et al., 2008) whereby movement coordination emerges under the influence of individual physiological characteristics and therefore multiple movement solutions are possible to satisfy identical task requirements. In this freestyle example, this may be characterised by swimmers making sub-scale adjustments to their limb position and orientation, and purposefully deciding through embodied feeling of water resistance, which movements serve to generate greater propulsion. Such movements are small, complex, highly dynamic and relative to what is referred to in the literature as organismic constraints (Davids et al., 2008). This prompted me to consider the value of instruction and demonstration in conveying the complicated intricacies of dynamic movement relative to the individual and their feeling of water resistance.

I began experimenting with pedagogical behaviours that provided students with greater decision-making in their movement performance. Using the freestyle example, I employed convergent questioning coupled with an inquiry focus. The learning objective was to couple perception-action to water resistance with a freestyle pull movement (within the S trajectory) which generated sufficient propulsion for students to complete 4 × 10 metre laps. I began with a relatable mnemonic (Scruggs & Mastropieri, 1991) to ask my students if they ever scooped frozen ice cream out of a container with a large spoon:

> Let's pretend the water is frozen ice-cream and we're inside the kitchen . . . I want you to try and scoop as much of this frozen ice-cream onto the (glass) wall as possible, seeing how high you can get the ice-cream to land.

My students thrashed their arms through the water, experimenting with various movements; skimming the water vs. dragging the arm completely under and up. After a short period, students were presented with questions to evoke cognitive consciousness around their performance. For example: How frozen did the ice cream feel? How do your arms feel? What movements did you use to scoop the ice cream? Were some movements better than others at scooping more ice cream? To further develop cognitive consciousness, I asked the students to lay their hands flat on the water surface with palms facing upward, and I moved through the group to each student, gently tapping their palms with my own:

> This feeling of how hard (resistant) scooping the frozen ice-cream was, I want you to have the same feeling for when you have to move through the frozen ice-cream and collect chocolate chips at the bottom of the container.

Chocolate chips were sinking toys that had been thrown to the deepest end of the lane. Some students opted to skim the surface of the water with their hands and arms in the initial activity, creating a thin wave of water spray on the glass wall. This game was used to reinforce feelings of water resistance, and to transition the skimming movement to a completely submerged pull as with freestyle. Prior to recommencing lap-swimming, verbal cues were used to signal reminders around the feeling of water resistance, encouraging students to make necessarily sub-scale adjustments to their pull mechanics in order to heighten this feeling in their hand and arm movements, thus generating greater propulsion. The time required to reach competency for the freestyle pull phase had significantly been reduced. Moreover, later the benefits were seen as far as propulsion generation for other stroke competencies, especially breaststroke. Unfortunately, my practices came under scrutiny by supervisory staff concerned that they did not conform to the curriculum that had been set. As a result, I ceased working as a swimming instructor and began to pursue my PhD with a focus on pedagogical behaviours within swimming.

## Conclusion

The experiences discussed in this chapter tell the story of an effort to shift away from dominant teacher-directed hegemony in learn to swim programs. Literature pertaining to the efficacy of athlete-centred coaching suggests that pedagogical considerations related to repositioning power discourses over decision-making in movement performance to value athlete experience may prove efficacious in skill acquisition for swimming (Light, 2016). This was my experience. In doing so, I understood good coaching practice hinges on the ability to not only manage organisation, training and competition but also consider athlete characteristics, the broader sporting environment and pedagogical actions (Côté, Young, Duffy, & North, 2007).

The story I have told in this chapter is one of dissonance created by the difference in coaching framed in my undergraduate teacher training and the learn to swim coaching where I worked. The athlete-centred coaching philosophy espoused in my teacher education was at odds with the coach-centred, highly prescribed and directed curriculum in the swim coaching setting. Although I perceived my attempts at student empowerment to explore movement mechanics to have been successful, they were not received well within the orthodoxy of the coaching setting, meeting resistance and challenge within the centre in which I worked and in conversation with other coaches from other centres.

## References

Abraham, A., & Collins, D. (1998). Examining and extending research in coach development. *Quest, 50*(1), 59–79.

Booth, D. (2001). *Australian beach cultures: The history of sun, sand, and surf.* London: Frank Cass.

Bunker, D., & Thorpe, R. (1982). A model for the teaching of games in the secondary school. *Bulletin of Physical Education, 10*, 9–16.

Cashman, R. (2002). *Sport in the national imagination: Australian sport in the Federation decades.* Sydney, Australia: Walla Walla Press, in conjunction with the Centre for Olympic Studies, University of New South Wales.

Cassidy, T. G., Jones, R. L., & Potrac, P. (2008). *Understanding sports coaching: The social, cultural and pedagogical foundations of coaching practice.* New York: Routledge.

Chow, J. Y., Renshaw, I., Button, C., Davids, K., & Keat, C. T. W. (2013). Effective learning design for the individual: A nonlinear pedagogical approach in physical education. In A. Ovens, T. Hopper, & J. Butler (Eds.), *Complexity thinking in physical education: Reframing curriculum, pedagogy and research* (pp. 121–134). London: Routledge.

Claxton, D. B. (1988). A systematic observation of more and less successful high school tennis coaches. *Journal of Teaching in Physical Education, 7*(4), 302–310.

Côté, J., Young, B., North, J., & Duffy, P. (2007). Towards a definition of excellence in sport coaching. *International Journal of Coaching Science, 1*(1), 3–17.

Crisfield, P., Cabral, P., & Carpenter, F. (2005). *The successful coach: Guidelines for coaching practice* (n.p.). Leeds: National Coaching Foundation.

Cross, N., & Lyle, J. (1999). *The coaching process: Principles and practice for sport*. Woburn, MA: Butterworth-Heinemann.

Cushion, C. J., Armour, K. M., & Jones, R. L. (2006). Locating the coaching process in practice: Models 'for' and 'of' coaching. *Physical Education and Sport Pedagogy, 11*(1), 83–99.

Davids, K., Button, C., & Bennett, S. (Eds.) (2008). *Dynamics of skill acquisition: A constraints-led approach*. Champaign, IL: Human Kinetics.

den Duyn, N. (1997). Game sense: It's time to play! *Sports Coach, 19*(4), 9–11.

Drewe, S. B. (2000). An examination of the relationship between coaching and teaching. *Quest, 52*(1), 79–88.

Farrow, D., Baker, J., & MacMahon, C. (2013). *Developing sport expertise: Researchers and coaches put theory into practice*. New York: Routledge.

Find a Pool. (n.d.). Retrieved from www.swimming.org.au/Home/Swimmer-HQ/A-Sport-For-Everyone/find-a-pool.aspx

Hewitt, M. (2015). *Teaching styles of Australian tennis coaches: An exploration of practices and insights using Mosston and Ashworth's spectrum of teaching styles*. PhD thesis, The University of Southern Queensland, Queensland, Australia.

Jones, R. L. (2006). *The sports coach as educator: Re-conceptualising sports coaching*. New York: Routledge.

Kidman, L. (2010). *Athlete-centred coaching: Developing decision makers*. Auckland, New Zealand: IPC Print Resources.

Lacy, A. C., & Darst, P. W. (1985). Systematic observation of behaviors of winning high school head football coaches. *Journal of Teaching in Physical Education, 4*(4), 256–270.

Light, R. (2008). Complex learning theory-its epistemology and its assumptions about learning: Implications for physical education. *Journal of Teaching in Physical Education, 27*(1), 21–37.

Light, R. (2013). *Game sense: Pedagogy for performance, participation and enjoyment*. New York: Routledge.

Light, R. (2016). *Positive pedagogy for sport coaching: Athlete-centred coaching for individual sports*. New York: Routledge.

Light, R., & Rockwell, T. (2005). The cultural origins of competitive swimming in Australia. *Sporting Traditions, 22*(1), 21–37.

Magias, T., & Pill, S. (2013, November 27–29). Teaching swimming for movement variability: An application of Teaching Games for Understanding – game sense. In J. Quay & A. Mooney (Eds.), *Proceedings of the 28th ACHPER international conference* (pp. 93–101). Melbourne, Australia.

Nelson, L. J., & Cushion, C. J. (2006). Reflection in coach education: The case of the national governing body coaching certificate. *Sport Psychologist, 20*(2), 174–183.

Pill, S. (2012). Teaching game sense in soccer. *Journal of Physical Education, Recreation & Dance, 83*(3), 42–52.

Potrac, P., Brewer, C., Jones, R., Armour, K., & Hoff, J. (2000). Toward an holistic understanding of the coaching process. *Quest, 52*(2), 186–199.

Rupert, T., & Buschner, C. (1989). Teaching and coaching: A comparison of Instructional behaviors. *Journal of Teaching in Physical Education, 9*(9), 49–57.

Scruggs, T. E., & Mastropieri, M. A. (1991). Classroom applications of mnemonic instruction: Acquisition, maintenance, and generalization. *Exceptional Children, 58*(3), 219–229.

Shogan, D. A. (1999). *The making of high-performance athletes: Discipline, diversity, and ethics.* Toronto, Canada: University of Toronto Press.

Smith, R. E., Zane, N. W., Smoll, F. L., & Coppel, D. B. (1983). Behavioral assessment in youth sports: Coaching behaviors and children's attitudes. *Medicine and Science in Sports and Exercise, 15*(3), 208–214.

Stolz, S., & Pill, S. (2012). Making sense of game sense. *Active and Healthy Magazine, 19*(1), 5–8.

Swimming Australia: Olympic History. (n.d.). Retrieved from www.swimming.org.au/Corporate-Information/History/Olympic-History.aspx

Thorpe, R. (2005). Rod Thorpe on Teaching Games for Understanding. In L. Kidman (Ed.), *Athlete-centred coaching* (pp. 229–244). Christchurch, NZ: Innovative Print Communications.

Tinning, R. (2015). Commentary on research into learning in physical education: Towards a mature field of knowledge. *Sport, Education and Society, 20*(5), 676–690.

Wein, H. (2007). *Developing youth football players.* Champaign, IL: Human Kinetics.

Williams, A. M., & Hodges, N. J. (2005). Practice, instruction and skill acquisition in soccer: Challenging tradition. *Journal of Sports Sciences, 23*(6), 637–650.

Winterton, R. (2010). *'Feats of fancy "and" marvels of muscle': A social history of swimming in late colonial Melbourne.* PhD thesis, Victoria University, Melbourne, Australia.

# 15

# ATHLETE-CENTRED APPROACH – BEGINNING THE PROCESS IN JUNIOR TEAMS

*Greg Forrest*

Over the past decade, there has been a renewed call for increasing athlete independence in coaching in sporting environments. Central to this are athlete-centred approaches, which have been promoted as an innovative approach "enabling athletes to succeed in and enjoy their sport participation" (Kidman & Lombardo, 2010, p. 16). Advocates suggest an athlete-centred approach allows athletes to gain control over their own athletic lives and take greater ownership and personal responsibility for their decisions (Kidman & Lombardo, 2010). DeSouza and Oslin (2008) also suggest an athlete-centred approach provides better opportunities for individual growth in the physical, cognitive, social and affective aspects, leading to improved decision-making, engagement, communication, competence and motivation. It is postulated that this provision leads to improved athlete autonomy and allows them a greater range of choices in relation to learning experiences used in sport (Kidman & Lombardo, 2010). This is, in part, because an athlete-centred approach should enable athletes to develop their own solutions to the many variations in play via the pedagogical aspects used in the approach.

## Three key components of an athlete-centred approach

Kidman and Lombardo (2010) suggest those wishing to use an athlete-centred approach should incorporate three key components into coaching practices to allow the benefits of athlete-centred approach to occur. These are: 1. The use of *Teaching Games for Understanding (TGfU)* or a *Game Sense approach*; 2. Using *questioning* and question structures; and 3. *Establish a quality team culture*. TGfU and Game Sense are games-based approaches that fall under the banner of *Game Centred Approaches* (GCA), and have been aligned with improved motivation and engagement through the use of game play as a key learning tool (Oslin & Mitchell, 2006). Questions have close pedagogical links with a GCA and are used for cognitive and social purposes, such as stimulating thinking and developing independent learners (Oliveira, 2010). When using an athlete-centred approach, advocates suggest the importance of building a culture where athletes take responsibility for the direction of the team and suggest all stakeholders (players, coaches and administrators) be involved in developing team culture, allowing improved 'buy in' and improving the chance of success.

To strengthen the potential of an athlete-centred approach to achieve these key components, advocates suggest a range of other supportive measures. For example, De Souza and Oslin (2008) suggest coaches ensure athletes are in a positive and safe environment and encourage the prioritisation of the long-term view of developing the whole athlete over a short-term view of winning. McGladrey, Murray, and Hannon (2010) also recommend the importance of a two-way communication between stakeholders involved in an athlete-centred approach to ensure stakeholders feel included and all parties are accountable for maintaining and supporting the approach. Kidman and Lombardo (2010) argue that developing leadership within the whole team and the allocation of roles all contribute to the development of the athlete and therefore assist in achieving the outcomes of an athlete-centred approach.

Using an athlete-centred approach presents significant challenges to current coaching discourses, practices and expectations (Nelson, Cushion, Potrac, & Groom, 2014). Cushion (2013) notes implementation of an athlete-centred approach is often problematic and not necessarily as straightforward as supporters of the approach may suggest. These issues have led to authors such as Jones (2007) to call for a more in-depth exploration of athlete-centred approach practices in a range of different coaching contexts. While research into an athlete-centred approach has demonstrated potential in elite sporting environments (Hodge, Henry, & Smith, 2014), Romar, Saréns, and Hastie (2016) argue there is little empirical evidence supporting the implementation of an athlete-centred approach in a range of different coaching environments.

The study presented in this chapter takes up the challenge to explore athlete-centred coaching and examines the use of an athlete-centred approach in grassroots junior community sport (JCS). JCS is an important context of athlete-centred approach research in Australia, as at least 60% or 1.7 million 5–14-year-old Australian children participate in organised sport outside of school (Australian Bureau of Statistics (ABS) 2012). An athlete-centred approach can also represent a significant philosophical shift in coaching, which in Australia has a history of coach-centred, managerial approaches (Evans, 2015).

This study examines responses of the main stakeholders in JCS (players, parents and parent/coaches) to an athlete-centred approach in JCS in three different sporting clubs: football (soccer), cricket and Australian football (AFL). Stakeholders (including myself) were volunteers who chose to be involved in JCS because their children played, they had an interest in the sport and/or they had a desire to facilitate opportunities for children and adolescents through the sport. An athlete-centred approach had potential to cause discomfort and disengagement when the approach did not meet stakeholder expectations or was different to their understanding of involvement in JCS.

## Method

Data presented in this chapter were collected as part of a larger study into innovative games-based pedagogies in Physical Education (PE) and Sport. Ethics approval and informed consent were gained prior to the collection of data for involvement in the study and potential publication. Each club had a range of teams from 5 to 17 years of age of differing ability levels and motivations, and managed from 130 players (AFL and cricket clubs) to over 300 players (football). All three clubs had similar values, focusing on maximising participation, encouraging involvement and providing opportunity for all who registered. I was a volunteer in each club and a parent of two players and, as is common, volunteered to coach my children's teams. Each team was typical of teams in each of the clubs. Player ages range from 5–12 years in football, 9–17 years in cricket and 8–17 years in AFL. I followed my sons as they moved chronologically through the age groups, and I am presently still implementing an athlete-centred approach with my youngest son (12 years old) in the three sports. As is typical of most JCS clubs, I am also a member of each club's junior committee, conduct professional learning workshops for club coaches, mentor coaches and run voluntary whole club training sessions using an athlete-centred approach.

It should also be noted that I am not a typical 'grassroots' coach. My background as a high school teacher and coach, then researcher and senior lecturer in teaching and coaching in PE and Sport, is more aligned with the pedagogical knowledge of a professional coach rather than the volunteer parent. It should also be noted, my experience in the three sports is also very different. I regularly coached soccer prior to and during my secondary teaching career and played at a representative level when younger. While an avid spectator of AFL and cricket, I have never played either sport competitively, and only began coaching the sports at the commencement of the study.

I will use a selection of exchanges to explore the meaning of an athlete-centred approach through the eyes of stakeholders in relation to the two pedagogical aspects of the approach – GCA use and questioning. As part of an ongoing attempt to continually improve my coaching practice, I regularly use a journal to record observations, conversations and exchanges with various stakeholders, and self-reflections on my coaching, particularly in relation to pedagogical conditions of an athlete-centred approach, which is an area I also research. The study described is informed by an ethnomethological approach, which allows the empirical study of how members of groups (in this case, stakeholders in JCS) create meaning when they engage with what may be seen as *common sense*, everyday activities – such as an athlete-centred approach in actual practice. Lemke's (1990) theory of social semiotics was used to analyse these exchanges. Lemke argues that it is misleading to assume that something, in this context an athlete-centred approach, simply has the meaning attributed to it by advocates when used in practice. Meaning *for* and *of* an athlete-centred approach is made in the context of use, and through the analysis, better sense can be made of the approach from a global perspective.

## Stakeholder responses to a game-centred approach

All stakeholders involved with my coaching at a team or club level were generally very positive about the use of GCA as part of an athlete-centred approach. In most cases, improvements in play, regular training attendance and the retention of players in the sport were seen by stakeholders as indicators of better engagement and motivation, and were attributed to GCA use. Stakeholders felt the exploration of cognitive aspects of play through a GCA, and the use of purposeful games, played a key role in achieving the outcomes. For example, Parent J noted:

> B (son) loves coming to training and playing AFL. He enjoys the games in training because they suit how he thinks and he loves things like planning and strategy. He can connect the games used in training to the things the team is trying to do on the weekend.

The focus on more cognitive aspects of play through GCA use also allowed team members, especially the younger teams (under 10 years of age), to demonstrate understandings often not expected of children this age. Club President J told me after one game:

> I love watching your 'Mini Roos' (Under 7) team play; their style and understanding of game play is better than some teenage teams. Others just chase the ball like seagulls to a chip. What can we do to get all of our teams playing like this?

Here, the better play at weekends in small-sided games had led to curiosity about the coaching methods to develop this. More importantly, it could be argued that play itself indicated that exploring more cognitive aspects of play through as GCA allowed better transfer to weekend play. However, these characteristics were not always evident for all stakeholders in my teams. GCA became problematic at times, even for one who constantly uses and researches the approach. For stakeholders, GCA clashed with perceptions of what 'playing games' represented or should be. As Player S (9 years old) told me during one session, *Coach, games are supposed to be fun, not like being at school. I just want to play!* Player A (14 years old) was also quite forthright when struggling in a game designed to improve managing run chases: *Coach, this game is stupid. Why do I lose all of my runs for hitting it out of the circle on the full? It's not like that in the T20!* A parent of a more 'serious' athlete also discussed the following during a GCA session:

*Parent:*    Coach, do you have a moment? I understand the philosophy and all but I think S needs be involved in a more serious approach to training; more fitness work, more drills. These sessions are just games, he just cruises around and does not really get involved.

Greg: Do you think it is about the games or about his understanding of the game?

P: It is about what he thinks of games.

Athlete-centred approach advocates argue GCAs are integral to the approach because games make sessions more enjoyable, engaging and motivating and are *fun* (Kidman & Lombardo, 2010). In the exchanges like the one above, games or, more importantly, purposeful games did not mean this to some stakeholders. Some disengaged when the game did not replicate the 'real' sport where they could play on instinct and do as they pleased. For others, games were for fun, but learning was perceived to limit this. For another, games did not focus on the appropriate learning or were not a context for learning. Thus, the meaning of games and associated perceptions of fun and learning in the different sports did not always align with that presented by athlete-centred approach advocates.

As an experienced GCA practitioner with a strong level of content knowledge in games and coaching, I was able to provide explanations of the reason for these games and their intended outcomes. However, it was not always as easy for other coaches. Coach T raised deeper concerns. He was a parent of one of my cricketers coaching his daughter in soccer:

Greg, I can run a 'typical' (traditional) training session but the 'things' your games explore with J (his son) in cricket are beyond me in soccer. I am just an interested parent with a bit of a coaching background so I volunteered. I wish I could look at strategy and decisions but when I was playing, you just kind of . . . understood it. And that was in Rugby! I don't know or see these things on the weekend and the qualification the club paid for didn't address these things. It seemed we were given a list of games and encouraged to use them for fun and self-discovery.

This exchange was representative of a number of concerns and raises key complications for the community volunteer coach and athlete-centred approach components in JCS. As a parent, T saw the benefits for his child and the team, but could not replicate the same as a coach. Importantly, he did not feel he had the content knowledge in the sport and his own coaching background did not allow him to articulate the meaning of strategy and decision-making, or incorporate these aspects in his coaching. The content of accreditation courses was also not aligned with the pedagogical use of games in accreditation programs. Therefore, while some stakeholders (like this coach) saw value in the outcomes created through the pedagogy used in an athlete-centred approach which is game-centred, they did not have, feel they had, or were not supported in developing the content knowledge needed to implement it.

## Stakeholder responses to the instructional use of questioning

Responses to the use of questioning as part of an athlete-centred approach demonstrated that the process allowed players to engage in the sport more meaningfully and develop confidence in contributing to the team and making decisions. Parents in particular were encouraged by how questions allowed players to articulate their knowledge in the sport and, through this, demonstrate they were taking responsibility for learning and engaging with the sport. Questioning was conducted within hearing range of parents wherever possible, a deliberate policy on my behalf to meet McGladrey, Murray and Hannon's (2010) suggestion of keeping open and transparent actions in an athlete-centred approach.

Questioning processes gave players an opportunity to demonstrate their game play understanding in different ways than just the game play, which was, for parents and listeners, an indicator of their child's understanding, not always evident in play. As one parent noted:

> I love how your questions make the players think. I never knew that D (12-year-old son) knew so much. He really contributes to some of the bigger picture things, such as strategy and what is going well or what can be improved. It does not mean he can do it in the game but I now know he understands. And I watch him when you are asking; he is so focused! Can you get him the same with his school work?

The use of questioning and the dialogue structures associated with these as part of an athlete-centred approach allowed D (and players like D) to engage with a range of key concepts of the sport while allowing him to contribute to the team beyond just play. In this exchange, the questioning process achieved Kidman and Lombard's (2010) outcomes of players, such as: enhanced concentration and intensity and improved autonomy. This then led to a positive effect on his motivation levels and his contributions to the team. For the parent, the combination of the questioning and the open environment where it was conducted meant their son was demonstrating a developing knowledge and understanding of the whole sport and engaging in his sporting activity in a meaningful manner. However, as the following exchange demonstrates, the use of questions can evolve into very different scenarios than those demonstrated in athlete-centred approach examples (see for example DeSouza & Oslin, 2008). Consider the implications of the following exchange:

> At half time, I asked young J (11 years old) what I thought was a fairly simple question for him about offence and, as expected, he answered it confidently. However, he looked very upset a couple of minutes later as he went back onto the field. I asked him was he ok and he replied:
> 'NO! I just don't know what I have to do!'

As his answers indicated that he did, I asked him what specifically he did not know. He replied 'It's not that. I don't understand ANYTHING! Can I just come off?'

At this stage, I abandoned the questions, gave him three very specific things to do in the half. He said 'OK', wiped the tears away and, happily (for him and me), had a great second half.

Here, J's initial answers indicated he understood the purpose of the question and the associated content. However, this understanding came at a personal cost that was only revealed outside the group environment. Another question simply made things worse. Questioning, at face value, was successful and indicated similar outcomes modelled in athlete-centred approach literature, but the actual cost of questioning was contrary to positive outcomes suggested by athlete-centred approach advocates. Questioning meant J felt quite unsafe as the result of questioning, not because of the process, but because his own understanding did not demonstrate where he fitted in the play – creating a situation that was contrary to the positive and safe environment DeSouza and Oslin (2008) suggested should exist. While questioning is beneficial and players will feel that their opinion is valued (Kidman & Lombardo, 2010), as indicated by J's ability to respond, in this instance it did not necessarily lead to improved discovery, increased motivation and more excitement in the sport. It led to emotional turmoil and required my pedagogical experience and some content knowledge to give direct instruction to rebalance the young player.

The uncertain outcomes that resulted from questions were also an issue for coaches when exploring coaching methods. In an ACA workshop, Coach K noted:

> I avoid asking too many questions. I think it comes across to the players and parents that I don't know. It is just easier all round to tell them what I want. The players are comfortable, they don't 'muck around' and I get through the training sessions and everyone is happy.

Similar thoughts are expressed in the following exchange. Here, Coach M, a qualified teacher and a coach with an interest in different coaching styles, noted:

> I tried some of questions you use at the half time break on the weekend, to 'get' the player's perspective. As the players went back on, I heard two of the parents say 'Seems Coach doesn't know what to do!' And, you know what? They may be right! I never can ask any more than one question when I try this because I don't know whether what they were suggesting was ok. When you explore strategy or decision-making or whole team play, I am just as much a student as the players. I get the logic of what you are asking and the follow-ups, I see the value but I don't see it myself when they play and it makes the process really problematic for me!

Both exchanges reflect a common perception of questions. In some manner, the responses of stakeholders give weight to the problems that an athlete-centred approach user faces when they challenge conventional coaching discourses – the idea that questioning may be perceived as a weakness. This perception led to different approaches from the coaches: avoidance of questions to limit the personal cost of a perception that the coach 'doesn't know'; and use of questions at a personal cost of facing these types of comments. The reluctance to question did not relate to ego, noted by Kidman and Lombardo (2010) as a potential barrier to athlete-centred approach. Questioning to coaches meant 'unsafe' – unsafe in how they were perceived as the coach, but more importantly, perceived in their knowledge. Questioning led them to places where, for example, Coach M admitted he did not have the appropriate knowledge to manage the learning. Thus, while initial examination of the exchanges could align coach reasons with clashes with traditional discourses, the notion of specialised content needed to use this pedagogy so integral to athlete-centred approach emerges as a significant barrier.

In my coaching, I had a depth of content knowledge to manage the questioning with players and create meaning of these in the presence of stakeholders present. While this allowed the benefits created by an athlete-centred approach to develop, questions still had to be managed carefully as they had the capacity to create different outcomes to those that might be envisioned from the athlete-centred approach literature. Without this content knowledge, the scenario was the very opposite. Coaches either avoided questions completely or discovered they did not have the content knowledge to use them meaningfully, and exploration with other stakeholders became problematic. Even an experienced pedagogue (Coach M) felt he could not develop dialogue from questions because he was uncertain of whether he had the knowledge to actually manage it.

## Conclusion

I have drawn attention to both the benefits of an athlete-centred approach and the underlying complexities that impact on what an athlete-centred approach *means* in JCS. The discussion demonstrated that the qualities so valued by advocates of the approach were achievable when it was used by someone like myself who had deep knowledge, understanding and experience in the content and pedagogies associated with the key conditions of an athlete-centred approach: in my case, 'a professional' in coaching. When used by the typical coach in JCS, the results were at odds with the athlete-centred approach findings. Paradoxically, the very pedagogical aspects that provided the positives for stakeholders in an athlete-centred approach, GCA and questions, were the very methods that created perceived or actual problems. I, as the 'professional' coach, found that stakeholders needed very careful management and support when an athlete-centred approach was used to ensure the conditions of the approach were understood and had meaning, a skill set that the volunteer in community sport in this study did not have or want to develop.

Despite the paradoxes created by use of an athlete-centred approach, the potential benefits of the approach in my use were quite evident and worthy of further exploration. However, I have argued elsewhere (Forrest, 2014) that the capacity to deliver the benefits of pedagogies such as questioning requires attention not just to the pedagogy but the content knowledge of the user.

The achievement of outcomes associated with innovative pedagogical approaches, such as an athlete-centred approach, requires a balance of pedagogical knowledge and content knowledge. The deeper the level of both, the better the experiences of both coach and player. While the exploration of more innovative and inclusive pedagogies in coaching and teaching games and sport has expanded rapidly in the last twenty years, the underlying assumptions associated with content knowledge have largely been unexplored, unchallenged or assumed to be adequate to use these approaches in most of the scholarly literature. The exchanges in this chapter do indicate that the challenges associated with an athlete-centred approach implementation are, in some way, challenging dominant discourses of coaching. I also suggest that stakeholders are not well prepared to meet the challenge. This is because of the limitations associated with the content knowledge needed in an athlete-centred approach, and how it is developed (or not developed) in coach accreditation.

One important aspect of this study was my own level of content knowledge in relation to the three sports. I had no specialised content knowledge in AFL and Cricket but a deep understanding the concepts of strategy and tactics and decision-making. This meant I was able to transfer the specialised knowledge of *concepts common* to all sports into a new *sporting context*. Therefore, the study suggests the potential value of reconceptualising what coaching content knowledge is developed in coach education programs in games and sports, such as accreditation courses. I suggest that focus should shift from managerial and organisational content to concepts such as strategy, tactics and decision-making and other common aspects of game play required to play. The alignment of these concepts with games that specifically develop these concepts would also be valuable, as it would model the potential of purposeful game play. Reconceptualising the content of coach accreditation courses in such a manner may then allow stakeholders to better understand the value of pedagogies associated with an athlete-centred approach, such that coaches could begin to manage some of the underlying challenges that are barriers to more meaningful use.

## References

Australian Bureau of Statistics. (2012). *Sports and physical recreation: A statistical overview of children's participation*. Retrieved from http://www.abs.gov.au/ausstats/abs@.nsf/Products/4901.0~Apr+2012~Main+Features~Sports+participation?OpenDocument

Cushion, C. J. (2013). Applying game centered approaches in coaching: A critical analysis of the 'dilemmas of practice' impacting change. *Sports Coaching Review, 2*(1), 61–76.

De Souza, A., & Oslin, J. (2008). A player-centered approach to coaching. *Journal of Physical Education, Recreation & Dance, 79*(6), 24–27.

Evans, J. (2015). Coach-player relationships in game sense. In R. Light, J. Quay, S. Harvey, & A. Mooney (Eds.), *Contemporary developments in games teaching* (pp. 133–145). London: Routledge.

Forrest, G. J. (2014). Questions and answers: Understanding the connection between questioning and knowledge in game-centred approaches. In R. Light, J. Quay, S. Harvey, & A. Mooney (Eds.), *Contemporary developments in games teaching* (pp. 167–177). London: Routledge.

Hodge, K., Henry, G., & Smith, W. (2014). A case study of excellence in elite sport: Motivational climate in a world champion team. *Sport Psychologist, 28*(1), 60–74.

Jones, R. (2007). Coaching redefined: An everyday pedagogical endeavor. *Sport, Education and Society, 12*(2), 159–173.

Kidman, L., & Lombardo, J. (2010). *Athlete-centred coaching: Developing inspired and inspiring people*. Worcester, UK: Innovative Print Communications Ltd.

Lemke, J. L. (1990). *Talking science: Language, learning and value*. Norwood, NJ: Ablex Publishing Corporation.

McGladery, B., Murray, M., & Hannon, J. (2010). Developing and practicing an athlete-centred coaching philosophy. *Youth First: The Journal of Youth Sports, 5*(2), 4–7.

Nelson, L., Cushion, C. J., Potrac, P., & Groom, R. (2014). Carl Rogers, learning and educational practice: Critical considerations and applications in sports coaching. *Sport, Education and Society, 19*(5), 513–531.

Oliveira, A. W. (2010). Improving teacher questioning in science: Inquiry discussions through professional development. *Journal of Research in Science Teaching, 47*(4), 422–453.

Oslin, J., & Mitchell, S. (2006). Game centred approaches to teaching physical education. In D. Kirk, D. Macdonald, & M. O'Sullivan (Eds.), *Handbook of physical education* (pp. 627–651). London: Sage.

Romar, J. E., Sarén, J., & Hastie, P. (2016). Athlete centred coaching using the sport education model in youth soccer. *Journal of Physical Education and Sport, 16*(2), 380–391.

# 16

# COACH EDUCATORS AS ATHLETE-CENTRED PRACTITIONERS

*Ed Cope and Andy Lowe*

Over the course of the last 30 years, thinking about what constitutes effective coaching pedagogy has changed and evolved. It is now understood that for coaching pedagogy to be considered effective, it must account for the learning needs of players, within the specific coaching context that they participate (Jones, Armour, & Potrac, 2004; Côté & Gilbert, 2009). This thinking is in opposition to previous suggestions that posited learning as a linear process where, if a learning environment were created, certain learning would happen regardless of differences in individuals' developmental needs. For an example of this thinking: it has been considered that if a coach's practice were effective in one type of context (i.e. elite), it would be equally effective in a different context (i.e. recreational). The premise of the argument that coaching can remain constant within and between contexts yet remain effective was based on behaviouristic principles of learning (Lucas, Claxton, & Spencer, 2013). Behaviouristic thinkers position the coach as the 'expert', who has superior levels of subject-specific knowledge, which she/he is able to impart on their 'less knowledgeable' subjects. The type of learning environment created would be prescriptive with pre-conceived judgments made of what constitutes good or bad coaching.

A behaviouristic approach shares many similarities with what has been termed coach-centred coaching (Kidman, 2001). Historically, formal coach education in the form of National Governing Body (NGB) qualifications has endorsed a coach-centred approach (Nelson, Cushion, & Potrac, 2013). Nelson et al. (2013) referred to coach education as adopting a 'top-down' approach, as coaches were prescribed content to learn with little or no input into what or how this process happened, and the assessment of coaches' competencies were undertaken out of context (e.g. assessment of coaching happened on coaching courses rather than in the context of coaches' work). It is perhaps no surprise then that NGB qualifications have been widely criticised for their failure to suitably educate coaches for the realities and challenges they face in their day-to-day practices (Abraham & Collins, 1998; Chesterfield, Potrac, & Jones, 2010; Cushion, Armour, & Jones, 2003; Jones, 2000; Nelson & Cushion, 2006). However, over the course of the last five years, and in keeping with movements and discussions in academia (i.e. Jones & Turner, 2006), some NGBs, such as the English Football Association (EFA), have been immersed in a process of revising the structure and delivery of their qualifications. Consequently, the criticisms previously levelled at NGB courses are, perhaps, no longer valid in some cases.

The rationale behind the qualifications revamp in English football was born out of an acknowledgement that these did not suitably educate coaches to effectively undertake their roles. For example, the content of coach education courses did not prepare coaches for the copious number of roles they had to undertake (Gilbert & Trudel, 2004). The revised set of coaching qualifications have deliberately moved away from the behaviouristic underpinnings of the previous qualifications and shifted toward being based on constructivist principles, with the aim that coaches adopt the same principles in their own practices. In this new scenario, knowledge is developed as a consequence of collaboration between coach educator and coach, and coaches are provided opportunities to shape their own learning through discussing issues most relevant to those they encounter (Light, 2008). Therefore, where once coaches were subjected to a very rigid curriculum of content to study, the current approach makes an explicit attempt to remain flexible to the challenges individual coaches face within their own specific coaching contexts. Furthermore, assessment of coaches' competencies is now undertaken in situ, which has replaced the traditional assessment day that came at the end of the taught content. Additionally, instead of the entire course being delivered away from the confines of coaches' practices and the players they work with, the revised courses appreciate the need to work with coaches within their own settings. Consequently, courses appear to be better preparing coaches for their roles, although research evidence is still inconclusive regarding the impact these courses are having on coaches' learning and development (Stodter & Cushion, 2014).

Given revisions to the format, delivery, and assessment of football courses in English football, it would seem that if the aims and aspirations of these are to be realised, the role the coach educator undertakes is of fundamental importance. However, to date issues related to a coach educators' role and the coach educator's ability to develop coaches' knowledge and skills are rarely acknowledged in the research literature. Therefore, in this chapter we discuss the knowledge and skills required of coach educators for them to create and model a constructivist, athlete-centred learning environment. In doing so, this chapter is one of the first to attempt to address this critical yet under-researched area of coaching. To assist in meeting this purpose, an experienced football coach educator who has delivered both the old and new versions of football courses in England will offer his reflections on how his role in educating coaches has changed, and how he has learned the knowledge and skills to educate coaches differently. This commentary will then be understood through relevant theory.

## A reflection on learning to educate differently

Learning from experienced coaches has been commonplace in coaching texts (i.e. Jones et al., 2004; Jones, Potrac, Cushion, & Ronglan, 2010), with these insights providing rich accounts of the strategies coaches have employed, bound by the socio-cultural constraints of the contexts in which they work. In this chapter, we follow a similar method by sharing the learning and reflections of an experienced coach educator, who has perceived his coach education practice to have changed and evolved over the period of his career. Sharing these understandings is with the aim of highlighting the non-linear, challenging, and time-consuming nature of learning to educate coach educators, particularly during a period when thinking about learning in coaching has changed:

> *Thinking about my role as a coach educator now to what it was fifteen years ago, it could not be any more different. I feel I have been trying to deliver in the current contemporary way for some time, but there now appears a more widespread acknowledgement of moving away from coach-centric methods of coach education toward better appreciating the issues coaches face. I think that central to enabling this to happen has been the revision in course design, which encapsulates the holistic nature of coach development, which is now flexible in enabling the trials and tribulations that coaches face to be explored within a constructivist approach.*
>
> *It has not always been like that. My early years as a coach educator involved teaching coaches in an often prescribed fashion, in what appeared to be the 'right' way to coach at that time. This was heavily focused around developing coaches' technical and tactical knowledge and not fully appreciating the multifaceted focus we see in coach development today. A central part of football courses was giving coaches a curriculum of sorts, which were essentially a set of drills and skills that they could take and mimic in their coaching, as they had seen delivered on the course. My knowledge of 'what to do' almost entirely stemmed from my experiences as a coach, and the judgment on whether I was competent to educate pretty much resided in the fact I had attained my 'UEFA B' coaching qualification. While there was some tutor training involved, this was minimal, and so my competency to educate was based almost exclusively on the knowledge I had acquired as a coach.*
>
> *In my formative years as a coach educator, I now accept that how I educated coaches in my early years was more prescribed and generic, compared to the more individualised and context specific nature which is deemed good practice today, where the coach is at the forefront of the process, rather than the syllabus being the defining factor. I always felt the coach should be at the centre of the learning process and therefore always sought learning opportunities to develop my practice further in creating coach-centred course delivery. I was fortunate enough in my early career to have outstanding mentors and teachers, who acted with such humility and empathy. It was never the case that everyone had to follow or agree with their perspective, but instead, I was encouraged to think for myself and consider the notion of being innovative and strive to constantly learn and seek modern ways of operating to up skill oneself and the coaches I was*

*educating. I entered coach education with the view that much of what I was subjected to as a young coach was not the best way to educate coaches. At this point, from a very early stage, I knew I wanted to be more coach centred as a coach educator, rather than the often didactic tutor focused methods I had encountered as a young coach. To this end I explored a diverse range of learning opportunities away from football, which gave me a more integrated approach in understanding the learning and educating coaches.*

*As I continued on my learning journey, I took every opportunity to interact with people who practiced in coaching and education more generally. It was some of these informal discussions and a desire to continue to challenge my thinking that led me to undertaking an undergraduate degree in Education, PGCE and an MSc in Sports Coaching. Above anything else, the blend of these learning episodes accompanied with my role as a PE teacher, academy coach and coach educator, reinforced my view that thinking critically and beyond coaching alone was a key characteristic that coaches required. The difference now was that I perceived I had developed the knowledge and skills that enabled me to work with coaches in order to develop their level of criticality. This was encapsulated in a blend of context specific coaching knowledge and sound pedagogical underpinnings. I believed I had learnt to move beyond didactic coach education and was ahead of my time in creating empowering, coach-centred learning environments in my approach to better develop and up skill coaches for the modern demands of coaching young players.*

*Over the last few years, coach education in football in England has seen some dramatic changes, namely moving to constructivist, coach-centred delivery within courses, encapsulated in context specific theoretical and practical underpinnings, linked to both coach and player development. Courses are now focused on better appreciating the learning needs of coaches and supporting their learning within the contexts that they coach. Furthermore, assessment of coaching is no longer based on whether coaches are able to follow strict guidelines in terms of what and how they are expected to coach.*

*Reflecting back on my learning experiences and how I believe these to have contributed toward my perceived ability to deliver effective coach education, I feel there can be no doubt that the diverse range of experiences most contributed toward this learning. While this is not to say that all coach educators should follow a similar learning pathway to the one I followed, I would urge coach educators to seek advice and mentoring from educational experts, as much as coaching experts. This enabled me to develop a high level of self-awareness to confirm the ways in which I educated and educate now. My learnings have also taught me that forcing myself out of my comfort zone is crucial to viewing the world through someone else's perspective and the realization that you don't always know as much as you may think you do, until you step in to other contexts.*

## The re-positioning of the role of the coach educator

In Andy's commentary, he described the paradigmatic shift that had taken place in both his own thinking about coach learning and development, and that of the EFA's, from behaviouristic, coach–centred conceptions of learning to constructivist, learner athlete-centred principles. Central to permitting this learning movement was Andy's positioning of himself as a learner who sought opportunities to challenge his thinking. However, in his earliest days as a coach educator, Andy considered he had not developed the capacity to deliver in a constructivist manner, and attributed this to the learning culture in football. The consequence of such a controlled, coach-centred learning environment has led to highly structured coaching sessions and high levels of instruction, management, and feedback (Cushion & Jones, 2006, 2014; Cope, Partington, Cushion, & Harvey, 2016). It has been suggested that these types of learning environments stifle player learning, the development of independent thinking, creativity, and problem solving (Kidman, 2001).

In response to this positioning of the player as a subject to be managed, Andy noted the EFA has in the past few years created a new curricula and blueprint, which they refer to as the England DNA (The EFA, 2014). A component of these new curricula has been to focus on educating coaches in a manner that enables them to create learning environments that allow players to deal with the challenging demands of the game. The changes required for how coaches are expected to coach comes with the need for coach educators to reconsider how they develop coaches' knowledge. In other words, a different type of coach development for coaches is required if they are to be armed with knowledge for developing 'critical thinkers' as opposed to coach-dependent players.

It has been suggested that the creation of an athlete-centred learning environment, whereby players are provided autonomy rather than being controlled and players' perspectives are listened and responded to (as opposed to being spoken at), leads to the development of desirable outcomes (Kidman, 2001) such as those envisaged by the England DNA. For example, an increased motivation to participate, greater levels of enjoyment, and opportunities to learn knowledge and skills required to complete the task at hand (Cope, Harvey, & Kirk, 2015; Kidman, 2001; Light & Harvey, 2017). It stands to reason, therefore, that these are the type of learning environments coach educators should be developing in order to teach coaches ways in which they can deliver in an athlete-centred manner.

## Scaffolding the learning

If coach educators are to base their delivery on athlete-centred concepts, then they will need to think differently about their role within the learning process. As Andy stated, a key element that resulted in the way he perceived himself as educating coaches was his need to move away from telling coaches the right or wrong way to coach, to them developing the knowledge and skills that would allow them to work this out for themselves. A method with the potential to do is scaffolding the learning environment. Based on the work of Vygotsky (1978), scaffolding is the process by which learners are supported by teachers, who modify tasks in order that they are accessible to learners whilst maintaining a level of challenge that is within their zone of proximal development. The notion of scaffolding learning perhaps helps to clarify what a constructivist, athlete-centred learning environment is.

Far from an athlete-centred approach being an approach that is almost entirely 'hands off', it potentially requires a high level of coach educator input. However, rather than this being in an entirely prescriptive and instructional sense, it is through the means of problem setting and supporting that coaches solve their problems (Hmelo-Silver, Duncan, & Chinn, 2007). The extent of the coach educator's input will inevitably vary based on the coach and where they are at in their learning and development. For example, some coaches may need higher levels of support in solving problems than other coaches, and therefore require a different level of support. Consequently, there needs to be some level of mindfulness to not pre-determine what an athlete-centred approach looks like in a coach development setting.

What this means for the role of coach educators is that they need to understand the type of support coaches require, and act accordingly. Andy wrote about this and about how seeking opportunities to learn in the form of professional development was pivotal in his understanding of how to best support coaches. While a scaffolding approach has been suggested, the extent to which this happens will need to change in order to avoid a 'one-size' approach that will rarely be appropriate or effective (Nelson, Cushion, Potrac, & Groom, 2014; Jones & Ronglan, 2017). This is a challenge and entails that coach educators understand the learning needs and wants of each coach and are able to act accordingly. As such, we agree with Hmelo-Silver, Duncan, and Chinn (2007) that athlete-centred coaching is not 'unguided discovery', where coach educators leave coaches to their own devices in the hope that they learn how to deliver the type of environments the EFA espouse. As Dewey (2012) wrote, "Even when a child (or grown up) has a problem, to urge him to think when he has no prior experience involving some of the same conditions, is wholly futile" (p. 12). For coach educators to have the capabilities to scaffold learning appropriately necessitates that they have developed certain levels of knowledge and understanding of how to do this to meet the learning needs of coaches they are responsible for educating. What can be learned from Andy's reflections is that it is important that coach educators continue to see themselves as learners who strive to develop their knowledge and skills, so that they are well placed to understand how to most appropriately educate coaches.

## Developing coach educators' knowledge and skills

There have been suggestions that coaches' transitions into coaching have come as a consequence of a playing career (Blackett, Piggott, & Evans, 2017; Watts & Cushion, 2017). In fact, it seems that to become a coach in elite, professional soccer, playing is a prerequisite, and if this opportunity has been afforded, the process of 'fast tracking' coaches through coaching qualifications is a possibility (Blackett et al., 2017). This means that previous players bypass the entry-level qualifications. The problems with the 'fast-tracking' of players into coaching is that they are unlikely to have developed the underpinning knowledge of learning theory that is required to coach, or indeed the level of criticality to develop self-awareness, which Andy discussed as being so important. Because of this 'fast track', a situation emerges where coaches' practices are based on the practices of their coaches, or those that they have seen coach (Cushion, Armour, & Jones, 2003). Indeed, Andy's coach educator practices in his formative years were because of his socialisation into coach educating. Therefore, this process can also be applied to how coach educators have transitioned into this role.

It would seem the case that coach educators mainly find themselves in this role due to being highly regarded as a coach and having the highest NGB coaching qualifications (something that is normally a requirement in being able to apply for these roles). Just as coaching is not playing (Rynne & Cushion, 2017), coaching is not coach educating. In other words, it requires a different set of knowledge and skills to effectively develop coaches than it does to coach players, and so it should not be assumed that good coaches make good coach educators.

## Content knowledge

Often, the considered 'experts' in coaching are those that possess superior sport-specific knowledge (i.e. understand the technical and tactical components of the sport). However, Andy referred to the knowledge and skills needed to be an effective coach educator as extending well beyond this. As Hattie and Yates (2014) stated, "possessing a high level of knowledge about a topic does not automatically bring with it the ability to teach this topic well" (p. 11). Hattie and Yates (2014) further argued that those with high levels of content knowledge are at risk of not being able to relate to those with less knowledge, and discussed how it felt to be in their position. Pedagogical knowledge is necessary to enable the coach domain-specific content knowledge (football) to be packaged into useful learning experiences in coach education settings.

Borrowing from the work of Shulman (1986) in teaching, Cassidy, Jones, and Potrac (2008) argue that coaches need three types of content knowledge, which consist of subject matter, pedagogy, and curriculum:

- Subject matter content knowledge (SMCK) refers to the coaches' repertoire of knowledge related to the sport or game (Cassidy et al., 2008);
- Pedagogical content knowledge (PCK) is the ability of the coach to rationalise why and when certain practices should be used, and then how coaches transmit information to the learners they are coaching; and
- Curriculum knowledge (CCK) signifies the resources that are available to the coach, and their aptitude in being able to select the most appropriate practices for what they want their learners to learn.

It should also be considered these types of knowledge are also required to be an effective coach educator, and therefore the need to know more than content-related information is critical to this role.

## *Apprenticeships by observation*

Of course, there is no doubt that, just as playing develops a certain set of knowledge or skills that prepares coaches for their role, so too does coaching in preparation for the role of a coach educator. This "apprenticeship of observation", as termed by Lortie (1975), is the period prior to fulfilling a certain role, but when the learning to understand the requirements of the role starts. For example, players start to develop an understanding of the role of a coach by being coached (Pill, 2016). Research undertaken in physical education teacher education would suggest this period to be when beliefs first start to be formed and thus inform future thinking about the knowledge and skills needed to be a physical education teacher (Lawson, 1986; Curtner-Smith, 2001; Curtner-Smith, Hastie, & Kinchin, 2008). This process also happens in coaching and serves as a powerful filter through which all future experiences are conditioned (Cushion et al., 2003). It also serves as the starting point for the developments of the perceived knowledge prospective coach educators consider they require. For Andy, his early experiences were perhaps different to most, but even still, he considered his formative years as a coach educator as based on coach-centred methods of delivery.

The dominant discourse in soccer perpetuates traditional ideologies of coaching, which positions the coach as the primary decision maker and expert who imparts knowledge onto players (Cushion & Jones, 2006; Cope et al., 2016). In coaching, several writings have been underpinned by a Bourdieusian analysis of coach learning and practice (i.e. Christensen, 2009; Cushion et al., 2003; Townsend & Cushion, 2017), with it suggested that the dominant discourses of coaching follow a process of cultural reproduction, as a person's beliefs are constrained by their social worlds (Bourdieu, 1986). In the context of coaching, this means such things as coaches' previous playing careers and their interactions with other coaches inform their perceptions of what coaching is and how it should be done (Cushion & Jones, 2006). As these perceptions become embodied, coaches then start to view all future experiences through this perspective. For example, Harvey, Cushion, and Massa-Gonzalez's study (2010) found that coaches employed coach-centred pedagogies based on the coaching beliefs they formed during their playing careers. However, the same could easily be said for coach educators who have 'learnt' to develop through being developed in coaching. Depending on how coach educators were educated, this will then determine how they develop other coaches. Coaches who have experienced an athlete-centred learning environment are more likely to hold the belief that knowledge is personally constructed, and thus view learning as a complex, interpretive process (Light, 2008). On the other hand, coaches who believe knowledge is acquired dualistically from an external source will view learning as a one-way, positivist process (Light, 2008). Schommer, Crouse, and Rhodes (1992) give an example of how beliefs impact on learning:

If learners believe that knowledge is simple, that is, that knowledge is best characterized as isolated facts, then learners would engage in study that is consistent with this belief. They would plan to memorize the facts and avoid integrating the facts. Furthermore, this same belief would influence the ways in which learners assess their comprehension.

*(p. 435)*

The beliefs about learning that coach educators hold will then determine how they perceive they need to structure the learning environment. Once beliefs are formed, they are difficult to change (Light & Evans, 2013), and so attempting to move coaches from traditional modes of thinking that view coach educators as experts whose role is to transmit knowledge to coaches, towards an approach that sees coach educators and coaches as co-constructors of knowledge is challenging. Therefore, some form of learning development is required that serves to disrupt the induction to common practice. In the case of Andy, this disruption came about through investment in further study. While this may not be a realistic avenue for all coach educators, moving out of comfort zones and engaging people who challenge existing beliefs and practices would seem required.

## Recommendations for helping coach educators move toward an athlete-centred approach to coach educating

Here we provide some recommendations with the purpose of helping coach educators develop a constructivist, athlete-centred approach to their coach development work. These recommendations are not intended to be exhaustive, but rather some strategies which could be considered:

- Coach educators should involve coaches in their learning by asking them what they consider the knowledge they need to acquire to do a better job of coaching specifically in their contexts. This can be validated through having discussions or, better still, observing coaches' practice before they enrol in some form of coach development.
- Coach educators should listen to what coaches are telling them and plan a curriculum accordingly. Therefore, while a curriculum can be developed ahead of time based on the experience and expertise of the coach educator, there needs to be a level of flexibility to enable this to be adapted/amended.
- Coach educators should not assume 'right' or 'wrong' ways to coach, but instead enable coaches to think about what approach would work best, at what time, and why.
- Rather than focusing on developing coaches' knowledge of what to coach, coach educators should think about developing coaches' knowledge of how to think, so that they are able to work out what the most appropriate coaching approach might be and increase their levels of self-awareness.

## Conclusion

This chapter has discussed the role, knowledge, and skills of coach educators in football who seek to move toward developing a constructivist, athlete-centred learning environment as espoused by the EFA. To meet this purpose, we drew upon the reflections and experiences of one coach educator who has perceived himself to have developed an understanding of how to move from delivering coach education based on behaviouristic, coach-centred principles to delivering based on constructivist, athlete-centred principles. In order to learn to structure a learning environment based on constructivist principles, a great deal of time and investment in a multitude of different learning situations are required. As such, we suggest that training for coach educators and entry into this role needs to be more rigorous and systematic, if they are to have acquired the pedagogical, content, and curriculum knowledge and skills needed to develop the appropriate knowledge and skills coaches require to undertake their role effectively.

## References

Abraham, A., & Collins, D. (1998). Examining and extending research in coach development. *Quest*, *50*(1), 59–79.

Blackett, A. D., Evans, A., & Piggott, D. (2017). Why 'the best way of learning to coach the game is playing the game': Conceptualising 'fast-tracked' high-performance coaching pathways. *Sport, Education and Society*, *22*(6), 744–758.

Bourdieu, P. (1986). *Distinction: A social critique of the judgement of taste*. London: Routledge.

Cassidy, T. G., Jones, R. L., & Potrac, P. (2008). *Understanding sports coaching: The social, cultural and pedagogical foundations of coaching practice*. London: Routledge.

Chesterfield, G., Potrac, P., & Jones, R. (2010). 'Studentship' and 'impression management' in an advanced soccer coach education award. *Sport, Education and Society*, *15*(3), 299–314.

Christensen, M. K. (2009). 'An eye for talent': Talent identification and the 'practical sense' of top-level soccer coaches. *Sociology of Sport Journal*, *26*(3), 365–382.

Cope, E., Harvey, S., & Kirk, D. (2015). Reflections on using visual research methods in sports coaching. *Qualitative Research in Sport, Exercise and Health*, *7*(1), 88–108.

Cope, E., Partington, M., Cushion, C. J., & Harvey, S. (2016). An investigation of professional top-level youth football coaches' questioning practice. *Qualitative Research in Sport, Exercise and Health*, *8*(4), 380–393.

Côté, J., & Gilbert, W. (2009). An integrative definition of coaching effectiveness and expertise. *International Journal of Sports Science & Coaching*, *4*(3), 307–323.

Curtner-Smith, M. D. (2001). The occupational socialization of a first-year physical education teacher with a teaching orientation. *Sport, Education and Society*, *6*(1), 81–105.

Curtner-Smith, M. D., Hastie, P. A., & Kinchin, G. D. (2008). Influence of occupational socialization on beginning teachers' interpretation and delivery of sport education. *Sport, Education and Society*, *13*(1), 97–117.

Cushion, C. J., Armour, K. M., & Jones, R. L. (2003). Coach education and continuing professional development: Experience and learning to coach. *Quest*, *55*(3), 215–230.

Cushion, C. J., & Jones, R. L. (2006). Power, discourse, and symbolic violence in professional youth soccer: The case of Albion Football Club. *Sociology of Sport Journal*, *23*(2), 142–161.

Cushion, C. J., & Jones, R. L. (2014). A Bourdieusian analysis of cultural reproduction: Socialisation and the 'hidden curriculum' in professional football. *Sport, Education and Society*, *19*(3), 276–298.

Dewey, J. (2012). *How we think.* Boston, CT: D.C. Heath & Co Publishers.

The English Football Association. (2014). Retrieved from https://community.thefa.com/england_dna/

Gilbert, W. D., & Trudel, P. (2004). Role of the coach: How model youth team sport coaches frame their roles. *The Sport Psychologist, 18*(1), 21–43.

Harvey, S., Cushion, C. J., & Massa-Gonzalez, A. N. (2010). Learning a new method: Teaching Games for Understanding in the coaches' eyes. *Physical Education and Sport Pedagogy, 15*(4), 361–382.

Hattie, J., & Yates, G. (2014). *Visible learning and the science of how we learn.* London: Routledge.

Hmelo-Silver, C. E., Duncan, R. G., & Chinn, C. A. (2007). Scaffolding and achievement in problem-based and inquiry learning: A response to Kirschner, Sweller, and Clark (2006). *Educational Psychologist, 42*(2), 99–107.

Jones, R. L. (2000). Toward a sociology of coaching. In R. L. Jones & K. Armour (Eds.), *The sociology of sport: Theory and practice* (pp. 33–43). London: Routledge.

Jones, R. L., Armour, K. M., & Potrac, P. (2004). *Sports coaching cultures: From practice to theory.* London: Routledge.

Jones, R. L., Potrac, P., Cushion, C., & Ronglan, L. T. (2010). *The sociology of sports coaching.* London: Routledge.

Jones, R. L., & Ronglan, L. T. (2017). What do coaches orchestrate? Unravelling the 'quiddity' of practice. *Sport, Education and Society*, First article, 1–11.

Jones, R. L., & Turner, P. (2006). Teaching coaches to coach holistically: Can problem-based learning (PBL) help? *Physical Education and Sport Pedagogy, 11*(2), 181–202.

Kidman, L. (2001). *Developing decision makers: An empowerment approach to coaching.* Queensland: IPC Print Resources.

Lawson, H. A. (1986). Occupational socialization and the design of teacher education programs. *Journal of Teaching in Physical Education, 5*(2), 107–116.

Light, R. L. (2008). Complex learning theory – its epistemology and its assumptions about learning: Implications for physical education. *Journal of Teaching in Physical Education, 27*(1), 21–37.

Light, R. L., & Evans, J. R. (2013). Dispositions of elite-level Australian rugby coaches towards game sense: Characteristics of their coaching habitus. *Sport, Education and Society, 18*(3), 407–423.

Light, R. L., & Harvey, S. (2017). Positive pedagogy for sport coaching. *Sport, Education and Society, 22*(2), 271–287.

Lortie, D. (1975). *Schoolteacher: A sociological analysis.* Chicago: University of Chicago.

Lucas, B., Claxton, G., & Spencer, E. (2013). *Expansive education: Teaching learners for the real world.* Boston, MA: McGraw-Hill Education.

Nelson, L. J., & Cushion, C. J. (2006). Reflection in coach education: The case of the national governing body coaching certificate. *The Sport Psychologist, 20*(2), 174–183.

Nelson, L. J., Cushion, C. J., & Potrac, P. (2013). Enhancing the provision of coach education: The recommendations of UK coaching practitioners. *Physical Education and Sport Pedagogy, 18*(2), 204–218.

Nelson, L. J., Cushion, C. J., Potrac, P., & Groom, R. (2014). Carl Rogers, learning and educational practice: Critical considerations and applications in sports coaching. *Sport, Education and Society, 19*(5), 513–531.

Pill, S. (2016). Implementing game sense coaching approach in Australian football through action research. *Agora for Physical Education and Sport, 18*(1), 1–19.

Rynne, S., & Cushion, C. (2017). *Playing is not coaching: Why so many sporting greats struggle as coaches.* Retrieved from http://theconversation.com/playing-is-not-coaching-why-so-many-sporting-greats-struggle-as-coaches-71625

Schommer, M., Crouse, A., & Rhodes, N. (1992). Epistemological beliefs and mathematical text comprehension: Believing it is simple does not make it so. *Journal of Educational Psychology, 84*(4), 435.

Shulman, L. S. (1986). Those who understand: Knowledge growth in teaching. *Educational Researcher, 15*(2), 4–14.

Stodter, A., & Cushion, C. J. (2014). Coaches' learning and education: A case study of cultures in conflict. *Sports Coaching Review, 3*(1), 63–79.

Townsend, R. C., & Cushion, C. (2017). Elite cricket coach education: A Bourdieusian analysis. *Sport, Education and Society, 22*(4), 528–546.

Vygotsky, L. (1978). Interaction between learning and development. *Readings on the Development of Children, 23*(3), 34–41.

Watts, D. W., & Cushion, C. J. (2017). Coaching journeys: Longitudinal experiences from professional football in Great Britain. *Sports Coaching Review, 6*(1), 76–93.

# 17

# APPLYING THE GAME SENSE APPROACH AND MOSSTON AND ASHWORTH'S INCLUSION STYLE-E TO PROMOTE ATHLETE-CENTRED TENNIS COACHING WITH JUNIOR NOVICE PLAYERS

*Mitchell Hewitt, Ken Edwards, Machar Reid and Shane Pill*

Traditionally, the practices of tennis coaches have been characterised by high levels of direct verbal instruction with an emphasis on isolated skill development and technical mastery prior to the tactical aspects of the game (Crespo, Reid, & Miley, 2004). Under these instructional conditions, the coach has been responsible for the unidirectional transmission of this information to athletes who have adopted a largely passive role in the teaching and learning process (Jones, 2006). This coaching behaviour often leads to a highly controlled, coach-centred and structured environment (Byra, 2006). In contrast, we identify that tennis players should participate in activities which promote development in four central domains – the physical (technique), social (interaction), cognitive (decision-making) and affective (fun and enjoyment) domains – as part of an athlete-centred philosophy. Generally, this philosophy empowers players with greater autonomy and choice in the learning process. Within the tennis coaching context, coaching with an athlete-centred philosophy should lead to contexts that encourage players to use problem-solving to explore solutions to various movement challenges. The coach enacts this via appropriate questioning techniques and choice in a game-based environment. In using tennis as an exemplar, we demonstrate how the principles of the Game Sense approach (den Duyn, 1997), informed by Inclusion Style-E from the Spectrum of Teaching (Mosston & Ashworth, 2008), may be practically applied to a range of tennis activities to promote an athlete-centred approach with junior and novice tennis players.

## The complex nature of coaching tennis

A foremost function of sports coaches is to assist players in the development of skills required to perform effectively during game-play. A key feature of this pedagogical process is "the activities in which coaches have their athletes engage in and the instructional behaviours used during these activities" (Ford, Yates, & Williams, 2010, p. 483). The complex nature of coaching should be understood in order to design relevant programs to adequately meet the diverse needs of the player. Launder (2001) indicates that coaching is a highly complex discipline that requires a vast array of knowledge, capabilities, dispositions and skills to be brought together in a dynamic, flexible way to manage and orchestrate complicated learning environments that are socially situated. He also suggests that "above all the coach must be the master of the instantaneous response in which professional and personal skills are skillfully fused and rapidly applied in complex environments to attain quality learner outcomes" (Launder, 2001, p. 2). In essence, the sport coach in this definition is an educator, and the player a learner. The behaviour of coaches acts as an avenue to link player understanding to the content presented in the session (Hall & Smith, 2006). Consequently, we agree that it is crucial that coaches "consider the objectives of the session, so that he or she can determine whether given behaviors are relevant to the task" (Lyle & Cushion, 2010, p. 52). We also affirm that effective coaches have the ability to "tailor their content and instruction to the specific learning readiness and interests of their students, by integrating concepts and implementing teaching strategies that are responsive to the students' diverse needs" (Lyle & Cushion, 2010, p. 52).

## Instructional practices and tennis

Much has been written about the various instructional practices and behaviours available for coaches to employ during coaching sessions (Lyle & Cushion, 2010). Traditionally, the educational association between tennis coach and player has been predominantly autocratic and prescriptive. Under these instructional conditions, the coach has been considered as the "sole source of knowledge and has been responsible for the unidirectional transmission of this information to athletes who have adopted a largely passive role in the teaching and learning process" (Jones, 2006, p. 43). The coach usually explains, demonstrates, organises and conducts the lesson, in addition to providing explicit feedback in order to correct players' errors (Crespo & Reid, 2009). The term most commonly linked to this instructional practice is a 'direct coaching' style. This coaching style implies a "highly structured, teacher-centred and controlled instructional environment" (Byra, 2006, p. 452). Other terms that have been used to describe this style include: command, explicit, prescriptive, coach-centred and teacher-centred.

This coaching style (the coach *tells* and the players *do*) has traditionally been accompanied by the coach employing a variety of 'skill-drill' activities that focus on isolated skill development and technical mastery prior to the development of a tactical application (or an authentic and actual game-related context during practice). This is a practice described by Kirk (2010) as sport-as-sport-techniques. The emphasis is placed on "skill acquisition, measurement, and evaluation which promote the quantification of isolated techniques" (Oslin & Mitchell, 2006, p. 628).

Isolated 'skill-drills' are characterised by practicing the "same skill over and over with little adaption required" (Breed & Spittle, 2011, p. 56). This type of practice is also commonly referred to as a 'technique-centred' coaching approach.

Technique-centred approaches are founded on the analysis of particular 'ways' of movement coordination, commonly referred to as techniques, that are considered fundamental pre-requisites to playing games. These technical aspects of the particular sport are required to be sufficiently developed before being employed in game-play (Light, 2013). Breed and Spittle (2011) suggest that technique-centred approaches "encourage teachers and coaches to focus on *how* to do a skill, before they teach *why*" (p. 8). Traditionally, effective tennis coaching was commonly associated with this linear process of technique practice leading to game-play. Lessons would invariably commence with an explanation, demonstration, drill and practice of skills (invariably where the coach feeds balls) as lead-up activities to a game (often characterised by a full game of tennis) (Hoffman, 1971). Additional terms that have been used to describe analogous instructional practices include: traditional, technique-centred and skill-based.

## Athlete-centred approach

In contrast to the more traditionally common forms of tennis instructional practices just described, an athlete-centred approach outlines a process by which players are enabled influence over the decisions that impact on their learning and performance in sporting experiences (Kidman & Lombardo, 2010). With an emphasis on catering to individual needs, coaches informed by an athlete-centred perspective empower players with greater autonomy to afford "ownership of knowledge, development and decision-making that will help them to maximise their performance and their enjoyment" (Kidman & Lombardo, 2010, p. 13). An athlete-centred perspective does not relieve the coach from making decisions, but rather shifts their responsibilities to guide engagement in problem-solving in conjunction with the player as opposed to prescription (Hadfield, 1994) – prescription being a common behaviour in more traditional technique and coach-centred approaches. Benefits ascribed to employing an athlete-centred approach include: increased motivation to learn, an elevated understanding and retention of the tactical and technical elements of game-play, in addition to fostering self-awareness and self-sufficiency (Kidman & Lombardo, 2010).

The central pedagogical components associated with creating an athlete-centred tennis coaching environment are learning skills within the context of a game (at least initially), as opposed to developing technique in isolation and separate from the tactical application, and the practice of questioning players (Kidman & Hanrahan, 2004; Pill & Hewitt, 2017). Learning through play in situations that are representative of the game is postulated as providing players with an understanding of the game, and how to apply skill and technique under 'pressure' of competing with an opponent (Pill & Hewitt, 2017). It is assumed that when athletes are afforded the opportunity to play or practice in a situation that is "uncluttered by coaches telling them what to do and where to go, they are more productive in terms of learning in context, and become more motivated through challenges, social interactions and decision making" (Kidman & Hanrahan, 2004, p. 25).

Purposeful questions designed to promote problem-solving and player choice and engagement in the learning (Kidman & Hanrahan, 2004) are a key tenet of the Game Sense approach (den Duyn, 1997). The pedagogical prominence on the coach's use of well-considered questions to create reflective moments, a debate of ideas and the guided discovery of tactical and technical concepts distinguishes the Game Sense approach from the more historically common 'sport as sport techniques' (Kirk, 2010) – commonly referred to as coach-centred or teacher-centred. However, the purposeful use of questions designed to promote player dialogue that encourages skill learning in the context of the game makes Game Sense an athlete-centred approach (Kidman, 2005).

Research by Hewitt (2015) has shown that Australian tennis coaches still use a traditionally common technique-focussed and coach-centred approach. Even when coaches believed they were using a game-based approach, directive and command style coaching still formed the dominant verbal behaviour of the coaches.

## The Game Sense approach as athlete-centred tennis coaching

The Game Sense approach is the pedagogical preference for sport coaching promoted by the Australian Sports Commission (2017). The Game Sense approach (den Duyn, 1997) has been aligned to an athlete-centred instructional practice as a game-based practice environment that incorporates the concepts of inquiry and guided discovery (Thorpe, 2005). In this way, players learn how to search and select information from the game environment, solve problems and explore solutions to various movement challenges, in collaboration with the coach. Unlike traditional pedagogical framing of sport teaching as a technical-to-tactical progression, the Game Sense approach highlights the complementarity of tactical and technical components of skilled performance at all levels of game development in the original Game Sense equation: technique + game context = skill ('game context' refers to elements such as pressure, decision-making, timing, use of space and risk) (den Duyn, 1997).

The key conceptual elements of the Game Sense approach have significantly enhanced the successful implementation of Tennis Australia's modified tennis program – Tennis Hot Shots (Tennis Australia, 2012). Each activity in the program attempts to promote the central feature of the game of tennis – the rally (projection and reception) in combination with technical skills and relevant tactical elements. In this game-centred approach, all players 'play with purpose' (Pill, 2013a) and develop their skills by:

- Knowing what to do in the context of play (decision-making);
- Knowing how to do it (movement knowledge); and
- Being able to execute the 'how' and 'what' successfully (movement capability) (Pill, 2013a).

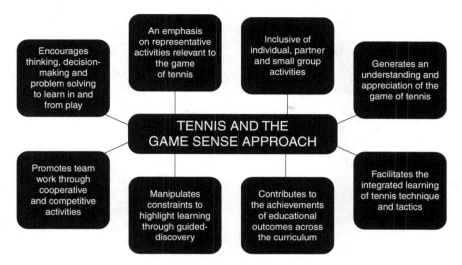

**FIGURE 17.1** Key conceptual features of the Game Sense approach featuring in Tennis Australia's junior tennis program – Hot Shots.

(Reproduced with the permission of Tennis Australia).

Tennis coaches and teachers are encouraged to adopt a variety of instructional strategies or a 'toolkit' of teaching processes (Pill, 2011). The key conceptual features of the Game Sense approach adopted by Tennis Australia's junior tennis program – Hot Shots – are summarised in Figure 17.1. The variety of instructional styles that may be used will be highlighted during the explanation of the games to follow.

## The Game Sense approach in practice

The game 'Groundstroke Scramble' in Figure 17.2 illustrates the key conceptual features of the Game Sense approach applied to tennis. The central feature of the game of tennis, the rally (projection and reception of a ball), in combination with the technical skill of striking with a racket and the relevant tactical elements associated with returning the ball and winning the point, are represented. Initially, the serve is simplified to a 'drop and hit'. The play space is reduced to make it easier for players to get to the ball and return it. The racket is modified to make it lighter and to bring the contact point closer to the hand, with a shorter head stem than a normal racket. A compression ball that is bigger and bounces more than a normal ball (while also not being able to be hit as far as a normal ball) is also used. These modifications represent the task and environment constraints changed to reduce the complexity of the game while maintaining the representation of the rally (projection and reception of a ball) in the game. The pedagogical use of problem-solving and questions to guide tactical and technical game development is also demonstrated by the 'Change It' feature (Schembri, 2005) in Figure 17.2.

## Game: 'Groundstroke Scramble'

**Organisational layout:** Players form pairs and are positioned at opposite ends of the court

**Tactical problem:** Players apply tennis stokes and explore ways to win the point using the width and length of the court

1   Players form pairs and are positioned at opposite ends of the court
2   Player 1 commences the rally with a drop hit or overarm serve
3   Players rally the ball until an error is made
4   Players are not permitted to volley the ball
5   The rally continues until the ball bounces twice before being hit, the ball lands outside the court space, the ball hits the net
6   Players alternate commencing the point
7   Play first to 10 points or until teacher calls "time"

### *Pause to ask questions (examples of focus questions)*

*   Identify the type of shots and positions on the court you may hit the ball to attack?
*   How may you reposition your opponent to win the point?
*   Where are the most desirable positions on the court to hit the ball?
*   If your opponent is forced wide on the court, where might you hit the ball? What about if your opponent is close to the net?
*   How do you position your body to control the direction of the ball?

## CHANGE IT (scale the challenge up or down to change the challenge point for players)

*   Reduce the player area
*   Use a smaller/lighter racket
*   Use a larger ball

The pedagogical use of questions to guide tactical and technical game development is shown in Figure 17.2 as a 'tactical time-out' in the game. Questioning from the coach can also occur in reflective moments created at the end of a defined period to debate ideas (Grehaigne, Richard, & Griffin, 2005) or when a 'teachable moment' is identified by the coach (Launder, 2001). The application of questions in preference to directive instruction is perhaps the pedagogical distinctiveness of the Game Sense approach and why it has been identified as athlete-centred coaching (Thorpe, 2005) by shifting the cognitive load for 'thinking' to the player (Light, 2013).

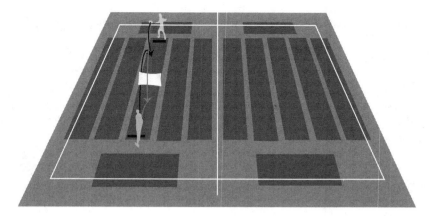

**FIGURE 17.2**   Game: 'Groundstroke Scramble' instructions and game illustration. (Reproduced with the permission of Tennis Australia).

## Guided discovery Style-F

The explicit process of using questions to purposefully build conceptual understanding of tactical concepts in a Game Sense approach (and other tactical approaches) has been described as guided discovery (Hopper & Kruisselbrink, 2001; Hubball, Lambert, & Hayes, 2007; Pill, 2008). Inquiry and guided discovery is often associated with Mosston and Ashworth's (2008) description of Guided Discovery Style-F. In this style, the development of questions led to a pre-determined learning objective such as an identified principle of play, strategy or technical aspect of movement performance. Certain teaching styles, such as Style-F, on *The Spectrum* (2008) are designed to empower players with increased autonomy in the learning process by shifting decisions from the coach to the player.

Like the Game Sense approach, the structure of *The Spectrum* (Mosston & Ashworth, 2008) is underpinned by the central premise that "teaching is governed by a single unified process: decision-making" (p. 8). Teaching decisions are organised into three sets that comprise the *anatomy of any style*. These sets are the *pre-impact set*, *impact set* and *post-impact set*. The *pre-impact set* involves making decisions in relation to planning the teacher–learner interaction. The *impact set* relates to implementing the decisions that occur during the teacher–learner face-to-face interaction. The *post-impact set* refers to assessment decisions that may occur at any point during the face-to-face interaction by either the teacher or the learner and to assessment decisions about the overall learning experience that occur after the face-to-face interaction (Mosston & Ashworth, 2008). By identifying who (i.e., the teacher of the learner) makes which decisions, the actual teaching styles emerge. The Inclusion Style-E teaching style located on *The Spectrum* (2008) affords coaches with an instructional practice that promotes the empowerment of the player in selecting tasks that cater to their specific developmental readiness, interest and motivation – features that are representative of an athlete-centred approach.

Illustrating these points in practice, the game of 'Three Point Play' depicted in Figure 17.3 includes the same pedagogical features of questioning, manipulation of task, performer and environment constraints to develop play with purpose and game simplification (while retaining the key representative rules of the game of tennis) used in Groundstroke Scramble (Figure 17.2). However, in this game, tactical appreciation of transitioning to the net and performing a volley to the opponent's court space, and then further development of understanding when to transition to the net and where to place the volley is fostered through manipulation of scoring. In this case, three points are awarded if the player wins the point as a result of a volley.

## Game: 'Three Point Play'

**Organisational layout:** Players form pairs and are positioned at opposite ends of the court

**Tactical problem:** Players explore ways to win the point by transitioning to the net and performing a volley

1  Players form pairs and are positioned at opposite ends of the court
2  Player 1 commences the rally with a drop hit or overarm serve
3  Players rally the ball until an error is made
4  Players are awarded 3 points if they successfully win the point as a result of the volley
5  Players alternate commencing the point
6  Play first to 12 points or until teacher calls "time"

### *Pause to ask questions*

- What are the benefits of hitting an approach shot and moving to the net to perform a volley?
- Where are the most desirable positions on the court to hit an approach shot? Why?
- How do you prevent your opponent from approaching the net?
- Where should you stand at the net after hitting an approach shot? Why?
- How do you determine where to hit the volley?

Pursuing the pedagogical concept of game modification by manipulation of task constraints to develop 'play with purpose' (Pill, 2013a), the scoring system of 'Three Point Play' has been varied to include (for example) an exaggeration of scoring. Three points are accrued if the player wins the rally as a result of a

**FIGURE 17.3**    Game: 'Three Point Play'.

(Reproduced with the permission of Tennis Australia).

volley, while maintaining one point for a shot landing elsewhere in the court. This constraint invites a debate of ideas around the strategy of attempting a one point play and a three point play, and the potential for tactical 'if–then thinking' being encouraged. Bell and Penney (2004) explained that this type of thinking is encouraged when the player is able to be involved in problem-solving where there is an appropriate association between certain game conditions and an action (solution).

The lens of Inclusion Style-E to the game 'Three Point Play' may be used to explain the constraints placed on the players within the task. For example, the players could be offered a range of choices and task entry level decisions to create their own challenge point (see Figure 17.4). Whereas in the common form of tennis, the ball is only permitted to bounce once in court, players may be offered the choice of one or two bounces to play the ball based on where they believe their challenge point lies in the game. Similarly, players may be afforded the choice to substitute rackets to use their hands to catch and throw the ball during the game. Alternatively, players may also have the option of first tapping the ball with the racket to first control the ball, with or without letting the tapped ball bounce after being hit for control, before hitting the ball back over the net. *The Spectrum*'s Inclusion Style-E (Mosston & Ashworth, 2008) describes this differentiation of challenge point by allowing the players to make decisions in relation to where they select the level of task performance (Mosston & Ashworth, 2008).

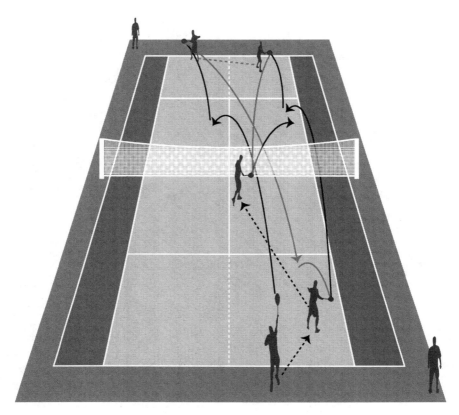

**FIGURE 17.4** Game: 'Three Point Play' – Inclusion Style-E with player choice.

(Reproduced with the permission of Tennis Australia).

## Player choice

- Players decide to let the ball bounce once or twice during the game
- Players decide to substitute rackets for hands to throw and catch during the game
- Players decide to trap the ball on their racket during the game before continuing the rally
- Players decide to tap the ball on their racket during the game before continuing the rally

## Differentiated instructional model

The objective of *The Spectrum*'s Inclusion Style-E (Mosston & Ashworth, 2008) is for players to participate in a task and learn to select an appropriate level of difficulty at which they may perform the task and to examine their performance. Entry level decisions, and, if necessary, adjustment decisions and self-assessment decisions (guided by specific teacher prepared criteria) are made by the players. The role of the player is "to survey the available levels in the task, select an entry point, practice the task, if necessary make an adjustment in the task level, and check performance against criteria" (Mosston & Ashworth, 2008, p. 15).

One concept that advocates the development of coaching content, practices and behaviours specifically designed to cater to player needs is the notion of differentiation (Graham, 1995; Tomlinson, 1995; Tomlinson, 1999). According to the differentiated instructional model (Tomlinson, 1999), coaches "respond to the needs of all learners, with consideration being given to the student's readiness, interest, and capabilities" (Whipp, Taggart, & Jackson, 2012, p. 2). Implementing a more individualised and context-dependent approach is linked to the notion of athlete-centred coaching.

## Conclusion

Reid, Crespo, Lay, and Berry (2007) suggested that historically, tennis practice has typically consisted of activities devoid of discernibly specific goals or objectives and unlikely to optimise a player's long-term performance development. It is considered that drill-practice based activities where sport is essentially presented as sport-as-sport techniques (Kirk, 2010) is problematised for its potential to engage, sustain and hold enthusiasm for sport participation in the long-term (Pill, 2013b). However, contrary to the educational convictions of Australian sport coach education materials, tennis coaches in Australia by and large still do not offer players developmental opportunities beyond a limited technical range due to a narrow pedagogical mix in their coaching (Hewitt, Edwards, Ashworth, & Pill, 2016; Hewitt, Edwards, & Pill, 2016).

In this chapter, we have argued for 'play with purpose' to guide the tactical and technical development via a practice workspace that is game-based and athlete-centred. This is achieved via the pedagogical emphasis of guided discovery and the fostering of player reflection and choice through the well-considered use of questions to develop tactical and technical game performance. We have also illustrated how the pedagogical 'toolkit' of the Game Sense approach can be applied to tennis coaching, and how Mosston and Ashworth's Inclusion Style-E provides coaches with a conceptual tool to understand the impact of their pedagogical decision-making, so that coaches can be responsive to an athlete-centred philosophy. While we have focussed on tennis, the descriptions provided may be applied to other games in the net/court/wall category, such as badminton, squash, table tennis and volleyball.

## References

Australian Sports Commission. (2017). *Legacy of the active after school communities Program*. Clearing House for Sport. Retrieved from www.clearinghouseforsport.gov.au/knowledge_base/sport_participation/community_engagement/community_sport_coaching

Bell, T., & Penney, D. (2004). PlaySmart: Developing thinking and problem-solving skills in the context of the national curriculum in physical education in England. In J. Wright, D. MacDonald, & L. Burrows (Eds.), *Critical inquiry and problem solving in physical education* (pp. 49–61). New York: Routledge.

Breed, R., & Spittle, M. (2011). *Developing game sense through tactical learning: A resource for teachers and coaches*. Melbourne, VIC: Cambridge University Press.

Byra, M. (2006). Teaching styles and inclusive pedagogies. In D. Kirk, D. Macdonald, & M. O'Sullivan (Eds.), *The handbook of physical education* (pp. 449–446). London: Sage.

Crespo, M., & Reid, M. (2009). *Coaching beginner and intermediate tennis players*. Spain: International Tennis Federation (ITF).

Crespo, M., Reid, M., & Miley, D. (2004). Tennis: Applied examples of a game-based teaching approach. *Strategies: A Journal for Physical Education and Sport Educators*, *17*(4), 27–30.

den Duyn, N. (1997). *Game sense: Developing thinking players workbook*. Canberra: Australian Sports Commission.

Ford, P. R., Yates, I., & Williams, M. (2010). An analysis of practice activities and instructional behaviours used by youth soccer coaches during practice: Exploring the link between science and application. *Journal of Sports Sciences*, *28*(5), 483–495.

Graham, G. (1995). Physical education through students' eyes and in students' voices. *Journal of Teaching in Physical Education*, *14*(4), 364–371.

Grehaigne, J-F., Richard, J-F., & Griffin, L. (2005). *Teaching and learning team sports and games*. New York: Routledge.

Hall, T. J., & Smith, M. A. (2006). Teacher planning and reflection: What we know about teacher cognitive processes. *Quest*, *58*, 424–442.

Hadfield, D. C. (1994). The Query Theory: A sports coaching model for the 90s. *The New Zealand Coach*, *3*(4), 16–20.

Hoffman, S. (1971). Traditional methodology: Prospects for change. *Quest*, *15*, 55–57.

Hewitt, M. (2015). *Teaching styles of Australian tennis coaches: An exploration of practices and insights using Mosston and Ashworth's spectrum of teaching styles*. PhD Thesis, School of Linguistics, Adult and Specialist Education, The University of Southern Queensland.

Hewitt, M., Edwards, K., Ashworth, S., & Pill, S. (2016). Investigating the teaching styles of tennis coaches using the *Spectrum: Sport Science Review*, *25*(5/6), 321–344.

Hewitt, M., Edwards, K., & Pill, S. (2016, November 19–20 2015). Teaching styles of Australian junior tennis coaches. In J. Bruce & C. North (Eds.), *2015 Game sense for teachers and coaches conference: Proceedings* (pp. 40–52). New Zealand: School of Sport and Physical Education, University of Canterbury.

Hoffman, S.J. (1971). Traditional methodology: Prospects for change. *Quest*, *23*(1), 51–57.

Hopper, T., & Kruisselbrink, D. (2001). Teaching Games for Understanding: What does it look like and how does it influence student skill acquisition and game performance? *Journal of Teaching Physical Education*. Retrieved from http://web.uvic.ca/~thopper/WEB/articles/JTPE/TGFU.htm

Hubball, H., Lambert, J., & Hayes, S. (2007). Theory to practice: Using the Games for Understanding approach in the teaching of invasion games. *Physical and Health Education Journal*, *73*(3), 14–20.

Jones, R. L. (2006). *The sports coach as educator: Re-conceptualising sports coaching*. London: Routledge.

Kidman, L. (2005). *Athlete-centred coaching: Developing decision makers*. Worcester, UK: IPC Print Resources.

Kidman, L., & Hanrahan, S.J. (2011). *The coaching process: A practical guide to becoming an effective sports coach* (3rd ed.). London: Routledge.

Kidman, L., & Lombardo, B. (2010). *Athlete-centered coaching: Developing decision makers* (2nd ed.). Worcester: Innovative Print Communications Ltd.

Kirk, D. (2010). *Physical education futures.* New York: Routledge.

Launder, A. G. (2001). *Play practice: The games approach to teaching and coaching sports.* Champaign, IL: Human Kinetics.

Light, R. (2013). *Game sense: Pedagogy for performance, participation and enjoyment.* New York: Routledge.

Lyle, J., & Cushion, C. (Eds.) (2010). *Sports coaching: Professionalisation and practice.* Edinburgh: Churchill Livingston Elsevier.

Mosston, M., & Ashworth, S. (2008). *Teaching physical education* (1st ed.). Online: Spectrum Institute for Teaching and Learning. Retrieved March 10, 2009, from http://www.spectrumofteachingstyles.org/e-book-download.php

Oslin, J., & Mitchell, S. (2006). Game-centred approaches to teaching physical education. In D. Kirk, D. Macdonald, & M. O'Sullivan (Eds.), *The handbook of physical education* (pp. 627–651). London: Sage.

Pill, S. (2008). Teaching Games for Understanding. *Sport Coach, 29*(2), 27–29.

Pill, S. (2011). Seizing the moment: Can game sense further inform sport teaching in Australian physical education. *Physical and Health Education Academic Journal, 3*(1), 1–15.

Pill, S. (2013a). *Play with purpose: Game sense to sport literacy.* Hindmarsh, SA: ACHPER Publications.

Pill, S. (2013b). Teaching Australian football in physical education: Constraints theory in practice. *Strategies: A Journal for Physical and Sport Educators, 26*(1), 39–44.

Pill, S., & Hewitt, M. (2017). Tennis coaching: Applying the game sense approach. *Strategies, 30*(2), 10–16.

Reid, M., Crespo, M., Lay, B., & Berry, J. (2007). Skill acquisition in tennis: Research and current practice. *Journal of Science and Medicine in Sport, 10*, 1–10.

Schembri, G. (2005). *Playing for life coach's guide.* Belconnen, ACT: Australian Sports Commission.

Tennis Australia. (2012). *MLC Tennis hot shots in schools.* Melbourne, VIC: Tennis Australia.

Thorpe, R. (2005). Rod Thorpe on Teaching Games for Understanding. In L. Kidman (Ed.), *Athlete-centred coaching: Developing and inspiring people* (pp. 229–244). Christchurch, NZ: Innovative Print Communications.

Tomlinson, C. A. (1995). Deciding to differentiate instruction in middle school: One school's journey. *Gifted Child Journal, 39*(2), 77–87.

Tomlinson, C. A. (1999). *The differentiated classroom: Responding to the needs of all learners.* Alexandria, VA: Association for Supervision and Curriculum Development.

Whipp, P., Taggart, A., & Jackson, B. (2012). Differentiation in outcome-focused physical education: Pedagogical rhetoric and reality. *Physical Education and Sport Pedagogy, 7*(12), 1–11.

# 18

# ATHLETE-CENTRED COACHING

## Tensions and opportunities arising in the masters context

*Chris Zehntner and Dawn Penney*

There is growing impetus for critical reflection into the application of athlete-centred coaching in order to advance research in the area and more meaningfully outline the ways in which this coaching practice is currently enacted and how it may be developed (Kidman & Penney, 2014). This chapter reflects on the paucity of empirical research that investigates athlete-centred coaching, and particularly research that frames athlete-centred coaching theory and practice as it relates to swim coaching and the masters athlete context. The chapter therefore presents a conceptualisation of athlete-centred coaching that foregrounds philosophical and cultural perspectives and provides ethnographic insights into coach and athlete experiences of athlete-centred coaching being enacted in masters swimming. It thereby seeks to extend understandings of how athlete-centred coaching is framed and practiced within the culture of masters swim coaching.

As a discrete sporting culture, masters swim coaching provides a unique field in which researchers can consider how athlete-centred coaching is interpreted and enacted as well as the various impacts of an athlete-centred approach (McMahon & Zehntner, 2014). In the first section of the chapter, we therefore address the philosophical underpinnings of athlete-centred coaching in the masters context, elaborate on the masters athlete identity and critically examine the relationship between athlete-centred coaching and contemporary sporting and coaching cultures (particularly associated with masters swimming). This provides a basis from which to turn attention to the practical challenges and opportunities of enacting athlete-centred coaching with masters swimmers. In the second section, we draw on ethnographic representations to examine the pedagogical enactment of athlete-centred coaching and explore how various pedagogical practices arise in support or sit in contradiction to the contemporary culture(s) of masters swimming. Brief evocative accounts of the experiences of the authors are used to illuminate the philosophical, cultural and practical elements of athlete-centred coaching in relation to masters swimmers from both a researcher–coach and researcher–athlete perspective. The accounts serve to bring to the fore points of tensions and alignment between the culture(s) of masters swimming and the culture(s) of masters swim coaching. Our discussion points to a need for extended understanding of culture to inform reflection on the meaning and prospective future enactment of athlete-centred coaching in contexts of masters swimming.

## What is athlete-centred coaching in the masters swimmer context?

The philosophical underpinnings of athlete-centred coaching are developed in Kidman's (2001) progression of Lombardo's (1987) work on humanistic coaching to elaborate on how athlete empowerment links to an increased motivation to learn, understand and internalise the athletic skills critical to success. Kidman (2001) called on coaches to consider such an approach and critically reflect on traditional and disempowering coaching styles that they may have experienced as an athlete. The athlete-centred approach to coaching is relatively well represented in research with reference to both sub-elite and elite athletes (Mallett, 2005; Light & Robert, 2010) and sporting organisations such Sport Canada (Thibault & Babiak, 2005). However, there is an absence of application to the coaching of older or masters athletes (Young, Callary, & Niedre, 2014). This lack of research presents issues for coaches and providers of coach education, as the drivers of participation in masters athletes vary considerably from the fun, fitness and friendship model for youth swimming espoused by Gould, Feltz, and Weiss (1985). Indeed, Stevenson (2002) reported that masters swimmers were most likely to swim through a need to become involved in something with "perceived fitness and health benefits" (p. 132). Further, Hastings, Kurth, Schloder, and Cyr (1995) found sociability, achievement and fitness were important to masters swimmers in the US and Canada. Young, Callary, and Niedre (2014) suggest that coaching approaches that are utilised with masters athletes should be subtly and distinctly different, and that coaching in this context demands "novel and innovative considerations" (p. 2). These authors found that one of the main considerations when coaching masters athletes was the development of self-determination and an engagement with learning. This is of particular relevance to athlete-centred coaching, as self-determination is central to its philosophy.

Athletic identity in masters athletes with particular reference to ageing and health has been the subject of much investigation. Masters athletes, unlike their younger counterparts, do not have persistent extrinsic motivators such as involvement through school to provide impetus, and this speaks to the high level of self-determination exhibited in the field of masters swimming (Medic, 2009). In addition, Stevenson (2002) demonstrated that masters athletes place a high value on how their athletic identity is seen by others and actively sustain particular role identities "because of the social, material, emotional, etc., benefits which they can see themselves deriving from their involvements" (p. 132). The centrality of athletic identity and the importance placed on it by masters swimmers presents both challenges and opportunities for the athlete-centred coach.

In Stevenson's (1999) case study of masters swimming, he recounted conversations that have been replicated in almost perfect detail in the most recent masters squad that I (Author 1) coached in 2016. In particular, Stevenson (1999) described how the hierarchical organisation of the lane was inhabited by swimmers with strikingly dissimilar attitudes to involvement in the decision-making. The knowledge, skills and abilities of swimmers at the front of the lane tended to be held in high esteem, and they were regularly involved in discussions surrounding stroke improvement. In contrast to this, swimmers at the back of the lane were at times classified as weaker, were unlikely to give advice, and would generally follow:

> my favourite spot is the last person in the lane, because then you don't really have to listen to, you know, 200 of this and three of that, and then do this. You just follow whatever the person ahead is doing – assuming they are listening.
>
> (Stevenson, 1999)

This illustrates clearly how athletic identity through the organisation of training sessions can be hierarchical in nature, and how this in turn might influence athlete-centred discussions between swimmer and coach. It should also be recognised that there are a number of practical and social reasons that a swimmer might gravitate to the back of the lane. For example, injury or fatigue is an often cited reason to move down the order; the practical capacity to hear and interpret coach instruction can impact on position in the lane. From an athlete perspective, I (Author 2) also highlight, however, that an emphasis of 'just following' when at the back of a lane may, in some instances, be the outcome of a swimmer being unable to hear and/ or understand a coach's instructions. 'Just following' is sometimes not so much a choice, but the only approach to take in a situation where you feel excluded from or unable to be involved in coach–athlete dialogue. Intuitively we can see that the coach will need to modify how s/he approaches these distinctly different athletes and how athlete involvement in decision-making could also be seen as a practical challenge.

The contemporary swim coaching culture encompasses the particular field where the coaching is undertaken, the particular group of athletes (junior, sub-elite, masters etc.) and a relationship with the sport's governing and educative body (in this case, Swimming Australia). In terms of educating coaches of specialist subgroups of swimmers (masters), Swimming Australia elaborates the formal coach education pathway by first developing a coach's understanding of the needs of junior or developing athletes. Once this initial accreditation is achieved, there is scope for extension courses associated with subsets of swimmers such as masters swimmers, open water swimmers etc. (Swimming Australia, 2017). The field in which swimming coaches engage with masters athletes is nuanced and varies greatly between squads. Swim coaches commonly work with masters athletes wishing to develop aquatic skills that will enhance a number of disciplines, such as the swim leg of tri-athlon or other multi-sport event, open water swimming, fitness swimming, swimming as cross training (non-weight bearing fitness for runners), competitive pool based swimming and fitness for other pool based sports (water polo and underwater hockey). It is rarely the case that a masters swim club is made up of members solely interested in the Olympic swimming disciplines, though there is often a tendency toward one particular genre of aquatic pursuit. This variation provides a number of challenges for both coaches and athletes, as the varying and competing discourses shape the field. Green (2017) encourages us to remember that the athlete as an autonomous individual also brings unique and individual traits that may have been shaped by their experiences in sport. For a squad with numerous masters athletes, this might be compounded by their collective experience of coaching approaches accumulated across a number of sports and over a long period of time. So if the athlete is transitioning into an athlete-centred program, then this change will be affected by both the coach, through the level of athlete-centredness practiced, and the athlete and their willingness to make the significant change "from simple obedience to critical thinker" (Green, 2017, p. 132).

## The challenges and opportunities of utilising athlete-centred coaching in the masters swimmer context

This section focusses on the practicalities of athlete-centred coaching in the masters swimmer context. Vignettes are used to contextualise the masters swimmer experience of coach- and athlete-centredness and how one coach responds to the opportunities and challenges of undertaking this approach with athletes.

### *The swimmer–researcher*

Recognising experience and valuing an athlete's perception in the learning process is integral to athlete-centred coaching. In this vignette, Author 2 describes how her learning came ostensibly from her experiences *in the water*, even though she had been trained to consider 'tactical and technical' aspects of this race; *I recognise that I have learnt things 'about' open water swimming technique and tactics* (Penney, 2017, p. 11). This comment reflected that coaches of masters swimming squads have often introduced specific drills with the explicit intention of bringing to the fore adaptations to stroke and technique that are invariably needed in open water conditions. The most common has been a drill designed to assist swimmers in practising sighting while also taking a breath, and therefore adjusting their breathing technique every few strokes to incorporate a head lift to check direction. In many instances, coaches have also emphasised the need to concentrate on 'feel' for the water (in both pool and open water contexts) and/or have talked of 'getting hold of it' as a critical part of the stroke. In an attempt to assist understanding of what this involves, coaches have often mirrored the desired stroke pattern while standing in an upright position. As an athlete who came to swimming late, I (Author 2) have struggled to grasp the notion of 'feel' for the water and have also struggled to try to translate a vertical demonstration into movement in a horizontal plane.

> I am in the water, looking up at the coach on the poolside. They go through the path they want our arms to follow, starting from the top, involving some sort of a curved pattern in front of their body and ending with a push back at the side of the thigh. All the time I am trying (but failing) to get a clear picture of what this is meant to look like when you are actually swimming. I can't get a clear sense of the depth or plane my arm is meant to follow at various points in the stroke – and I know I definitely have not got any clear feel for what I am aiming for.
>
> Not for the first time I'm at a loss as to how to respond. I try a smile and as ever commit to trying to make my best attempt something I really 'don't get'. I'm not at all confident I ever will!
>
> *Author 2, athlete–researcher*

Drills such as one-arm swimming or catch-up are also things that I (Author 2) have had plenty of exposure to in squads over the years. They have often highlighted to me more about my lack of feel for the water and/or inability to 'get hold of it' (particularly on my left side) than anything. At the same time, the masters swimming context and sessions structured around set schedules for each lane have typically not supported questioning or extended conversations that might help me make a meaningful connection between the task, the goal (better feel for the water) and kinaesthetic feedback. After many years of participation, I recently reflected on a new awareness in and for the water:

> it is Arnold's concept of education 'in' movement that many years on, I now feel captures the sort of learning and 'embodied consciousness' (Brown, 2013, p. 26) that only the experiences of swimming in all sorts of open water conditions over a considerable period of time, could provide. I didn't have those experiences as a child. I've very much enjoyed them later in life.
>
> *(Penney, 2017, p. 11)*

Author 2 came to this realisation on her own and after an extended period of time, and goes on to elaborate how this extended her skill set in a way that was once hard to imagine.

> this time when I take to the water my body and movements aren't constrained by fear. I'm not fighting the waves. I wouldn't say I'm really confident in these conditions, but I'm comfortable. I've learnt (somewhat) to 'relax with the waves', swim with them not against them, enjoy their momentum and try to use it. It is a swim where I smile at an experience I couldn't have had a few years ago – an experience of my body and movements being in sync with the water. I have gained a new appreciation of open water swimming that isn't about physiology, or biomechanics or tactics. It is about my body in relation to the water. It's about that thing I've heard coaches talk

about but that I've taken years to be able to understand; 'feel for the water' and 'in' the water.

*(Penney, 2017, p. 11)*

Author 2's reflections provide us with a snapshot of the learning process experienced by one masters athlete from a coach-centred background. They give impetus for us to consider a more athlete-centred approach that might stimulate and support learning. In particular, this vignette illustrates how the coaching experiences of Author 2 align with Kidman and Hadfield's (2000) assertion that athlete-centred coaching, using tactical questioning for higher order thinking, would have allowed her to "increase kinaesthetic (body and sensory) awareness of appropriate skill execution" in such a way that she would be able to "make decisions about what strengths to keep and what weaknesses fix" (p. 14).

## *The coach–researcher*

Perhaps the most persistent challenge as a swim coach in the masters context is the ethereal nature of quality technique in the water. Improvements cannot be optimised just by pushing harder, going longer or hurting more. Optimising stroke technique for the individual masters swimmer that might come with limitations of flexibility and strength, or with differing amounts of deliberate practice undertaken in their childhood (Ericsson, Krampe, and Tesch-Römer, 1993), would seem to fit the athlete-centred approach promoted in this publication. The truth is a much more complex and unwieldy reality. Compounding factors influencing the manner in which a coach can individualise a particular training session include: lane space and allocation within the lane; the way that training is organised into group tasks; and the massive variation in skills and abilities of squad members. These combine and can result in a coach undertaking the role of directing traffic rather than providing quality coaching. This is illustrated in detail in the vignettes that follow.

> Dealing with individuals was never more intense than coaching in the masters swimming context. I constantly battled (internally) with some athletes' need for continuous personal feedback and correction of stroke, my understanding of best practice stroke development and maintenance of some semblance of coherent direction in each session.
>
> *Author 1, coach–researcher*

Assuming that a masters swimmer is not self-aware despite coming into the sport from a non-swimming background is a mistake I (Author 1) have made on numerous occasions. In particular, with swimmers new to the squad, if I have failed to make a connection with them and forge an understanding of how they learn in the water I can fall into the trap of telling rather than asking.

> I can remember once when I offered stroke correction to a masters swimmer, only to be told on the following lap: "Now you have wrecked my stroke. I am going slower than ever. I think I will just stick with what I was doing before".

> To contrast this, at a recent annual general meeting of the masters club that I coached, I received a lot of feedback along the lines of; "the coach doesn't to do stroke correction anymore". Which necessitated a lengthy discussion about how I focus on stroke development by using key drills or modified strokes rather than just telling the swimmer what to do. This was further compounded by a committee member stating that; "most times I would rather just keep swimming, when I stop and we talk about my stroke I get cold and can't concentrate anyway!"
>
> *Author 1, coach–researcher*

In many ways it is not just the diverse experiences that masters athletes bring to the table that affect the practical implementation of athlete-centred coaching in the masters context; it is also the ingrained experiences of the coach and habitual nature of our approach when under pressure (Hadfield, 2005). The challenges of undertaking an athlete-centred approach in swimming, where pool space and the squad-based nature of many activities might at first seem to encourage a coach-centred approach, must be resisted. The technical nature of the sport, where the "advantage faster swimmers have over slower swimmers is derived more from technique than strength" (Havriluk, 2010, p. 321), speaks to the individual nature of this sport and the value that coaches should place on personal kinaesthetic feedback when building technique and stroke capability with masters swimmers.

### So where to for the athlete-centred masters swim coach?

We must first heed Hadfield's (2005) call for patience during the change process. This can refer to change from the coach's perspective and change in the way that a masters athlete experiences 'training' and becomes a part of the coaching dyad that is central to athlete-centred coaching. It should come as no surprise to the reader that developing a relationship with the athlete becomes the cornerstone of enacting an effective athlete-centred approach. In a masters context, this might include knowledge of an individual's sporting, academic and work background so that a common language can be developed and interactions between coach and athlete are purposeful and effective.

Becoming self-aware in the water can be closely linked to an athlete being able to articulate what they are feeling in such a way that the coach can interpret and, conversely, with a coach being able to articulate what s/he wants to see. To illustrate this, we build on Hadfield's assertion that "if you can't feel it, you can't change it" (p. 20) and suggest that if an athlete can't describe what s/he is feeling and a coach can't describe what s/he sees or wants to see, then there is an impasse in which the athlete-centred coaching effect is diminished. Therefore, when utilising a questioning approach, or query theory (Hadfield, 1994; Martin & Gaskin, 2004) as a bridge to athlete-centred coaching, the coach–athlete dyad must first agree to terms. That is, they must define a common dialogue so that meaning can be made and knowledge and skills produced on both sides. To illustrate this dialogue, we reference a recent coaching point with a masters swimmer, who is also a golfer:

*Coach:* So when you swing your driver aiming to achieve maximum distance with your golf ball, do you need to care about what happens with your body after you strike the ball?

*Swimmer:* Of course, I concentrate on as fluid a follow through as my back will allow.

*Coach:* Why?

*Swimmer:* Well so the club head is at maximum speed at the point of impact, rather than slowing down.

*Coach:* OK, can you see how this can relate to your hand speed at the end of your freestyle stroke just before it exits the water?

*Swimmer:* So it needs to be fast not slow?

*Coach:* Yes, I should be able to see water being pushed backwards forcefully as your hand exits, but what will that feel like?

*Swimmer:* I suppose I should feel the water pressure on my palm right through and into the air?

*Coach:* Yes, let's see what that feels like on the next 50 then . . .

In this way, we follow Hadfield's (2005) suggestion that the coach must first provide leadership in their role as a guide to "athlete self-discovery and self-improvement" (p. 41) and subsequent self-reliance.

## Engaging with health and wellbeing discourses

We recognise that adopting athlete-centred coaching in a masters swimming context requires coaches to consciously engage with the complex and varied ways in which discourses of wellbeing and culture mix with performance discourses in masters squads. This brings us back to the mix of athletes and interests that often come together in a masters squad. We suggest that effective athlete-centred coaching involves a challenging and complex task of mediating and negotiating individual and group interests that exist across a squad and within any given lane. A masters swimmer identity can be synchronously linked to past and current athletic performance discourses and current healthy and fit discourses, even if they are not considered to be one of the top swimmers in the squad. Stevenson (2002) suggested that this can be due to reputation attributed by others. Work colleagues and family members see the masters swimmer as active and fit, and potentially experts "in matters to do with health, fitness and exercise" (Stevenson, 2002, p. 14). Masters swimmers can value their position within the health and wellbeing discourse in a competitive manner (Young, Callary, & Niedre, 2014) and in some instances feel a greater connectedness to this discourse than their substantive career (Stevenson, 2002).

> In a squad situation I'm destined to be in the lower lanes. That's fine, but I don't want lane hierarchies to frame how a coach views me. Will the coach understand that irrespective of where I swim I'm still committed to doing my best, training as well as I can, and setting myself up to do as well as possible in events? Do they even know what I'm aiming for? Will they understand that sometimes running is what I'm focused on and I'll be pretty shattered coming to swim training? Do they know what else is going on in my life and that while I want to push myself in the pool I'm also after relief from mental stress and a fun supportive environment?
>
> *Author 2, athlete–researcher*

Catering for this is inextricably linked to the athlete-centred approach, as individuals at all levels within squad and lane hierarchies must be allowed to retain their individuality within the hurly-burly of competing athlete interests and needs.

> Acknowledging competing discourses was a strategy that I subconsciously adopted when I (Author 1) first started coaching masters swimmers. Late in the session or during a particularly hard set, a swimmer might stop at the wall and pull out of the line to give themselves a rest. You could see their tension as they battled for breath and resisted the performance discourse that would seem to suggest they should battle on, make the set, and finish the lap. They would try to hide against the wall, sitting low in the water to avoid attracting attention. I would grab this chance to engage them about something entirely unrelated to the session but centred on them.
>
> Mick, a self-employed builder, was often 'on the wall' during long freestyle sets. I would catch his attention and ask about what he was working on at the moment.
>
> "I had to pull out two bathrooms today, not the best part of my job!"
>
> We would banter back and forth as the swimmers from his lane filed past again, then I might suggest that he use a pull buoy for the last few repeats if he felt that might give him more support in the water and give his legs a break.
>
> *Author 1, coach–researcher*

Athlete buy-in and ownership of their path through the training session might be enacted by the athlete, but in a tightly structured and scripted swim session it must be facilitated by a coach who has a strong understanding of how to utilise an athlete-centred approach. In this chapter, we have shared insights from our contrasting experiences to illustrate why we see a need for more engagement with the approach in masters contexts particularly, and greater understanding of the approach from both athlete and coach perspectives.

# References

Brown, T. D. (2013). A vision lost? (Re) articulating an Arnoldian conception of education 'in' movement in physical education. *Sport, Education and Society*, *18*(1), 21–37.

Ericsson, K. A., Krampe, R. T., & Tesch-Römer, C. (1993). The role of deliberate practice in the acquisition of expert performance. *Psychological Review*, *100*(3), 363–406.

Gould, D., Feltz, D., & Weiss, M. (1985). Motives for participating in competitive youth swimming. *International Journal of Sport Psychology*, *16*(2), 126–140.

Green, D. (2017). On athlete centred coaching: Empowering the athlete. In D. J. Svyantek (Ed.), *Sport and understanding organisations* (pp. 127–143). New York: Information Age Publishing.

Hadfield, D. C. (1994). The query theory: A sports coaching model for the 90's. *The New Zealand Coach*, *3*(4), 16–20.

Hadfield, D. C. (2005). The change challenge: Facilitating self-awareness and improvement in your athletes. In L. Kidman (Ed.), *Athlete centred coaching: Developing inspired and inspiring people* (pp. 31–43). Christchurch, NZ: Innovative Print Communications.

Hastings, D. W., Kurth, S. B., Schloder, M., & Cyr, D. (1995). Reasons for participating in a serious leisure career: Comparison of Canadian and US masters swimmers. *International Review for the Sociology of Sport*, *30*(1), 101–119.

Havriluk, R. (2010). Performance level differences in swimming: Relative contributions of strength and technique. In Per-Ludvik Kjendlie, Robert Keig Stallman, & Jan Cabri (Eds.), *Proceedings of the XIth international symposium for biomechanics and medicine in swimming* (pp. 321–323). Oslo, Norway: Norwegian School of Sport Science.

Kidman, L. (2001). *Developing decision makers: An empowerment approach to coaching*. Christchurch, NZ: Innovative Print Communication.

Kidman, L., & Hadfield, D. (2000). Athlete empowerment. *New Zealand Coach*, *8*(4), 14–15.

Kidman, L., & Penney, D. (2014). Promoting and supporting coaches' professional learning: Developing a community of practice. *The Journal of Athlete Centered Coaching [E]*, *1*(1), 6–31.

Light, R. L., & Robert, J. E. (2010). The impact of game sense pedagogy on Australian rugby coaches' practice: A question of pedagogy. *Physical Education and Sport Pedagogy*, *15*(2), 103–115.

Lombardo, B. J. (1987). *The humanistic coach: From theory to practice*. Springfield, IL: Charles Thomas Publisher.

Mallett, C. J. (2005). Self-determination theory: A case study of evidence-based coaching. *The Sport Psychologist*, *19*(4), 417–429.

Martin, A. J., & Gaskin, C. J. (2004). An integrated physical education model. *New Zealand Physical Educator*, *37*(1), 61–69.

McMahon, J., & Zehntner, C. (2014). Shifting perspectives: Transitioning from coach centered to athlete centered. *Journal of Athlete Centered Coaching*, *1*(2), 1–19.

Medic, N. (2009). Understanding masters athletes' motivation for sport. In J. Baker, S. Horton., & P. Weir (Eds.), *The masters athlete: Understanding the role of sport and exercise in optimizing aging* (pp. 105–122). New York: Routledge.

Penney, D. (2017). Valuing movement: Learning *in* open water. *Active and Healthy Magazine*, *24*(1), 10–11.

Stevenson, C. L. (1999). The influence of nonverbal symbols on the meaning of motive talk: A case study from masters swimming. *Journal of Contemporary Ethnography*, *28*(4), 364–388.

Stevenson, C. L. (2002). Seeking identities: Towards an understanding of the athletic careers of masters swimmers. *International Review for the Sociology of Sport*, *37*(2), 131–146.

Swimming Australia. (2017). *Coach accreditation pathway for swimming in Australia.* Retrieved from www.swimming.org.au/Home/ClubCloach/Coaching.aspx

Thibault, L., & Babiak, K. (2005). Organizational changes in Canada's sport system: Toward an athlete-centred approach 1. *European Sport Management Quarterly, 5*(2), 105–132.

Young, B. W., Callary, B., & Niedre, P. C. (2014). Exploring novel considerations for the coaching of masters athletes. *International Sport Coaching Journal, 1*(2), 86–93.

# INDEX